This Land Is Not For Sale

This Land Is Not For Sale

Canada's Original People and Their Land
A Saga of Neglect, Exploitation, and Conflict

Hugh and Karmel McCullum

ANGLICAN BOOK CENTRE
TORONTO, CANADA

The Anglican Book Centre
600 Jarvis Street
Toronto, Ontario
Canada M4Y 2J6

ISBN 0-919030-10-6

PRINTED & BOUND IN CANADA BY
THE JOHN DEYELL CO.

for
Tony and Russ
whose commitment encouraged us
to write this book and
whose support got us through it

PRINCIPAL INDUSTRIAL DEVELOPMENT AREAS IN CANADA
AFFECTING THE ENVIRONMENT AND ABORIGINAL PEOPLE

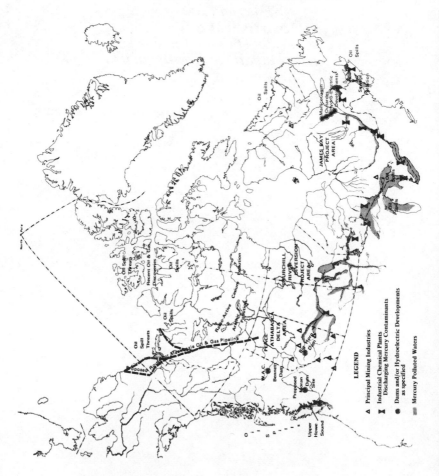

*The above illustration shows only the approximate location of development areas in Canada.

Contents

Foreword

In the course of the history of any nation, as in the lives of individual people, focal issues which call for difficult value decisions arise from time to time. The decisions that are made reveal the values that have become primary values in national life and point the direction for the nation's future development.

I am convinced that this book deals with two interlocking concerns which constitute focal issues for Canada at this time. These are the pattern for Northern development which we adopt, and the way in which we respond to the aboriginal rights of Canada's Native peoples, particularly to land claims.

The authors of this book, Hugh and Karmel McCullum, have researched a number of concrete situations in Canada where these issues are confronting different federal government departments, different provinces and territories, and a variety of corporations and tribal groups, and for the first time have brought the findings together into one publication.

Because of their common conviction that the issues are of vital concern, six churches in Canada—namely the Anglican, Lutheran, Mennonite, Presbyterian, Roman Catholic, and United Churches—have supported this undertaking. Whereas they do not necessarily endorse all the opinions expressed by the authors, they are convinced that the issues being dealt with need to be better understood by

Canadians, and believe that the information provided in the book will be a valuable contribution in promoting deeper understanding of the complexity of the decisions to be made, and will facilitate greater citizen involvement in policy making. They are grateful to the authors for undertaking both the research and the writing, and hope that the publication will have a wide circulation.

Edward W. Scott
Primate
The Anglican Church of Canada

Introduction

This book is about Indian, Inuit[1], and Metis land claims and
Northern development. It is about energy, government, and the
church. Already that covers a lot of ground and makes us tired just
thinking about the complexity of the task we took on—especially
because it changes every time we pick up a newspaper or turn on the
radio.

It's also a book about people. About Native people who live on
reserves, in towns, and in Arctic settlements. And about white
people. It's about politicians who are committed to their constitu-
ents and politicians who are knaves, committed to themselves. It's
about industrialists and businessmen who act predictably and use
Canada's colonial approach to the North for multi-national profiteer-
ing. It's about church people who use the liberating teachings of the
gospel to help free men and women, and it's about church people
who use the institution's waning power and prestige to stubbornly
maintain the status quo for "our Natives." It's a microcosm of
Canada.

We were encouraged to write the book because we believe that
the future of Canada, the quality of its democracy and its reputation—real or invented—for justice, rests on how it acts on the legitimate demands of its Original People who are trying, in the face of
enormous energy-development projects, to attain a just settlement
of their land rights and compensation for past wrongs.

The subject matter bores some people to death because to them, the rights of a few hundred thousand Indian and Inuit are unimportant beside the needs of an inflated, uneasy, consumer society. Many politicians agree, and wish the "Indian problem" would go away and stop disrupting progress. The issue angers others, especially Northern whites, who are bewildered by the changes in attitude of the Natives who used to passively accept the white man's paternalism and standards and now find great pride in their new-found—because it was almost extinct—Native-ness.

The key to it all is land. Land and what it means to Indians, Inuit, and Metis is almost indefinable to the North American mind. It is not ownership in the sense of subdivisions, industrial complexes, parking lots, and high-rises. It is not exploitation of trees, minerals, animals, fish, and birds. It has become some of all these things though, because Native people are using our criteria for reparations and compensation.

The closest definition we can come to is that, for Natives, land is for use; it is like a Mother. It is a breadbasket, protector, and friend. It is something you live with easily, you don't fight. It is something you cherish and return to when you are sick, frightened, or lonely. It has always been there and it always will be there. And out of it comes your being, the reason for your existence, the only power you have in a white man's world. If you lose it or sell it or have it taken away from you, then you are dead, or at best, a second class white man.

So this is a book about land too. But this land, north of the 60th parallel and across the tops of the provinces, is enormously rich, especially in terms of oil, natural gas, hydro power, and minerals. And guess who faces an energy crisis? And guess who's going to solve it? Why, the same good old guys. The United States has the crisis and Canada has the answer. Simple. Dam up a bunch of rivers, string a few transmission lines, build a couple of pipelines, drill a few holes, and presto—instant energy.

The fact that Northern Quebec looks like a war zone and Northern Manitoba may become one huge lake is irrelevant. The fact that Northern British Columbia looks less and less like "Beautiful British Columbia" and the only certainty in our two colonies, the Yukon and Northwest Territories—emphasis on *territory*—that no one has any idea what will really happen to the delicate balance of the ecology, is also irrelevant. The fact that fewer than 100,000 people live in the only real wilderness left in North America—and maybe in the world—is nothing more than an annoyance that has to be dealt with.

So there you have it. It's called Native Affairs and Northern Development. Sounds suspiciously like the name of the federal department whose vast (some 14,000 employees) and unaccountable bureaucracy administers the affairs of many Indians and forms all Northern development policies from their 15-storey complex in downtown Ottawa, several thousand miles from the action. Its minister, presently the Honorable Judd Buchanan, is charged by law with the administration of the Indian Act, which makes him the Native peoples' trustee or guardian. He is also minister of Northern Development and as such is responsible for everything north of the 60th parallel, which is nearly half of Canada's land mass, and probably the richest half in terms of resources. And his senior development bureaucrats know that.

Native land or Northern development—can the twain ever meet? That perhaps, in the final analysis, is the reason for this book. We have tried to point out that there are valid alternatives open to governments: land claims can be settled in a just manner; native groups are not *per se* anti-development. But we have gone further and suggested that a settlement of land claims, an appreciation of Native culture and values, and a slower, more planned human orientation in Northern development will enrich all of Canada. But it requires a new approach, and that threatens mandarins, whether they be Ottawa mandarins or Quebec, Victoria, Winnipeg, or Yellowknife mandarins.

"Mandarins," a labor boss in Terrace, British Columbia, told a conference of natives, workers, and environmentalists, "think all people are like mushrooms. They should be kept in the dark and fed a lot of manure." He was talking about the propensity of planners —especially those of government and Crown corporations who should be most accountable to the public—for formulating their projects in secret, announcing them with little or no consultation with the people to be affected, and starting work almost immediately.

It's called progress and knowing what's best for Canada. Others call it sheer arrogance and shortsightedness. But in the North, where there are vast tracts of land which no one was interested in until our alleged energy crisis broke, the lives and culture of Native people, already in serious jeopardy, are at stake. Even then, Natives are not saying "no development" but rather are saying "no further development until our land claims are settled."

Or put another way, they are saying: "Look, a gas pipeline, for example, is not our priority. We don't need it. We don't particularly want it. But we understand you want it and think you need it. So, since we are part of Canada, we'll listen to you. But we want our land, and we want recognition of our rights, and we want to be part of the process that looks into all the aspects of large industrial projects. Then, when that process is completed and you still all think the project is needed, okay, as long as our rights are guaranteed and our involvement clear, we'll go ahead."

It's not just a case of blocking progress—however you define progress. It's a case of putting it all out in the open, taking time to plan and examine all the available data, guaranteeing the rights of the Original People, and developing new and more just patterns of growth. One Canadian Prime Minister, a Liberal at that, called it "participatory democracy". But he shall be nameless because it's never happened, and besides, it's too costly in terms designed for us by the multi-national corporations.

Finally, we think this book is really about a struggle for survival. It is not overstating the case that, should Northern colonial development continue as it is, Native people will not survive as a race. It is essential too, to see that our nation's survival hinges on their future, for if we, as members of a democracy dedicated to justice, cannot deal justly with them, then we cannot expect justice for anyone.

Notes

1 Inuit is the designation for the people who originally inhabited the Arctic regions and became known as Eskimos—an Indian word roughly translated, "eaters of raw meat," but in their own language, simply meaning "the people." Inuit is common to all dialects of the aboriginal people who live on the Arctic coast and islands north of the tree line.

Indian people have their own society in which their relationship to the land is crucial. The meaning of ownership is very important to this Indian idea.

Cabinet ministers and most white people do not understand this Indian concept of the way we see ourselves in relation to the land. They are stuck inside their own society and concepts, and they try to impose their view on us. We cannot compromise, because it means giving up our concept and accepting theirs.

We are not talking only about land, but also about Dené people, and how we see ourselves as a group.

How Indian people view land, trees, animals, minerals is difficult to describe.

If we are told we have to live inside certain boundaries, we will not see ourselves the same way. We are defined by our relationship to these things. The government view will destroy this. Here, in the Northwest Territories, we cannot accept this. This is not the way we look at land (in terms of boundaries) or ourselves. It does not matter how much money they give us. Money goes down—never goes back up. Land is always there . . . will grow back . . . its value is always there. Land is more valuable than money. If we give land up for money, we will not survive as a people.

Alexis Arrowmaker
Head Chief of the Dogribs at the
First General Assembly of the
Indian Brotherhood of the Northwest Territories
at Fort Good Hope, June 1974

I

The Land

*A Century of
Unfinished Business*

You have to run when you follow Flora MacDonald through the tunnel that connects the Centre Block of the Parliament Buildings with the West Block where her cramped, chaotic office is located. You have to balance a notebook and pencil as you trot along, because the ideas and statements come bursting at you in a stream of facts and proposals that is mind-boggling. Flora is Member of Parliament for Kingston, and expert—although no longer Conservative party spokesman—on Native Affairs and Northern Development. She talks about land and treaties and aboriginal rights with deep conviction.

"I don't question the constitutional and legal rights of the Native people of this country to a just land settlement. But I'll go a lot further than he will," she muttered nodding at Judd Buchanan, the lanky federal minister of Indian Affairs and Northern Development, as we swept by the government lounges. "I think we have a moral right to help them achieve recognition of their aboriginal rights. More important, we have to recognize that their concept of land, rooted in their belief in aboriginal title, is vastly different from ours."

And that's the crux of an issue that threatens to overshadow every other domestic problem that faces Canada today. The question of Native land, aboriginal rights, treaties, Northern development—the question of the survival of a race of people, of nations within a nation. It is a moral question, a legal question, a political question.

The last great scandal that rocked Ottawa and brought down the Liberal government of Louis St. Laurent involved a pipeline. Energy development in the North and across the tops of the provinces threatens to engulf the government of Pierre Trudeau and several provincial governments in a controversy that could spell doom for their futures as well, unless they are prepared to deal fairly with Indians, Inuit, Metis, and other Native groups about their land. It is land they have held "from time immemorial," or about 10,000 years as anthropologists believe. It is the very mystical and spiritual quality of their lives.

Right now, Canada's ruling politicians of various stripes and hues are acting towards the 500,000 or more Natives in Canada in a most cavalier fashion. It has been said that civilizations are often judged by how they treat people in prison. And while, by stretching a point, this could have special meaning for Native people, it seems clear to us that, in North America, governments should be evaluated according to their principles in dealing with the continent's indigenous people—the Natives.

There is no doubt they are a minority in terms of population, and through that incredibly paternalistic piece of legislation known as the Indian Act, they are isolated and divided from each other. Of the 500,000 Natives, only about 125,000 are treaty Indians, those people under the Indian Act who live on the Prairies and most of Ontario where land cession, numbered treaties, were signed between 1871 and 1923. There are another 125,000 people, also under the Indian Act, who are called status Indians but who live in areas like British Columbia, the Yukon, the Northwest Territories, and Northern Quebec, who have never signed treaties or whose treaty agreements have never been fulfilled.

So you have treaty status Indians and non-treaty status Indians. The other 250,000 people of Native blood who do not have status (because for a whole variety of reasons they lost the status they originally held under the Indian Act) are the Metis people who are often called half-breeds or non-status Indians. There are also about 17,000 Inuit or Eskimo, 13,000 of whom live in the Northwest Territories, and about 4,000 in Arctic Quebec and Labrador.

The Indian Act regulates almost totally the life-style of the 250,000 status Indians, both as individuals and as communities. It is a terribly misguided policy based on the assumption, made years ago and never really changed, that the Native is a lazy bum, incapable of handling his own affairs, and that the values, culture, and life-style of Native people are vastly inferior to white society. Sound familiar? Try the foreign policy of the United States in Vietnam, the apartheid doctrines of South Africa, or British colonialism (from where the Indian Act originated) until the 1960's.

The sole though unwritten purpose then of the Indian Act was to promote assimilation of the Native into white society, and after four or more generations of this not-so-benevolent policy, Indian culture has been virtually destroyed. But ironically, it never resulted in the unstated hope of total integration or assimilation—some would charge genocide—of Indians. It merely succeeded in creating dependency, welfare, and isolation, thereby widening the educational, economic, and social gap between Indian and non-Indian.

It is only recently, with a resurgence among young people and the excellent memories of the old, that Native people are again looking to the land and their rights as the first inhabitants of North America, as the means to survive as a special minority within Canada. Flora MacDonald understands this. The slim redhead from Cape Breton talks with deep understanding about the land. "You know, just because we have chosen to become a mobile, transient population, living in high-rise apartments or moving from one faceless part of suburbia to another, cutting off our roots, shifting our loyalties, is no reason to assume we should seek to enforce these values on others. Land to many of us is a piece of property we own until we can move on to something better". In contrast to this utilitarian approach, Miss MacDonald points out the Natives' regard for the land as a personal inheritance. "The Native people have a very different concept of land. . . . The Native person still has a concept of communal ownership and he is the custodian of that land for future generations. He has the use of it and its resources while he lives, but he has no right to destroy it in his daily use of it and thus deny its benefits to future generations."

After talking to literally hundreds of Native people in thousands of miles of travel across much of the North, the following is a synthesis of what they have told us, especially the old people who have so much influence on the young.

> We are telling you again and again that without the land Indian people have no soul, no life, no identity, no purpose. Control of the land is essential for our cultural and economic survival.
> We are people of the land. We love the land but the land is no longer what it was.

We see the land as having been taken into the white man's society, his economy. It is covered in asphalt, surveyed, scarred, tracked in the search for oil and natural gas and minerals that lie under it. Sadly we know that we cannot use it much in the old ways. The animals are hiding or dead, the fish are poisoned, the birds fly away. So we must seek a way to live in this new way, but we must not sell our land or allow it to be taken away. It is only for our use, even if the use is a new use. The land is for our children, not for sale. The land is still part of us and we are part of it.

In the Northwest Territories, where the Indian Brotherhood and the Metis Association work in a coalition to combat the imminent gas pipeline until land claims are settled, a philosophy of land has been developed and articulated that is probably more far-reaching and imaginative than most. It is called the Dene philosophy, a philosophy that means, as the translation for *Dené* suggests, people's land. It is not, as government and corporation bureaucrats would have us believe, a blanket return to pre-Christopher Columbus days, totally anti-development. It is a new concept that lies within the aboriginal philosophy of community development and community ownership.

Our thesis—"No pipeline before a land claims settlement"—is more than just a request designed to protect our bargaining position. It is the formal expression of a more fundamental issue. The issue is one which involves the struggle between two opposing concepts of economic development for the North. The pipeline proposal represents the "colonial" philosophy of development. Opposed to this notion of Northern development is the "community" philosophy of development as exemplified by the Native land claim.

What are the characteristics of these two concepts of development: the "colonial" philosophy and the "community" philosophy? The "colonial" school of economic development is the one which is promoted by the American multi-national corporations and their Canadian subsidiaries. They see the North as the storehouse of resources for the industrial centres of the south. Oil, gas, and minerals move south to these centres. The profits which they generate move south along with them. The North becomes a hinterland dependent on the south; it loses its resources and gets welfare in return. It is never permitted to develop an economic base which allows its people, and particularly its Native people, to enjoy the benefits of equality with the residents of the industrial south.

Is there an alternative to this dismal outlook? There is; and it is found in the vision of hope and dignity which characterizes the "community" philosophy of development and which is the foundation of the land claim advanced by the Native people of the Mackenzie District.

By claiming ownership of the land, what the Native people are saying is this:

As much as possible we want to be able to control our own destiny. We want to be the ones who decide what directions our society should take. We also want to participate in Canadian society, but we want to participate as equals. It is impossible to be equal if our economic development is subordinated to the profit-oriented priorities of the American multi-nationals.

Therefore, the Native people are saying, we must have a large degree of control over our own economic development. Without that control we will end up like our brothers and sisters on the reserves in the south: continually powerless, threatened, and impoverished.

Only community ownership of the land, land which has belonged to our people for thousands of years, can give us the ability to determine and follow our own way.[1]

With varying degrees of emphasis, this is the philosophy which lies behind the Native search for equitable settlement of their land claims. But the present situation is steeped in complexities. Parts of Canada are covered by treaties and parts are an open book. Treaties have been obtained by fraud, or provisions within them totally ignored or violated, all with the tacit approval of government. Settlements are often forced to clear the way for imminent development; governments openly practice a policy of divide-and-conquer, and legal action often seems the only recourse, other than violence, open to the Native people. For the most part, land claim and treaty negotiation processes look long and tedious.

In some areas there are strong pockets of white backlash and outright racism. Some groups such as the American Indian Movement and the Ojibway Warriors Society are accused of being openly militant. Such an explosive situation can only be resolved when governments are prepared to negotiate openly, immediately, and in good faith without the pressures of hydro projects, pipelines, or industrial programs.

Historically, the land question dates back to the seventeenth century or earlier. Then it involved aboriginal rights and treaties— now, land claim settlements. Governments have tried various ways of dealing with this crisis of survival. They can continue as at present with no clear policy, in a manner totally unsatisfactory to anyone; they can negotiate in good faith, or they can face court action. All of these methods have been tried with varying degrees of success. In the remainder of this chapter we will examine how Canada got into this mess, and what some of the historic decisions were that lie behind present ineptitude and lack of cohesive policy.

Aboriginal rights, or the claim by Native people to ownership of the traditional lands they have always occupied "since time immemorial," is a key element of British and Canadian law. Basically this means that a conquering or discovering nation takes sovereignty over lands, but the aboriginal people—in this case, Indian and Inuit people and their blood relatives, the Metis—retain property rights. Under the Royal Proclamation of 1763, during colonization by the British of North America, this concept was enshrined in law and has never been questioned by any Canadian government until Trudeau shrugged in 1969 and said, "No." He has since modified his position slightly.

There are two components to aboriginal rights or aboriginal title: first, land occupied and used by Native people can only be surrendered to the Crown (in Canada the provincial or federal governments in the case of the Yukon and Northwest Territories) and cannot be sold privately, since the Crown legally must extinguish title either by purchase or conquest (expropriation); secondly, the concept is one of communal rather than individual ownership.

The basic intention of the Royal Proclamation was to create a vast tract of land (which became known as Indian Land) for the hunting, trapping, and fishing rights of Native people, and white settlers were to stay out. That this never worked is due solely to the greed of early settlers, later to be succeeded by colonial developers, later to be succeeded by multi-national oil, gas, and energy companies, all aided and abetted by government. The decision to "sell" Indian land to the Crown for resale to settlers resulted in the extensive treaty-making process that took place until 1923 and covered most of Ontario and the Prairies.

The areas this book is primarily concerned with—the area north of the 60th parallel, Northwestern British Columbia, and Northern Quebec—were never under treaty. Northern Manitoba has been the subject of so many treaty violations by a whole series of provincial governments, and the clear fraud involved in obtaining signatures and adhesions to Treaties 8 and 11 in the Northwest Territories makes those areas ripe for renegotiation. While the treaties signed in the 50 years between 1871 and 1923 constitute one of the greatest rip-offs in the history of Canadian land dealings—even more devastating than the CPR grab—they at least clearly acknowledged the Native peoples' communal right to own their land.

Usually the treaties allowed 1 square mile of land—160 acres in Manitoba—per family of 5, $5.00-a-year per head, a little ammunition and twine, and hunting and fishing rights. These provisions still obtain and have extinguished claims to some of the best land in Canada, leaving most reserve Indians in a position of dependency, degradation, and hopelessness. Even with poor land and reservations, governments feel no compunction about flooding, polluting, or otherwise invading Indian land if it suits the purposes of groups such as Manitoba Hydro.

The treaties are really an extension of the aboriginal title principle, and rather than denying the existence of aboriginal rights —as some members of the judiciary and the prime minister have alleged—they actually support the concept. Treaties were signed by the federal government, which under the British North America Act —Canada's unrepatriated constitution—is empowered to legislate in regard to "Indians and lands reserved for Indians" and various Indian nations. Parliament, also under the BNA Act, can abrogate treaties and expropriate Indian land. It can also deal with Indians— and lawyers generally agree that, under the BNA Act, Indians means aboriginals—outside treaties.

All this means, according to Professor Peter Cumming, associate dean of Osgoode Law School in Toronto, that Native rights are derived from a person's racial and cultural origins rather than strictly from the Indian Act, thereby allowing the government to treaty with Inuit and Metis, as it has with Indians. Also, he says, Parliament can "regulate, settle, deny, or expand" aboriginal claims.[2]

The treaties, meagre as they were in terms of what Indians received, have been violated time and again. The Migratory Birds Convention between Canada and the United States, passed as a wise conservation measure, simply ignored the fact that hunting and fishing rights of Indians were guaranteed. Provincial and territorial game laws are usually in contravention of the treaties, and while most Natives are conservationists, the point is that any law thought to be in the interest of the white man can quickly supersede an Indian treaty. It matters not whether the contravention is in the area of game laws, pollution, or mineral and energy extraction. For the "greater good" of the nation, Indian and other Native rights are quickly forgotten.

Other treaties have been so fraudulently obtained and so poorly implemented that their validity in law—and in fact—is seriously in doubt. Two such treaties, both affecting the Northwest Territories, resulted in a landmark legal opinion in 1973 which, while still under appeal on technical grounds, clearly supports aboriginal claims. Treaty 8, signed in 1899, ceded the greater portion of Northern Alberta and a small part of the Northwest Territories to the Crown — coincidentally just after gold was discovered in the Yukon. Treaty 11, signed in 1921, allegedly ceded the Mackenzie Valley to the Crown and was signed just after oil was found at Norman Wells.

The deal included the usual provisions of $5-a-year and 1 square mile per family of 5, along with some twine for nets and ammunition for hunting. The reserve lands were never set aside, and now the Indians claim none of the more than 400,000 square miles involved was ever ceded. They also have produced evidence that they had been tricked into signing both treaties.

The Indians, some 7,000 of whom have Indian Act status, launched a court action early in 1973 by applying to Mr. Justice William Morrow, the only judge in the Northwest Territories' Supreme Court, for a caveat (or legal declaration) on their claim to the land. Ottawa, in the form of the Indians' legal protector, the Department of Indian Affairs and Northern Development (DIAND), was clearly worried. If the caveat was allowed—and it subsequently was—all development in the area could be halted until land claims were settled.

The government tried a number of legal manoeuvres to prevent Morrow from hearing the case. They wanted nothing to stop exploration for oil and natural gas in the Mackenzie Delta or to stand in the way of the Mackenzie Valley pipeline so urgently desired by the Energy Department. Four hundred or more thousand square miles of land in Native hands? Unthinkable to Ottawa's colonially-minded bureaucrats. Never mind that, legally, they are the Indians' paternal trustees and guardians. Some parents!

Ottawa said that Morrow was exceeding his authority in hearing the caveat application.[3] Morrow declared that an insult to his authority as a federal judge. Another judge ruled against DIAND, and Morrow took his court to the people of the communities along the Mackenzie Valley and talked with those who remembered signing the treaties. He wanted to find out, among other things, if the Indians at the time had known they were signing over their land to the white man or, as the Indian Brotherhood contended, had merely thought they were signing treaties of friendship and peace. Ottawa's next ploy in "protecting" Indian rights was to huffily withdraw its lawyer from the case. Morrow promptly appointed a Yellowknife barrister to act for the government and placed a temporary freeze on all land transactions in the disputed area.

Essentially, the Indians had six point of argument, all of which relate to disputed areas across the nation. These points were summarized for us by members of the Northwest Territories Indian Brotherhood.

(1) Treaties 8 and 11 do not surrender Indian land to the Crown because "the Indian people did not understand or agree to the terms appearing in the written version of the treaty."

(2) Indian land rights to the Mackenzie valley were recognized by the Royal Proclamation of 1763, by the Imperial Order in Council of 1870, and by the early Dominion Lands Act, all of which transferred this land to the northwestern Territories of Canada.

(3) The land in question has been used and occupied by Athabascan-speaking Indians "from time immemorial."

(4) The land has been occupied by distinct groups of Indians, organized into societies from the time of the first non-Indian entry into the area.

(5) Aboriginal people have a legal title to the land if they were in occupation of that land prior to colonial entry.

(6) The 7,000 treaty Indians of the Northwest Territories represented by the Indian Brotherhood "have a legal title and interest in the lands, and their interest can be protected by the filing of a caveat."

Morrow moved through the Arctic by plane for six weeks and his hearings were alive with the natural poetry of the Indian people. He visited 15 communities and heard from 34 witnesses, including 11 chiefs. He heard testimony from 2 old people in their homes. Then he wrote his historic decision. In 59 pages Morrow supported his "uneasy feeling" that the treaty negotiations were not at all aboveboard, and because of this he ruled that the Indians had a right to file claims to the land—although he ordered them not to do so until all appeals had been exhausted. This left the clarity of title seriously in doubt—a major barrier for anyone wishing to build a pipeline.

"Clearly," Morrow wrote, "there exists a clear constitutional obligation on the part of the Canadian government to protect the legal rights of the indigenous people in the area."[4]

Key to much of Morrow's judgment was the research of a Roman Catholic priest-historian, Fr. René Fumoleau, and the testimony of people who recalled the treaty talks. In Fort Providence, Chief Vital Bonnetrouge recalled a treaty signer saying flatly that if the $5.00 treaty money was for land, "I won't sign it."

At Fort Norman, near where oil was first discovered, 88-year-old Julian Yendo told Morrow that he had arrived for the signing at Fort Wrigley after it was all over. He said he hadn't signed any papers and hadn't ever found out what the $5.00 was for. In fact, he said, it was the first time he'd ever seen a white man. When the court showed him a copy of the treaty (number 11) with his signature in syllabics, Yendo identified it but said it must have been a forgery, because he couldn't read or write at the time.

Louis Caesar, 70, from Fort Good Hope quoted the treaty party as saying that the paper should be signed to protect the Indian people from whites who were going to come in and overcrowd the land. By signing the treaty, the Indians were told, the white men would be forced to stay off Indian land. "Ever since, they've been coming. They sure fooled us," Caesar testified.

Fr. René Fumoleau, an Oblate priest of long-standing in the Arctic, knows the Indians well, speaks their language, and has spent two years researching Indian treaties in the Northwest Territories. His findings, as related to those of Morrow, present a fascinating if predictable story of a federal government that looked on the North as worthless until gold and oil were found but then went on a "signing binge" that was neither honest nor legal, in his opinion. Fumoleau, a native of France, set out to write a few pages for the Indian Brotherhood about treaties. His research extended to two years and 500 pages of material, including the fact that most of the 75 signatures (X marks) on Treaty 8 were made by the same person, obviously from the facility of the penmanship, a white man.

"The treaties were unjust then; they were never fulfilled; they were never explained, and the real point is they are even more unjust today," Fumoleau testified.

Morrow's decision on aboriginal rights is not final. He said the whole question of treaties and their validity must be examined by a wider tribunal, but his ruling makes it clear, as did the Migratory Birds Convention and a host of other legislation, that Indian rights, be they under treaty or not, can be and have been abrogated any time federal or provincial governments have seen the gold or oil of 50 years ago or the natural gas and hydro of today in the "public interest."

The Inuit, who have never entered into treaties with the federal government, clearly have aboriginal rights too, but despite the formation of branches of the Inuit Taparisat who claim land rights, the government has thus far ignored all Inuit land claims and blithely issued exploration permits across the Arctic. This may soon come to confrontation, for in the Mackenzie area the Inuit are allied with the Metis and Indian associations in demanding no development, no pipeline before a land claim settlement.

There are numerous examples of seismic exploration by oil companies having disturbed the whale and seal populations and white fox trapping on places like Banks Island and Southampton Island. But there is rarely, if ever, any consultation with Inuit people about the possible effect of exploration or establishment of drilling sites on the very delicate balance of the Northern ecology, although the Inuit have survived in one of the harshest climates of the world by being the most expert of environmentalists. Inuit people have survived largely through their close relationship to the land, and like the Indians, their culture is based on one of the most superb functional civilizations known to man. But by the very acts of a paternalistic government, they are being herded into larger and larger settlements, being provided the same welfare benefits as their southern brothers, and ultimately being further isolated from the land.

Recent outbreaks of violence due to the abuse of alcohol, coupled with the frustration of leaving a land-based society, indicate to many Northerners that the Inuit face the cultural genocide that Indians have been trying to cope with for nearly a century. A proud, self-reliant, energetic, and happy people, the Inuit is being faced with the same colonial approach, the same indifference to culture, as was historically perpetrated against the southern Indian.

But despite all the treaty violation, the Canadian governments have always paid lip service to the concept of aboriginal rights—accepted it, at least, until 1969 when the present prime minister, unilaterally and without consultation with the people most affected, declared that what had been an integral part of the Canadian constitution was no more. It was in August, and significantly in British Columbia, that Prime Minister Trudeau stated:

> By aboriginal rights, this really means saying, "We were here before you. You came and you took the land from us, and perhaps you cheated us by giving us some worthless things in return for vast expanses of land, and we want to reopen this question. We want you to preserve our aboriginal rights and to restore them to us". And our answer—it may not be the right one and may not be the one which is accepted, but it will be up to all of you people to make your minds up and to choose for or against it and to discuss with the Indians— our answer is "No."

And then he wondered why the Native people were outraged, why they rejected this denial of their history and culture, why they utterly refused to accept his government's White Paper of the same year—surely an appropriate color in view of the utter lack of consultation in its preparation. Trudeau told them to abandon their legal and historic claims, join the just society and enjoy "full and equal participation in the cultural, social, economic, and political life of Canada"—as the White Paper so grandly put it—and then a few paragraphs later unilaterally decided which obligations the government would honor and which it would not. Clearly, insofar as the Liberal government was concerned, aboriginal rights were anachronistic, and the real problems of the Native people were educational, social, and economic. These they were prepared to discuss, aboriginal rights, never.

The White Paper, although largely ignored and rejected after the enormous outcry against it, did appoint a commissioner to look into Native claims, but clearly, he was to stay away from the question of aboriginal rights. Dr. Lloyd Barber, vice-president of the University of Saskatchewan, took on the job despite its restrictive terms of reference. He was to simply consider appropriate methods of adjudicating claims arising from the treaties and the administration of lands and money.

Understandably, the Indian people rose up in righteous indignation, and led by Harold Cardinal, president of the Indian Association of Alberta, denounced the whole White Paper and its exclusion of aboriginal title as unacceptable. Moreover, they asserted it was stupid to inquire into the performance of treaties without considering the very basis on which the treaties were negotiated—expressed in such traditional treaty language as to "cede, release, surrender and yield up" their lands.

But hope springs eternal, and subsequent events indicated the Liberals were softening their position, albeit with typical reluctance. In April of 1973, the issue actually got to the floor of the House of Commons, although not to a vote. The National Indian Brotherhood had produced a document for the Standing Committee on Indian Affairs, asking for recognition of aboriginal rights in non-treaty areas and in areas where treaties are deemed unfair by the Indians. The NIB also wanted hunting, fishing, and trapping rights restored or their loss compensated for as part of any aboriginal rights settlement. Since that time the Liberal government has revised its stand to the point where some forms of aboriginal rights, still to be defined, are tacitly accepted by Ottawa.

More than any other single event, the tireless attempts of the Nishga Indian Nation of Northwestern British Columbia to have their aboriginal rights recognized swayed the federal Liberals to a recognition that aboriginal title was not an anachronism. The Nishga had hunted and fished along the banks of the Nass River for centuries before the white man arrived, but as in other parts of Canada, it has been unclear whether the 2,200 people had any legal right to the 4,400 square miles of land they have always occupied. As far back as 1913, the Nishga nation petitioned the King of England for recognition of their right to the land, claiming they had never surrendered it. From mountaintop to mountaintop the valley running northeast from the Pacific Ocean was Nishga land, they said. The British monarch politely received their petition and took no further action.

In 1969, the same year Trudeau's government was issuing its White Paper, the proud and independent Nishga went to court and sued the province of British Columbia, demanding recognition of their aboriginal rights. They went alone. No federal funding. No support from the rest of the British Columbia Indians who thought a loss would jeopardize the whole movement towards aboriginal rights, as treaties had never before been signed in the province (except for a few small areas on Vancouver Island). The provincial supreme court ruled against them, and in 1970 the British Columbia appeal court upheld this ruling.

The Nishga's lawyer was Tom Berger, NDP leader in British Columbia, later to become Mr. Justice Thomas Berger of the provincial Supreme Court. In March, 1975, he convened the massive and historic commission of inquiry into the Mackenzie Valley natural gas pipeline. Berger's contention that the Nishga had a right to recognition was based on the Royal Proclamation of 1763 under the reign of King George III. The pertinent section declared:

> Such parts of our dominion and territories, as not having been ceded to, or purchased by us, are reserved to (the Indians) as their hunting grounds.[5]

The defence countered that this never applied to British Columbia, since the monarch at that time was not even aware of the province's existence.

Berger went to the Supreme Court and there earned a 3–3 split decision on January 31, 1973 when the seventh judge, Mr. Justice Louis Pigeon, ruling against the Nishga on a technicality, said a fiat allowing the province to be sued had never been obtained.

The inconclusive decision was hailed immediately as a moral victory by the very Indians in British Columbia who had discouraged the Nishga, and they rushed to Ottawa to meet Trudeau and Chrétien whose Indian policies of 1969 were clearly shaken.

Had the Supreme Court upheld the two lower courts and ruled against the Nishga, the statements of Trudeau that his government would recognize claims well based on treaty rights but not on aboriginal title would have been valid. In fact, the minority government of that day, pressed hard by the NDP holding the balance of power, reacted swiftly, and Trudeau conceded to the Nishga delegation that came to meet him after the decision, "Perhaps you have more legal rights than we thought you had when we did the White Paper."[6]

He also referred—although in typically tentative fashion—to the rights of Inuit and Indians in all the non-treaty areas. It was clear that the modification of his views was a direct result of the strong opinion in favor of the Nishga, written by Mr. Justice Emmett Hall (now retired) and supported by Bora Laskin, now chief justice, and Wishart Spence. According to Hall, the Royal Proclamation was "declaratory of the aboriginal rights"[7] a clear statement disregarding the opinions of the British Columbia government lawyers.

And that is where the situation remains today in Canada. Treaties have been made—in some cases fraudulently—and broken. Aboriginal right is clear in our constitution, no matter how reluctantly held by the government. Indian, Inuit, and Metis people are demanding just settlements of their claims. The land is all they presently have.

Perhaps it remains for the Indian Claims Commissioner, Lloyd Barber, the 41-year-old academic from Saskatoon, to express what the basis for native claims is in Canada. Walking fearlessly into alien country, Barber, in 1974, told the Rotary Club of Yellowknife that his view of Native Affairs for many years had been unrealistic and that during that time he had favored integration as the only realistic approach. He supposed, as did many others, that while the game was loaded against the Native people, given enough assistance, they could compete as effectively as ordinary citizens in Canadian society.

But it had become clear to Barber that Indians do not buy this assumption, because they feel they have, as owners of the land, a right to participate in resource development and a right to political autonomy within the larger Canadian framework. What's that we hear? Separatism? Coming from a resident of Western Canada? Sheer heresy. But Barber explained further.

> They are saying that they are distinct and in some ways, separate people who must have a special status within our country. I also think they are saying that as a practical matter, no matter how hard we try, it is simply not feasible to think that Native people can be brought into our game just like us when they start from such basic differences in culture and so heavily disadvantaged from the standpoint of political and economic power.[8]

To compound this heresy in the eyes of white, English-speaking Canada, Barber suggested that there is a direct analogy with the aspirations of French Canadians who also insist on a substantial resource base for the opportunity to run their own affairs as much as possible. After all, Indians and Inuit are not just one of the founding races in Canada, but in fact, are *the* founding race. Barber asked his audience to face clearly the implications for non-Native Northerners and non-Native people across Canada.

> If we are to deal fairly with Native people, it must mean that they are given the type of power in economic and political terms which will make things more difficult for us in some ways. Notably the development of the North and other remote parts of Canada may become more difficult from the standpoint of non-Native people. But we have to face this. And I think it can be argued that there are ultimately benefits to us as well, in that we will be living with much healthier, more viable, and contributing Native communities.
>
> If we don't face up to it, I think it is clear that Native people will feel forced into extreme action in order to achieve what they believe to be, and what seems to an increasing number of Canadians to be, a very legitimate aspiration . . .
>
> I want to make it absolutely clear that I am in no way advocating militancy and certainly not violence, but I think that the degree of militancy and extremist measures around the world should tell us that if we don't take the legitimate concerns of Native people seriously, we should not be surprised if extremism, which we smugly feel is the problem of the Irish or the Americans, becomes our problem in a real and direct way. We have had a relatively placid, peaceful history in Canada but it is not impossible to imagine the frustrations of a re-awakened people leading to extremes that could make Canada a less pleasant place to live.[9]

It is not formally recorded how the predominantly white, predominantly business-oriented Rotarians of Yellowknife felt about this speech which placed the Native problem squarely where it belongs—in the laps of white people. The reaction was undoubtedly—

given personally observed reactions by many Northern whites—the one expected by Barber. When we stand on the other fellow's toes for so long, we become indignant when he wants to pull his foot out.

Notes

1 *The Native Press* (Yellowknife, Northwest Territories), March 13, 1975.

2 Peter Cumming in *Arctic Alternatives* (Canadian Arctic Resources Committee: Ottawa, 1973) Page 94.

3 An appeal by the Federal government against Judge Morrow's decision was heard in the Northwest Territories Court of Appeal in June 1975, on two technical counts. A decision on this appeal had not been handed down when this book went to press.

4 Reasons for the judgment of Mr. Justice W. G. Morrow (No. 2) in the Supreme Court of the Northwest Territories, in the matter of the application of Chief Francois Paulette et al, to lodge a certain caveat with the Registrar of Titles of the Land Titles Office for the Northwest Territories, September 6th, 1973, Page 56.

5 Royal Proclamation of King George III of Great Britain, issued in 1763 at Westminster, England.

6 Prime Minister Pierre Trudeau speaking in his Ottawa office, February 7, 1973, to a delegation from the Nishga Tribal Council.

7 The dissenting opinion of the Supreme Court of Canada, January 31, 1973, on an Appeal by the Nishga Tribal Council against the Government of British Columbia, written by Mr. Justice Emmett Hall.

8 "The Basis for Native Claims in Canada", an address to the Rotary Club of Yellowknife, Northwest Territories, by L. I. Barber, Indian Claims Commissioner for Canada, October, 1974.

9 Ibid.

We know that the white man does not understand our ways. One portion of the land is the same to him as the next, for he is a stranger who comes in the night and takes from the land whatever he needs.

The earth is not his brother but his enemy, and when he has conquered it, he moves on. He leaves his fathers' graves behind and he does not care. He kidnaps the earth from his children. He does not care. His fathers' graves and his children's birthright are forgotten. His appetite will devour the earth and leave behind only a desert.

The sight of your cities pains the eyes of the redman. But perhaps it is because the redman is a savage and does not understand . . .

Portion of a letter written in 1855 to the
President of the United States by
Chief Seathl (Seattle)
Chief of the Suwamish Tribe in the State of Washington
regarding the proposed purchase of the tribe's land

2

Energy

Our Most Non-Renewable, Non-Returnable
Throw-a-Way Product

Up in Northwest British Columbia along both sides of the Nass Valley, the ugly scars of clear-cut logging pock the base of the mountains, making them look like some disease-ravaged giant. Euphemistically called "tree-farming," this is just an indication of bigger things to come. A huge, secret development scheme, promoted and backed by Victoria and Ottawa, threatens to change the northwest from a beautiful wilderness into a $500 million industrial complex.

In Northern Manitoba great rivers are dammed, diverted, or dried up to create massive amounts of electricity for the lucrative markets of the United States. The Manitoba government—yesterday's social activists and today's social entrepeneurs—have just borrowed from a Swiss bank another $40 million dollars (one of many foreign loans) which will be earmarked for Manitoba Hydro's Northern capital programs.

In Northern Quebec, Premier Robert Bourassa's "Project of the Century," which has been plagued by lawsuits, labor strife, and money problems, has also been plagued by Parti-Quebecois charges that label it the "multi-billion-dollar bungle of the century." Scary, when you think that much of Quebec's economic future depends on the success of this grandiose scheme of harnessing enormous amounts of "cheap" power from the rivers that flow into James Bay.

And so it goes. In the past, the vast wilderness of the Canadian North was virtually ignored—in terms of resource development—but now these regions have become the promised land of fuel, mineral deposits, and hydro-electric potential. The unrelenting drill continues to probe for oil and natural gas in the High Arctic. In a few short years, after decades of almost total obscurity, the Arctic has become a major resource area. And as our voracious consumption of energy —and that of the United States—continues to grow, the development of Northern resources will fall increasingly into the hands of multinational corporations and other profit-oriented developers, for the most part not accountable to the Canadian public.

These giant, mostly American companies have invested billions of dollars to find oil and gas in the far reaches of the North and to eventually transport it to our southern markets and the United States. The need is merely to provide cleaner heat and better light, to provide more horsepower for our cars, to turn on our gadgets, to maintain industry that provides goods and services that in turn contribute to our affluent comfort—and whose indiscriminate use produces incredible waste.

The United States and Canada are ranked as the highest users of energy in the world today. We contain little more than 6.5 percent of the world's population, yet we consume more than 43 percent of the energy on this planet. Worse still, we cause more than 40 percent of the earth's industrial pollution, and no less than 48 percent of total energy ends up in waste. In the last 25 years, Canada's consumption of fossil fuel and hydro-electric power has increased four times and is expected, by the end of this century, to multiply four more times. There is every reason to believe that, as the world continues to increase its population, even these figures will become obsolete. Surely, even to the most myopic, it is clear that the non-renewable resources of this planet are limited, that the time will soon be upon us when we must make some hard decisions about who should own and manage our energy resources and who should dictate our national energy policy.

The so-called energy "crisis" in the Western world has caused us to focus on the energy resources of the Canadian North, posing new threats to the Native people in their struggle for survival. Governments and large corporations combine to secretly plan and suddenly announce the construction of large scale industrial projects, without prior consultation with the people who will be most directly affected. The Churchill River Diversion plan (mentioned earlier in this chapter and discussed later in greater detail) is a perfect case in point.

From the very beginning, the grand design to divert the Churchill River into the Nelson River in Northern Manitoba made no provision for the wishes or rights of the people who live in the area. The huge project, expected to create enormous amounts of hydro-electric power for southern-based interests and the United States, was given approval by the federal government and has been doggedly backed by the present (as well as the former Conservative) government of Manitoba. Manitoba Hydro's own calculations show that there is enough energy in the Nelson River alone to meet the needs of *Manitoba* for at least the next 20 years, even if consumption continued to grow at the predicted rate of 7 percent a year.

Why the project now? So that excessive power consumption can continue in the south. So that Hydro can sell its excess summer supply of power to the United States at a handsome profit. Later on, Hydro could always add a couple of uranium enrichment plants and sell the uranium to Britain, France, and the United States, to feed their nuclear reactors, as Quebec wishes to do.

Cheap power in the south requires destruction of the lives of the Native people in the North, who have always lived within the means afforded them by their environment. Some say a short-sighted, even cowardly sellout. It would appear that Manitoba Hydro, a Crown corporation, has outgrown any need to be accountable to the public, and not unlike the giant multi-nationals, embodies one law only—the law of growth. But more and more public attention is being drawn to the fact that concentration of economic resources is ending up in the hands of large corporations. In Canada the problem is particularly acute. By 1970, only 229 of the 207,424 corporations in Canada (.1 percent) owned 53 percent of total corporate assets. In manufacturing, 62 of the 21,000 firms (.3 percent) owned 40 percent of the total assets.[1]

Just who are these companies who enjoy the approval and the blessings of governments in their all-out campaign to gobble up public resources?

In the case of the multi-national petroleum companies, the world's seven largest oil companies—known as the International Oil Cartel—have a virtual monopoly on the non-Soviet bloc of the world-wide industry. Sometimes called the "seven sisters," they are Texaco, Exxon, Mobil, Standard Oil of California, Gulf (United States controlled), Royal Dutch Shell (British and Dutch controlled), and British Petroleum. Their holdings include pipelines, exploration and producing facilities, refineries and transportation facilities. They own your local service station and they decide how much the next tank of gas is going to cost you. Besides that, according to Statistics Canada, Imperial Oil, a subsidiary of Exxon, controls 49 Canadian companies, and two cents of every Canadian dollar spent in Canada ends up in Esso's bank account. Operating in more than 100 countries, Exxon grossed the whopping sum of $20.3 billion in 1972.

Because of the tremendous size of the energy industry, it is almost impossible for the average citizen—or the average government for that matter—to comprehend it, and it is not our purpose to de-mystify the complexities of the international oil and gas companies here. It is obvious, however, that the name of the oil companies' game is "gouge the consumer", while enjoying the protection of federal policy. Their purpose is always to search out profit. An oil company will often co-operate rather than compete. It then becomes a monopoly and withholds oil to increase profit, and "in addition to assisting in maintaining high prices, its exchange agreements enable a firm to sell in a market area even when it does not have a refinery nearby to furnish gasoline."[2]

In an article written for *Spokesman Pamphlet, 1971*, Malcolm Caldwell points out that Standard Oil, under its present name, Exxon, has the kind of budget that ranks it behind only the United States and the Soviet Union.

> Standard Oil of New Jersey alone had sales of $14,000 million in 1968, which is not far short of the combined GNP's of Indonesia, Malaysia and Singapore put together. The thirty-three oil companies featured in *Fortune* magazine's top five hundred account for one-third of their joint earnings. "It is estimated that through such sectors as transport, roads, plastics, hotels, garages and a multitude of other activities shaped and dominated by petroleum supply, the oil companies may directly and indirectly share up to 45–65 percent of the American GNP.[3]

The energy "shortage" which caused long lineups and short tempers at the gas pumps in the summer, fall, and winter of 1973 caused many people to believe there was indeed a world-wide energy "crisis" caused, in part, by the Middle East War. It would seem now that either the oil companies failed to be aware of the increased demand for oil, or they deliberately contrived the shortage to increase profit by restricting supplies. It is a generally accepted fact that there was not, at that time, a physical shortage of energy supply in the United States, even though that country has been using up energy at an unprecedented rate. The shortage, it would appear, was of a totally political and economical nature, foisted on an unsuspecting American public, and the reverberations were felt in Canada as well.

In July of 1973, Democratic Senator, Henry Jackson, a 1976 United States presidential nominee, made public a Federal Trade Commission study of the petroleum industry. The report, released over the objections of the FTC noted "this growing and widespread conviction that the fuel shortage is a deliberate, conscious contrivance of the major integrated petroleum companies to destroy the independent refiners and marketers, to capture new markets, to increase gasoline prices and to obtain the repeal of environmental protection legislation."[4]

Back in 1960, The Organization of Petroleum Exporting Countries (OPEC) was founded. These include all the major Arab oil producers and African and South American exporters. Canada and the United States do not belong, although Canada is a major exporter to the United States. The purpose of this organization was to stop the declining price of oil on international markets. Slowly, it began to dawn on these oil producing countries that on each gallon of gas the consumer bought for $56\frac{1}{2}$ cents, they were in some cases receiving only $7\frac{1}{2}$ cents or less than 14 percent. At the same time, company profits on the same gallon amounted to 14 cents or almost 25 percent.

In 1971, the Tehran and Tripoli Agreements were signed by the OPEC countries, establishing a four-step price rise that would increase from $6.7 billion-a-year in 1969, to $41.2 billion-a-year by 1980. This meant, of course, that the giant oil companies would have to take a cut in profit by paying higher royalties to OPEC members or somehow bring prices up to a level that would ensure their previous enormous profits.

By 1973 the domestic production of oil in the United States was failing to keep up with the demand. The timing of the Middle East War in that year and the subsequent oil embargoes was perfect. The oil companies cried "shortage" and blamed the Arabs. The United States government acquiesced. Prices went up ostensibly to finance exploration for new sources of supply, and the oil companies have been reaping handsome profits ever since. In the third quarter of 1973, Exxon increased profits by 80.7 percent, Mobil by 64.1 percent, Texaco by 58.2 percent, Gulf by 90.9 percent, and Standard of California by 50.7 percent.[5]

There have been other benefits for the oil cartel as a result of the phony energy "crisis". By claiming to have only enough supplies for their own franchised operators, major oil companies were able to knock out thousands of independent operators who had bought gasoline and sold it at prices below those ordained by the cartel. It provided the opportunity to slow down gains made by ecologists and environmentalists.

On November 18, 1973, President Richard Nixon signed, under what were considered to be crisis conditions, a bill permitting a consortium to begin work on a 789-mile-long pipeline that would stretch from the oil wells at Prudhoe Bay on Alaska's north coast, to the deep water, ice-free port of Valdez near the Panhandle. This action effectively swept away environmental lawsuits by people who felt the building of this 2 million-barrel-a-day pipeline would be a disaster and an ecological tragedy. The pipeline, costing $6 billion, is now well under way with a completion date set for 1977.

We are not suggesting that, because the energy shortage was contrived by the big oil companies, we in Canada can now breath a sigh of relief and continue to use energy with our former gay abandon. In fact, John Turner, former Federal Minister of Finance, legislated moderation and constraint when, in his June 1975 budget, he hiked the prices by slapping higher excise taxes on gasoline, heating fuel, and natural gas.

> We must [Turner said] accept the fact that our existing supplies of both oil and gas from Western Canada are limited. They are so limited, in fact, that Canada's capacity to supply its own requirements will likely diminish steadily from now until the early or mid-1980's. We shall only be able to increase our self-reliance if we are prepared to pay the high prices required to meet the high cost of finding, developing, and transporting petroleum from new sources of supply. Neither the tar sands nor the frontier will yield up their treasure without a massive commitment of human and material resources.[6]

How can Canadians be sure that the $350 million they coughed up to the federal government in this fiscal year will end up in exploration? Well, they can't. Any more than they can be sure that foreign oil companies are not deliberately underestimating Canada's oil reserves to create visions of shortages, thus raising prices to finance more Northern exploration and thereby creating profits. James Laxer, in his book *Canada's Energy Crisis*, echoes this sentiment.

> In 1973, the Canadian petroleum industry entered a new and mysterious phase in its development. The industry dropped its traditional rhetoric about expanding production and began predicting petroleum shortages for Canada.
> In 1973, the oil companies told us that Canada could produce

more than enough oil to meet her domestic needs for the next 80 years. In 1974, they told us that Canada would face domestic oil shortages in only eight years.

This dramatic change in estimates took place at the same time as the international price of oil increased from $3 a barrel to $11 a barrel. The coincidence of these two developments—the change in the estimates of Canada's reserves and the international oil price revolution—must give pause to any serious observer.

Projected oil shortages in Canada are welcome news to the oil industry. They serve to prod governments to raise the domestic price of Canadian oil to the world price.

Despite the disturbing coincidence of these events, the Canadian government has gone along unquestioningly with the new estimates of the industry. Government agencies and the public are prisoners of a small group of petroleum companies who have a monopoly on this information and whose top level decision-making is located outside Canada—in American and European offices.[7]

On a cold, wintery day back in December, 1973, less than a month after the United States Senate and President Nixon approved the Alaska Pipeline Bill, Prime Minister Trudeau rose in the House of Commons and made clear his Liberal government's position on one of the most gigantic and costly private enterprise schemes of all times—the proposed Mackenzie Valley Pipeline, which his colleagues have compared with the construction of the Canadian Pacific Railway. No wonder the Natives recoil in horror!

"The government believes," the prime minister said, "that it would be in the public interest to facilitate early construction by any means which do not require the lowering of environmental standards or the neglect of the Indians' rights and interests."[8]

It has been the government's policy to woo foreign investors into the Canadian North by making exploration and extraction costs incredibly cheap. The federal government's royalty policy on oil and natural gas virtually gives away these non-renewable resources to petroleum companies whose financial gains are extremely high. For example, the government collects 5 percent of the available royalty amount for the first 3 years, and 10 percent thereafter, leaving the petroleum industry with 95 and 90 percent respectively. The industry now has 50 years of contracts covering 80 percent of the 544 million potential Northern producing acres.[9] And now, Mr. Trudeau, the greatest wooer of them all, has given approval to the most Herculean project in history—the transportation by pipeline of Arctic natural gas to southern markets in Canada and the United States.

In March, 1974, Canadian Arctic Gas Pipeline Limited, a consortium of 27 major petroleum, pipeline, and transportation companies (mostly American)[10] filed applications in Ottawa—as did its sister company, Alaskan Arctic Gas Pipeline Company in Washington—to build an estimated $8-billion, 48-inch, natural gas pipeline from the oil and gas fields of Prudhoe Bay across the Yukon and Northwest territories, where it would take on Canadian gas from the Mackenzie Delta. Plunging south, up the Mackenzie Valley and into Alberta to a point just northwest of Calgary, the pipeline would fork, with one artery aimed southwest and one artery aimed southeast. The gas would be relayed by existing facilities, as well as by new lines, into Canadian and United States' consumer markets.

When the proposed pipeline idea was first aired before the public, two questions most often asked were: why foreign interest, and why Arctic gas, now? Some people see the scheme as allowing more foreign domination of our non-renewable resources. Arctic Gas would have us believe it is a co-operative venture between two countries that would mutually benefit. Originally, Arctic Gas promoted the pipeline as a joint carrier for Alaskan and Canadian gas on the grounds that this system of delivery could not be justified in terms of the Canadian market alone. The plan was devised, according to Arctic Gas, as follows:

> Alaska has rich gas fields and Canada also has fields in the Mackenzie Delta, although less extensive. The gas Arctic plan is premised on a basic concept: Canada could gain worthwhile access to its own reserves by seeking to make transportation of gas from the Mackenzie and Alaska a co-operative "piggy back" venture. The advantages to Canada and the U.S. are as obvious as a car pool. Both nations will be assured of adequate energy supplies at the lowest cost possible, sharing talent and facilities to benefit their respective populations. The Study Group formed two companies, Canadian Arctic Gas Study Ltd. and Alaskan Arctic Gas Study Company to carry out the feasibility engineering, environmental, and financial work needed to prepare applications for the pipeline to Canadian and U.S. regulatory authorities . . .[11]

But Eric Kierans, former Trudeau Government cabinet minister, now a McGill economist and leading opponent of the pipeline, was not impressed. He put it this way.

> The incorporation of Canadian Arctic Gas Study Ltd. seemed to resolve the Canadian government's political problems. It could say to the Canadian people that it was concerned about foreign ownership of our resources and that it could prove it because it was insisting

on 51 percent Canadian ownership of this pipeline. At the same time it could say to Washington that, while the government was more internationally-minded and good-neighborly, it had to contend with a contagious nationalism at home and a group of virulent, but articulate xenophones . . .[12]

But the real arch-enemy of Arctic Gas and its affiliate, Alaskan Arctic Gas, is the El Paso Company of Houston, Texas, and if its scheme is adopted, it could spell the end for Arctic Gas. On May 5, 1975, a tense hearing began in Washington, D.C. at the headquarters of the Federal Power Commission, to determine who would win the grand prize—licence to build the world's largest gas pipeline.

Under El Paso's plan, the gas would be piped from Prudhoe Bay to the south coast Alaska town of Valdez, along the same route as the Alaskan oil pipeline, where it would be liquified and loaded into specially built tankers and shipped along the west coast of Canada to United States' ports in Washington, Oregon, and California. El Paso claims that the proposed line would deviate no more than a mile from the Alyeska (oil) line, and the same environmental factors would apply. Arctic Gas disputes this, saying that El Paso may have to reroute its line as much as 100 miles, because many of the mountain passes are too narrow for two lines. Separate studies would have to be done, delaying the project and adding to its cost.

El Paso argued that, because of the varied components of its system, the capital cost of $6.7 billion, spent mostly in the United States, would benefit a wider section of the American economy. Arctic Gas countered that its system would save United States' consumers $600 to $800 million. The Arctic Gas Consortium believes it has the more economically viable proposal, and this view is supported by the major utilities in the United States.

In the aftermath of the Viet Nam war, with the United States becoming more isolationist in its foreign policy, El Paso has one more ace-in-the-hole, and that is, don't trust American natural resources to foreign control, no matter how friendly the power is or even if its natural resources are American-owned.

> It [El Paso] is talking of the "dire consequences" of moving Alaskan gas through Canada, consequences "so threatening to the reliability of Alaskan gas service that they compel a rejection of the trans-Canada concept."
>   At the pre-hearing conference, El Paso eloquently established its position.
>   "A Canadian pipeline would commit Alaskan gas reserves inevitably and irretrievably to a measure of Canadian control."[13]

On the other hand, Foothills Pipeline Limited, owned by Alberta Gas Trunkline Limited of Calgary, has also filed an application with the National Energy Board, and it is for a 42-inch pipeline that offers complete Canadian control. It would run along much the same line as Arctic Gas, but there would be no "piggy-back" line from Alaska. Called the "MapleLeaf Line," it would deliver only Canadian gas to only Canadian markets—it says.[14] Arctic Gas huffily accused its competitors of "nationalistic bias."

But the fight is on and the battlefield is the Arctic, where the people have the most to lose. Along with the oil scare there is now a gas scare, and the big oil companies are putting enormous pressure on the government to build a pipeline to get Arctic gas south as quickly as possible. But is now the time to start tapping Canadian Arctic gas supplies?

If you listen to Arctic Gas, they will tell you that natural gas shortages will occur in Canada as early as 1980 and the "country has no more than six or seven years in which to get additional reserves to its markets . . . to avert shortages such as those now facing the United States."[15] They will say, as they do in their handsomely printed Arctic Gas "Profile," that:

> Reserves of natural gas in western Canada are not now growing at a rate as fast as the growth in demand. The result has been a gradual decline in the relative supply of proved remaining reserves of marketable natural gas. This has not yet reached a critical point. But the trend will continue until we can gain economic access to the 85 percent of our potential gas resources which lie outside of western Canada. . . . Long before the gas reserves in western Canada have been depleted they will be incapable of production at a rate sufficient to supply continually increasing demand. It is at this point that Canada will require supplementary supplies of natural gas from new source areas, initially at a modest rate, but in steadily increasing volumes. Studies by Arctic Gas suggest that this may start to occur by about 1980.[16]

Eric Kierans doesn't buy that argument. Kierans maintains that the Arctic Gas consortium represents essentially the same international oil firms that make up the Canadian Petroleum Association which in 1970 successfully urged the National Energy Board to approve export of 6.3 trillion cubic feet of western natural gas to the United States. Declares Kierans:

> I will never know by what twist and tortuous processes of thinking it can be concluded . . . that Delta gas is urgently needed for Canadian consumers while cheaper Alberta gas continues to flow south.[17]

And John Helliwell, University of British Columbia economist, has added his voice to the growing skepticism concerning the
need for Arctic gas supplies now.

The consortium [Arctic Gas] argues that Arctic gas will be required
for Canadian use before 1980. Our independent research at the end
of 1973 indicated the contrary—that even if natural gas demand were
to grow at the improbably fast rate of eight percent until 1980 and
four percent beyond, Canadian non-frontier gas supplies would be
sufficient to deliver enough gas to cover Canadian demand and existing export contracts until the late 1980's. If account is taken of
the energy conservation measures being induced by higher oil and
gas prices, and being encouraged by various government and private
groups, it is even less likely that any Arctic gas would be needed in
the next 15 years.[18]

The federally-appointed National Energy Board (NEB), in
the most complex hearing it has ever undertaken, will decide later
this year whether or not to tap Mackenzie delta Arctic gas supplies.
Canadians have had to rely on the NEB to make findings that would
bring the whole question of oil and gas supplies into a true perspective. The truth, as it were, should emerge from these hearings—the
truth about conflicting claims of dwindling gas reserves and whether
or not petroleum companies have been deliberately misleading the
public when they say that Arctic gas is urgently needed now for
Canada. Since the NEB is virtually an arm of the federal government,
and in particular the energy department, and since the decision
regarding the pipeline will ultimately be made by cabinet, there
need to be some serious questions raised about the impartiality of
this regulatory body.

It has been no secret to anyone that Trudeau and some other
members of his cabinet have publicly supported the building of a
pipeline. In March of 1975, then Acting Prime Minister Mitchell
Sharp said in the House of Commons that he "could imagine circumstances" in which the government would have to make a decision
about the pipeline before Mr. Justice Tom Berger's report on the
project was presented. And there is rising skepticism on the part
of some people. The New Democratic Party's energy critic, Tommy
Douglas, asserts bluntly that the government has already made up its
mind in favor of the pipeline and that the Berger Commission is
irrelevant.

If assurances to the contrary are only a "sop to pacify the general public and the Natives," as suggested by Douglas, then we can
only view the hearings of the NEB, as well as the high sounding

phrases of Trudeau's "participatory democracy," with some suspicion. It would seem the time has come—and is long overdue—for
Canada to turn its energy policy right-side-up.

Canada has for years been enticing multi-national corporations
into this country to explore, develop, extract, and transport our non-
renewable resources. She has been making herself more and more
attractive by providing low royalty payments, special federal tax
privileges, and exploration concessions. The favorable tax climate
for the petroleum companies has produced billions of dollars for
them, increasing their size and non- accountability to the Canadian
public. The exploitation of our national resources has taken on
night-marish proportions in the light of damage to the environment,
the economy, and the rights of Native peoples. It is imperative that
Canada create some kind of sane policy before time runs out.

Since Canadians are the second highest per capita energy users
in the world, we need to question the goals of an industrial system
that encourages people to consume and waste in such incredible
amounts. The government has offered legislation that encourages
voluntary constraints yet, at the same time, supports large industrial
projects designed to meet our insatiable demands. We should encourage our government to create public education programs on the
conservation of energy and take appropriate measures to regulate
advertising and other forms of social pressure which prompts wasteful consumption.

We live in a country whose wealth comes primarily from its
natural resources. We need a policy, therefore, that involves putting
back into our own hands these resources that are now largely controlled by multi-national corporations. This would include the
creation of a just royalty and tax climate that would reduce the
excessive profits now made by large companies. The United States'
demands for our oil and gas are becoming louder and more strident.
We must be prepared to make firm decisions that are in Canada's
interest, even if those decisions include the stoppage of oil and gas
exports to the United States. An energy policy should also include
a concerted effort to seek and develop alternative sources of energy.
For example, the potential of the sun's energy is immense. We suggest that some of the money and research, now used for pipelines
that in a few decades will be obsolete, could well go into developing
the technology to utilize this potential source of energy.

Finally, if Canadians are to become responsible stewards of
their own resources, they must insist that any energy policy must

include exporting energy, below international prices, to Third World countries that now pay 20 percent more for oil and gas than do industrial nations. Because of the high prices charged by industrialized countries, people of the less developed nations have precious little left over for badly needed goods and services. For example, high prices for oil prevent poorer countries from buying fertilizer needed for production of food, thus causing widespread starvation. The struggle of people in the so-called Third World offers Canadians a chance to stop and consider the reality of what is happening in our own northlands to the Native people there. Perhaps we still have a chance to turn around and build a society built on justice rather than greed.

Notes

1 Eric Kierans, "Arctic Gas and the National Purpose" *Gas from the Mackenzie Delta: Now or Later?* May 23–24, 1974, (Ottawa, Canadian Arctic Resources Committee; 1974), Page 73.

2 *Toronto Star*, July 9, 1973.

3 Malcolm Caldwell, "Oil and Imperialism in East Asia", *Spokesman Pamphlet*, No. 20, Partisan Press, Nottingham, U.K. Page 6.

4 Permanent Subcommittee of the U.S. Senate, Report on the Petroleum Industry, Washington, D.C., 1973.

5 *Ramparts Magazine*, New York, March, 1974.

6 The Honorable John Turner, Finance Minister, introducing the Federal budget in the House of Commons, Ottawa, June 23, 1975.

7 James Laxer, *Canada's Energy Crisis*, (Toronto; James Lorimer and Co., 1975), Page 137.

8 *Time Magazine*, Montreal, Que., April 1, 1974.

9 Peter H. Pearse, editor, *The Mackenzie Pipeline: Arctic Gas and Canadian Energy Policy*, (Toronto, McLelland and Stewart; 1974), Page 82.

10 "Some Facts About Arctic Gas", (Toronto; Canadian Arctic Gas Pipelines Ltd., 1975).

Some of the participants in the Arctic Gas Project are:

Majority-owned Canadian Companies
    Alberta Natural Gas Company Limited,
    Canada Development Corporation,
    The Consumers' Gas Company,
    Northern and Central Gas Corporation Limited,
    Numac Oil and Gas Limited,
    TransCanada PipeLines Limited,
    Union Gas Limited,

Minority-owned Canadian Companies
    Canadian Superior Oil Limited,

Canadian Utilities Limited,
Gulf Oil Canada Limited,
Imperial Oil Limited,
Shell Canada Limited,
Non-Canadian owned companies
   Atlantic Richfield Company,
   The Columbia Gas Transmission Corporation,
   Michigan Wisconsin Pipe Line Company,
   Northern Natural Gas Company,
   Natural Gas Pipeline Company of America,
   Pacific Lighting Gas Development Company,
   Sun Oil Company Limited,
   Texas Eastern Transmission Corporation.

[11] "The Pipeline That Came in from the Cold" (Toronto; Canadian Arctic Gas Study Ltd., 1974), Pages 13-14.

[12] Eric Kierans, "Arctic Gas and the National Purpose", Page 70.

[13] *The Globe and Mail* (Toronto), May 5, 1975.

[14] Robert Blair, president, Foothills Pipelines Ltd., Calgary, Alberta, said in an interview with the *Toronto Star* on August 6, 1975, that if Foothills was granted permission to build the Mackenzie Valley Pipeline, he would ask the National Energy Board for a delay in its construction until Indian land claims were well on the way to being settled.

[15] "Why Canada Needs the Arctic Gas Pipeline", *Arctic Gas Profile* No. 1 (Toronto; Canadian Arctic Gas Study Ltd., October 3, 1973).

[16] Ibid.

[17] *Time Magazine*, Montreal, Que., April 1, 1974.

[18] John Helliwell, "Policy Alternatives for Arctic Gas", *Gas from the Mackenzie Delta: Now or Later?* May 23-24, 1974, (Ottawa; Canadian Arctic Resources Committee, 1974), Page 2.

Dear fellow members of the mushroom society: I address you in this fashion because I am sure that when you think about the growth of a mushroom, you will agree this is how our governments see us. You know how the mushroom grows best, don't you? In the dark and fed a lot of manure! So, fellow members of the mushroom society let us proceed to examine how it is that participatory democracy really works . . .

John Jensen
President of the
Terrace and District Labour Council
in a speech to the
Northwest Study Conference at
Terrace, British Columbia, 1975

3

The Mushroom Society

*Paternalism, Colonialism, and the
Department of Indian Affairs and
Northern Development*

It's enormous, complicated, remote, expensive, and contradictory. It has a federal cabinet minister at its head, aided and abetted by a parliamentary assistant and run by a deputy minister, no less than four assistant deputy ministers, two territorial commissioners, and almost 15,000 bureaucrats in various classifications. It had a total budget in 1975 (never forget for a moment that the government's fiscal year ends March 31 and must be spent) of just over $842 million, making it one of the more substantial items on the list in Ottawa. It has its share of bunglers, political hacks, hangers-on, and its share of highly competent, visionary, dedicated, and frustrated employees. In between these extremes it is made up of many faceless, usually unaccountable, bureaucrats who carry out, interpret, and we suggest, make policy from a 15-storey architecturally drab building known as Centennial Towers in beautiful downtown Ottawa.

It also has branches across the country made up of people bearing all the above descriptions. They would fit almost any ministry within our federal and provincial governments. But this one has a difference, and right now, in case you haven't already guessed, we're talking about a two-headed monster whose name alone expresses a conflict of interest—the Department of Indian Affairs and Northern Development (DIAND), the Honorable Judd Buchanan, minister.

The conflict of interest is its first difference. How, to ask the most elementary question, can one man be charged in one breath with preserving the rights of Canada's more than 500,000 Native people and in the other with pushing and promoting Northern resource development across the very lands he's supposed to be protecting? In between breaths, he's also in charge of national parks and a few sundry Crown corporations like the Northern Canada Power Commission. The Opposition finds this state of affairs, not surprisingly, unreasonable, and according to the latest policy statement of the Conservative Party, they would move to "end this dichotomy by a suitable re-arrangement of ministerial responsibilities."[1] Whatever that means is suitably vague.

However, Flora MacDonald, the former Tory critic of DIAND, who still makes Canada's Native people one of her prime concerns, sees it quite clearly as a preoccupation with southern (i.e. south of the 60th parallel) reserve Indians, under the present Indian Affairs branch and its assistant deputy minister, Mr. Peter Leseaux. Whereas Mr. Digby Hunt, assistant deputy minister of Northern development, is committed to a style of development in the North that can only be described as colonial.* This could result, in some situations, in creative tension, except that, insofar as public statements are concerned, the two divisions are not in open conflict, and Miss MacDonald thinks they should be, or else they should remain separate.

Speaking to Traffic Clubs International in Montreal two years ago, the Member of Parliament for Kingston and the Islands stated:

> Northern development, whether it involves transportation systems or harvesting natural resources, must be conditional upon settling the land claims of the Native people who have lived there from time immemorial. The longer political decisions about land claims are deferred, the longer will development of all kinds be delayed. This situation is especially applicable to the Mackenzie River corridor. It would be senseless for firms to spend millions or billions of dollars constructing transportation systems through land where the ownership is still in question. Development in the North must await the outcome of the Native peoples' land claim.[2]

What the Conservatives would do with DIAND is less clear. Whether they would place Native Affairs by itself with a full minister or whether they would amend, abolish, or replace the notorious (although still better than nothing) Indian Act is also unclear. We are often reminded of the attempts made by the last Progressive

*Hunt was recently appointed chief negotiator for Native land claims.

Conservative administration to ballyhoo the North into a vision that deteriorated into "roads to igloos" and has the dubious distinction of having foisted the instant town of Inuvik upon the Mackenzie Delta. Certainly, putting Indian Affairs in with Citizenship and Immigration was an even greater conflict of interest than is presently the case.

Government's role in the affairs of Native people in Canada goes back prior to Confederation. Many Native leaders are emphatic in their claim that Canada has a fully developed policy on Indians (because all Natives were at one time looked upon as Indians) that was formulated in Britain during its colonial administration of Canada and has never changed. The names have been altered, the faces are different, the bureaucracy remains.

In one word, that policy is assimilation. It is based on the inherent white, arrogant assumption that Native people must effect a transition from the Native way of life to the way of life of the white majority and with that basic assumption the belief that Indians (again read Natives) required then, and require now, assistance (more quickly now because of resource development) and paternal protection in making that transition. Hence, the Indian Act and whatever subsequent portfolio administered that act followed the assimilation policy down to the last Indian.

Only this year, the slick, professionally-written annual report of the Northwest Territories reiterated this policy of assimilation. Entitled *Arctic Today*, the hardcovered, multi-colored report, which is presented annually to the minister in charge of DIAND by the commissioner of the Northwest Territories, Stuart Hodgson, contains a highly positive account of the previous year's events. This issue, which would make any multi-national corporation green with envy, starts off with some emotive prose written by Ed Ogle, *Time Magazine's* bureau chief in Vancouver, who travels extensively with Hodgson and other Northwest Territories officials.

Ogle, a lucid writer, normally sensitive to Native Northerners, falls into the same trap as the Indian Act and its policy of assimilation. After outlining in some detail the events leading up to our present need for resource development, he writes:

> Few would quarrel with objectives which include higher standards of living for all northerners, a higher quality of life and greater equality of opportunity through methods compatible with the preferences and aspirations of the people themselves. The least hidden and potentially greatest resource of the north, its Native people, is at last being recognized.[3]

No one could argue against such a motherhood statement except to plaintively ask what standards of living? whose quality of life? and where do the preferences and aspirations come from — white or Native? Messers Ogle and Hodgson might also explain who thinks the Natives are the North's greatest resource? Certainly not the multi-national resource developers or their arch-supporters in DIAND. The assimilation policy, à la Northwest Territories '75, continues:

> Indians, Eskimos and Metis have lost generally and forever a way of life which they understood and to which they were uniquely adapted. Whatever the white man's responsibility for this, neither he nor the native northerner can turn back. In spite of sporadic and scattered attempts by some "to go back to the land" the old way has been seriously disrupted and in the main will gradually disappear.[4]

This is precisely the policy of DIAND toward all Canadian Natives. But it can be safely argued that they will not disappear, and if they are to live in white man's society, it will be on their own terms. "We are all Northerners alike. We are all Natives, those of us who were born here" — catch phrases used over and over again to promote the melting-pot theory that has worked in the United States with such disastrous results. Canadians are not assimilationists. Minorities have always had rights, at least in theory.

We are *not* all Natives, any more than we are all Anglophone or Francophone Canadians. There is a unique place in Canada for its Original People and the federal government is their guarantor. And the guarantee is the Indian Act, the British North America Act, and the Royal Proclamation of 1763, despite the built-in paternalism and unwritten policy of assimilation. Until a new Indian Act is forthcoming — and the White Paper of 1969 was no substitute — that is written in a clear and integrated fashion by the Native people of Canada, that old act is the only safeguard of Native communities and culture that there is.

A new Indian Act, which includes Inuit and Metis people, must be written by the Natives. It must also include maximum involvement by them and maximum implementation by them in order to safeguard their rights. This reform is now underway by Native people, but in the meantime, and in the face of rapid resource demands, present government policies must be shaped to interpret the act, regardless of how piecemeal and discriminatory it is, for the fullest protection of Native rights. Indeed, the present minister and his predecessor, Jean Chrétien, have been most articulate in this regard, but one wonders if their brave words have filtered down to the policy-implementation level as carried out by Hunt and Leseaux or if, as some Northern-watchers assert, control of DIAND has passed from the hands of the elected members of the government into the hands of the civil service. (Later in this chapter we will look at what is probably the most able of these Northern-watchers, the Canadian Arctic Resources Committee, a non-profit organization which attempts to pose alternatives and options for the Canadian North and as such, has kept a watching brief on DIAND, which has earned it an unenviable reputation at 400 Laurier Avenue in Ottawa.)

Mr. Chrétien, close friend of the prime minister, and now president of the Treasury Board, was perhaps in a more powerful position within the Liberal cabinet than rookie Judd Buchanan. As such, Chrétien carried more clout with his policy statements. Certainly the Native organizations felt more secure under his ministry than they do now. Chrétien, they claimed, being a French-Canadian, a small-town lawyer, and originally not very fluent in English, better understood their position as a minority in Canada. Whether or not this was the case, they felt this way until they began to see how little impact his speeches had on the people responsible for carrying out policy, because assimilation and integration continued to run hand-in-hand with Northern development.

Chrétien understood separate development as a Quebecois should, but he also understood the need for resource development if the traditional link between big business and the Liberal party coffers was to be maintained. He managed to balance both with greater finesse than his successor. Perhaps that is why he is cursed around the white beer parlors of Whitehorse in the Yukon as being in the Indians' back pocket. Certainly his speeches bear out a policy of land settlement before major development.

On August 8th, 1973, Chrétien issued a statement about the land claims of Indian and Inuit people which has never been repudiated by Mr. Buchanan. He said that the Liberals were pledged to honor "all lawful" obligations where Indian treaties were involved, although moral obligations were not mentioned. He made it clear that his government's policy was to recognize "its continuing responsibility under the British North America Act for Indians and lands reserved for Indians".[5] He expanded the federal government's jurisdiction, as the courts had earlier ruled, to include the Inuit. A clear statement some would say — one of acknowledged responsibility, one which could not easily be shifted or misinterpreted. He went on to guarantee some policies regarding the Native people not covered by treaty — in other words, Native land claims and aboriginal rights.

The Government is fully aware that the claims are not only for money and land, but involve the loss of a way of life. Any settlement, therefore, must contribute positively to a lasting solution of cultural, social and economic problems that for too long have kept the Indian and Inuit people in a disadvantaged position. It is basic to the position of the government that these claims be settled and that the most promising avenue to settlement is through negotiation. It is envisaged that by this means agreements will be reached and that these agreements will be enshrined in legislation, enacted by Parliament, so that they will have the finality of law.[6]

Holy head-dress! No mention of settlements being rushed by pipelines or hydro projects. No mention here of "unrealistic" demands. No mention here of extinguishment of land title. Just high-minded phrases about flexibility and concern.

But what's happened since then despite the fact that this policy statement has never been repudiated? Since then Mr. Chrétien has moved on to bigger and better things. But not before a settlement was imposed on the Cree and Inuit people of James Bay, despite a court ruling that they had aboriginal title to most of Northern Quebec (see Chapter 4). It was a settlement forced on Native people, because there was a massive hydro project which, the Quebec Appeal Court said, could not be stopped while the rights of a few thousand Natives were "enshrined in legislation." It isn't good enough for Mr. Chrétien or Mr. Buchanan to shrug the settlement off as a provincial responsibility. Native people are the sole responsibility of the federal government and so is their land.

Since that policy statement in 1973, the Native people of the Northwest Territories have been researching a land claim (see Chapter 8) that is based on the slogan "no pipeline before a land claim settlement." But only in June, Mr. Hunt, in a speech at Banff to the Canadian Mining Association, said that a pipeline down the Mackenzie Valley could be built before land claims were settled and it could start next year, despite the fact this was Indian land. His hypocricy is total when he says that no one wants to rush the Natives into doing their land claim research. No rush, just allow us to build on your land.

Mr. Buchanan has threatened to cut off the Northwest Territories' funding for land claim research, because "the Native claim is unrealistic." But where, gentlemen, does Mr. Chrétien's policy statement talk about "hurried" settlements or pipelines? Where does it talk about "realism" from the white man's point-of-view?

After that policy statement was publicly aired by DIAND, Native people have been told they must be prepared to settle within something called Canada's national interest. They must be prepared to have their lands expropriated either legally or as an accomplished fact, because it is deemed to be "in the greater good." By whom it is so "deemed" or in who's "greater good" is rarely subject to negotiation. Mr. Buchanan has described it publicly as something like taking 20 feet off his lot if the city says it is for the greater good of London to build a road where he owns land. The analogy boggles the mind when compared with all of British Columbia for example.

Two examples of what happens in the name of the greater good are the events in Northern Quebec and Northern Manitoba. Both will be examined in detailed chapters later on, but in the context of the Liberal policy statements of 1973, they are interesting illustrations of how policies can be bent.

Manitoba Hydro may flood thousands of acres of land for hydro projects involving the Nelson-Churchill River diversion scheme. Some of this land belongs to various Indian bands as reserves set aside under treaties with the federal government. Canadian law makes it clear that reserve land is Indian land and therefore cannot be expropriated by any level of government except with express permission of the bands involved and the action of the federal cabinet.

Mr. Chrétien's 1973 policy statement on reserve lands is equally as clear as his statements on aboriginal rights.

> Many Indian groups in Canada have a relationship with the federal government which is symbolized in Treaties entered into by those people with the Crown in historic times. As the government pledged some years ago, lawful obligations must be recognized. This remains the basis of government policy.[7]

Someone should have told Manitoba Hydro and the "people's" NDP government of Premier Edward Schreyer in Winnipeg. Thousands of acres of reserve land in Northern Manitoba are being threatened with expropriation by flooding, and no level of government has given its permission. After the fact, DIAND and some of the Indian bands involved may sue the province and its offspring, Manitoba Hydro. Where was DIAND, the department constitutionally charged with defending and protecting Indian land? It seems the hydro project was so far in the works that a few Indians were not even allowed to protest their few acres of reserve land. What about "lawful obligations?"

When Premier Robert Bourassa dusted off an old report on the James Bay hydro development back in 1971 and promoted his multi-billion dollar scheme into an election victory, it seemed as though no one even knew that 7,000 Cree and 4,400 Inuit lived in the area, that they had never been conquered in war, and that none of their land was ever ceded to the Crown. Their language and culture remained intact, and although Quebec had been required to negotiate a land settlement with them as one of the terms of the 1912 Boundaries Extension Act, successive governments had ignored the Natives. The province was to "recognize the rights of the Indian inhabitants . . . to the same extent, and will obtain surrender thereof" in order to have Northern Quebec become provincial land. Nothing was ever done; no treaty was ever made. But Bourassa was undaunted. He needed 100,000 jobs to win the 1971 election. Who were a handful of Cree and Inuit to stop him? and further, if you suggested that these people had rights, you were dubbed anti-Quebecois on the grounds that most of the Natives owed their allegiance to the Anglican church and used English as their second language.

Clearly then, the Cree and Inuit, under the Indian Act, were the responsibility of the federal government, but by late in 1971, Chrétien was doing everything in his power to evade the issue, and it was not until a year later that he even spoke for the Indians, suggesting to the Liberal Quebec Premier that a land settlement should be made. Eventually, money was forthcoming to help the now-famous Malouf court case, where for eight heady days the Indians and Inuit actually succeeded in halting the project until the Appeal Court injected a note of "sanity" and sent the construction workers back to their bulldozers.

The outcome was inevitable. A "settlement" was negotiated all too quickly (the terms of which will be discussed in the next chapter). It was a typical land extinguishment settlement, albeit with more generous terms than those negotiated earlier in the century. It was negotiated with construction well underway and violation of Indian land an accomplished fact. By November 1, 1975, James Bay had been disposed of and its terms touted as a model for the rest of Canada.

Where were the vaunted "lawful obligations" of Trudeau and Chrétien? Obviously during the height of the separatist crisis, with Trudeau's political future riding on federalism, there was no way any deterioration of relations between Ottawa and Quebec was going to be allowed. Ottawa kept a low profile in the dispute, even if it meant sacrificing the most primitive, the most Native of all its charges in the interest of expediency. It was politics at the highest level. Mr. Chrétien's policy statement of 1973 carefully skirted James Bay on the grounds that the matter was before the courts.

These two examples then, Northern Manitoba and Northern Quebec, one a treaty area, the other involving unextinguished land, clearly indicate that Indian Affairs has always been utterly reluctant to side clearly with its charges when it comes to land that is coveted by energy-hungry corporations or vote-hungry politicians. The policy remains the same — assimilate. And the method is the same. Plan projects in secret, announce them, then if the Indians object, settle for as little as possible and tell no one any more than you have to. If those pesky Indians would only do as they're supposed to and integrate, then the Indian problem could be solved once and for all.

After the Liberals had achieved a comfortable majority, Trudeau promoted the faithful Chrétien to the powerful Treasury Board portfolio, and a tall, lanky, Prairie-born former parliamentary assistant to Chrétien took over and moved into the cabinet. Judd Buchanan, 48, represents a London, Ontario riding, is a graduate of Western's prestigious business administration school, and an ambitious politician. He's going to solve the Indian problem, make a name for himself, and move onwards and upwards in the federal government. That's the scenario as many Indians see it. They fear this man and express little hope for fair settlements as long as he heads DIAND. Chrétien they understood, if they didn't always trust. He was from a minority. His English was always stilted. He liked Indians, and best of all, he seldom lost his temper — at least in public. Additionally — rightly or wrongly — the Native people suspected that Chrétien carried a fair amount of weight in the cabinet.

They see Buchanan as a WASP, an Easterner or worse, an Albertan by birth, Protestant, ambitious, and far down the totem pole in cabinet ranking. He has a reputation for impatience, indeed anger, at the slowness or intransigence of the Native position. They suspect, with his Bay Street credentials, that he's firmly in the hands of the DIAND development-oriented bureaucrats. Chrétien fought off the likes of Digby Hunt all the time he was minister, and he wasn't too successful. What chance do we have with a minister who's firmly committed to the cabinet's position on energy? a Prairie Indian leader asked us. This is how the Native organizations and their leaders see the situation today in DIAND.

They regularly boo or laugh at Leseaux, their own assistant

deputy minister. His reliance on public relations, rather than on developing new approaches to Indian Affairs, angers many leaders who insist there has been no consultation before the implementation of new policies. The department recently issued a set of guidelines about accounting for money and band level administration that has many of the Native organizations in fits, especially when DIAND officials insist they are to make band administrators more accountable. The implication here is that band money has been improperly diverted or mismanaged.

An open confrontation in 1975 between Saskatchewan Indians and Buchanan and Leseaux resulted in the latter being booed and Buchanan admitting there was a dearth of consultation. The National Indian Brotherhood (NIB) has repudiated the guidelines and claims they are a subtle attempt by bureaucrats in DIAND to rewrite the Indian Act. George Manuel, president of the NIB issued a statement on April 30 accusing Leseaux's "tyrants" of the following six violations of Indian rights:

1. The circulars (on local government and accounting of funds) are a blatant attempt to unilaterally revise the Indian Act.
2. The circulars seriously restrict the powers of band councils.
3. The circulars provide for the transfer of responsibilities for Indians to other agencies and/or provincial governments, therefore, in effect, a subtle attempt to implement the white paper policy of 1969.
4. The government of Canada and the N.I.B. position is that revision of the Indian Act is the right of the elected leaders of the Indian people, not civil service tyrants.
5. Negotiations on aboriginal and treaty rights will determine Indian rights' issues, not bureaucrats.
6. The government's intention is to force band councils to raise their own funds through taxation of Indian lands and band members, and force municipal status on Indian communities.[8]

According to the Native people, the real power in DIAND, the federal department charged with their protection, is the Northern Development branch, which they feel is more closely aligned with the Department of Energy, Mines and Resources than it is with Native Affairs. While the conflict of interest identified by the Tories at the ministerial level is real, the people most concerned — Canada's Natives — place the conflict at the senior administrative level.

Digby Hunt, the assistant deputy minister, is seen as the villian. In the North he's known as someone who's only happy when he's building something up there. Around Yellowknife he's seen as the man behind the Mackenzie Valley pipeline, whose career as an Ottawa mandarin is at stake if the natural gas pipeline should fail.

The whole thrust of the Northern development branch is towards this pipeline. People in his branch thought the Berger inquiry (the government commission headed by Mr. Justice Thomas Berger of B.C. into the Mackenzie Valley pipeline) would just be a little hearing stuck off in the North. It would be a good public relations gesture to Natives and environmentalists while the National Energy Board and the cabinet made the real decisions. But this backfired, and Berger has taken the spotlight and captured the imagination of the country. Hence the attempt earlier this year to downgrade the Berger hearing by cutting back on funds. Such a blatantly desperate ploy by frightened civil servants has rarely been seen. And if that's not bad enough the fact that they have been aided and abetted by Buchanan, (Mitchell) Sharp and (Donald) MacDonald shows how clearly the politicians are controlled by the mandarins.[9]

Hunt, a government representative on the consortium which is exploring the Arctic Islands for oil and gas, sits on the board of directors of Panarctic Oils Limited, which has a vested interest in pipelines and other Northern transportation programs. He's also on the board of Northern Canada Power Commission, which builds dams in the North. At the same time he's part of the whole Indian Affairs department and responsible for advising the minister on how these corporations will affect the lives of Native people and the environment they live in. DIAND officials predictably deny any conflict of interest and plead that they are merely interested in a rational policy.

A recent article in *the Globe and Mail* quoted Hunt on the conflict of interest between his side of the department and the Indian Affairs branch.

We try to approach it and look at the problem on both sides. There are pressures for economic development and pressures for the environment and pressures for the Native way, and you have to come down on the rational and reasonable argument.[10]

Asked by the *Globe* what the priority for the North is, Hunt said:

There is no absolute priority. What we try to do is maintain a balance between environmental protection, economic development, and concerns for the people of the North. It's no easy task . . . special interests will feel their particular interests are being sacrificed.[11]

This statement would appear to fly in the face of comments by politicians in the Liberal party, including the minister of DIAND,

Hunt's boss, that no further land claims where aboriginal rights are involved will have to be negotiated — under threat of imminent resource or other development.

In 1971 the tide for Northern development was running strongly in Canada, and a group, primarily with environmental concerns, got together to form what has today become the most important observer of DIAND this country has. Known as the Canadian Arctic Resources Committee (CARC), with headquarters in a dingy Ottawa office building, its prime function is to keep an independent watchful eye on the "handful of people who have carte blanche in dealing with the public domain north of the 60th."[12] These people, responsible for administering a vast area of Canada, are the same civil servants who account to no one and who have frustrated Canada's Native people for so long.

CARC started out hoping to encourage public involvement in the North and in the formation of policies affecting the North. It began with the hope that it could work with DIAND and the petroleum industry and get financial support from them. By their own admission they failed on both counts.

> What we learned in those early days is now widely recognized: conflicts between the federal and territorial governments, inter-departmental conflicts, squabbles within DIAND itself . . . there was a lack of normal checks and balances and to cap a dismal picture no provision for public participation. When various sectors of the public tried to participate, DIAND did everything to thwart them.[13]

Today, CARC is an independently funded, highly competent although understaffed organization of experts and part-time consultants that provides constructive and dynamic leadership in focussing public attention on social, cultural, environmental, and land-use concerns which are associated with Northern development. Because of its unrelenting examination of DIAND, it has borne the brunt of attacks from senior civil servants and ministerial assistants, but its conclusions bear so directly on the affairs of the North, on Native people, and indeed, on the suspicion with which a growing number of Canadians view their political institutions that a digest of some of CARC's more important observations on the DIAND concludes this chapter on government. We are indebted to Kitson Vincent, secretary of CARC, for permission to use material from two important papers he has presented. "The Citizen as an Obstacle to Efficiency" and "Cornelius Vanderbilt is Alive and Well: DIAND and the Public Interest".

CARC's central assumption, insofar as the Government of Canada and particularily the DIAND is concerned, is that senior levels of administration in our nation have become so large, so self-serving, so apart from the electoral process that they are unaccountable to anyone, including Parliament, in any significant manner. Further, they constitute a power bloc that is in reality the centre of decision-making as far as energy, Northern development, and the environment are concerned.

That this bureaucratic influence directly affects the lives of Native people and applies equally in provincial bureaucracies and Crown corporations makes it of urgent concern for Canadians who should distrust bigness and power, and see instead the need for a viable, involved, and independent citizenry as the key to a democratic society. Senior officials and ministerial assistants usually refer to these concepts of democracy as quaint, and point to the complexities of a technological age as too difficult for the "average" Canadian to understand.

> All three departments (energy, northern development, and environment) continue to press for legislation designed to facilitate administrative discretion; all three have delegated important areas of rule-making to their respective bureaucracies and regulatory agencies; and all three have closed ranks against the public in order to protect narrow agency interest. The justifications are never-ending: the growing complexity of government decision-making, they say, has made it necessary to delegate more power to the bureaucracy. And indeed, Parliament continues to yield its legislative responsibility to the civil service. Officials of these agencies are neither elected nor controlled by the people.[14]

Energy development policies in the North seem to be based less on factual evidence of need and more on the demands of multinational corporations. Not even Parliament has ready access to important matters on Northern Canada, which were discussed between industry and the DIAND bureaucracy. Minutes of meetings and resulting memoranda remain outside the scope of what is euphemistically called "the public interest."

CARC comes up with some interesting examples from major documents prepared for cabinet. They deal with how to get around the public rather than how to inform and involve the public. A memo on the disastrous Mackenzie Valley highway dealt with appeasement of Natives and how to isolate environmentalists from Indians. At inter-departmental meetings in 1970-71, senior officials urged immediate planning for a Mackenzie Valley pipeline, because

Canadian environmentalists were less organized than their American counterparts. The real value or need for these projects was never discussed.

Regulatory bodies such as the National Energy Board (NEB) are viewed with some justifiable suspicion by CARC. Originally these bodies were established as impartial agencies at a time when governments "regulated" rather than "did" things. The NEB is perhaps the most important regulatory body in Canada. It is supposed to be impartial, and it is supposed to remain at arms length from initiators of policy and from business groups which are involved in energy production, distribution, and retailing. Its purpose is to decide and advise cabinet on needs, supply, and transportation. It is not expected to endorse concepts in advance or to influence cabinet in certain directions but only to present impartial findings. Yet, CARC points out that NEB officials prepared the material that persuaded cabinet to endorse a Mackenzie Valley pipeline in 1970. CARC further shows how the powerful task force on Northern oil development in 1972 laid the groundwork for all oil development in Northern Canada, and its pipeline committee was chaired by the NEB, which will eventually hear and decide on the *need* for such a pipeline! These are further conflicts of interest which the voter "hopefully" should ignore, allowing "experts" to make the important decisions affecting our future and the future of Native people in the North. The impartiality of the NEB, which is presently hearing the applications for a Mackenzie Valley natural gas pipeline, must be forever seriously questioned.

Another administrative procedure that rouses CARC's wrath is "the agreement in principle," which is, in reality, a firm agreement to proceed. No oil or natural gas company would invest the millions of dollars needed for feasibility studies unless some commitment was forthcoming. For example, Canadian Arctic Gas Study Limited, with a budget of $100 million, has a whole infrastructure ready for the pipeline that cannot be built until a firm decision is made by the NEB. The Berger hearings are window dressing and cannot be considered as evolving any rational alternative to the pipeline.

CARC has produced the following classic "agreement in principle," involving a massive program for offshore drilling in the Beaufort Sea, one of the most hazardous parts of the world:

> In this major decision, where numerous elements of the public, including the Parliament of Canada, should have played a role, there was not a single mention that a whole new threshold of development

in Northern Canada had been given approval in principle. After the release of CARC studies on the offshore drilling program, Mr. Hunt stated to the press that there was no reason for concern because no firm decision had been made. All talk and discussion had been of a preliminary nature and the government had only given approval in principle for drilling in the Beaufort Sea. At the time of his announcement, drilling from artificial islands was already proceeding.[15]

It would appear that "approval in principle" means two things — a firm agreement to industry, and plans to win support through public relations for a few years.

Prime Minister Trudeau, who used public involvement in politics as a slogan for the Just Society, deplores the lack of trust that citizens have in democracy. And he's right. For all the messiness and inefficiencies that discussion and participation by the great unwashed hordes may involve, it beats the alternatives, which are totalitarianism and rank corruption. But if the administrative mandarins, who are accountable to no one, misuse the "impartial" boards, "arms-length" regulatory bodies, and "agreements in principle," how can the abused citizenry have any trust or respect for Trudeau's slogans like "participatory democracy."

DIAND, along with the energy department, operates as though the rights of the individual or minorities were an affront to its intelligence. Policies, such as Mr. Chrétien's statements of 1973, are ignored, and no one is accountable for failing to follow or implement policies. Policies, it seems, are only for voters or dissident Native groups. The numerous reassurances that Native people and the environment come before Northern development are simply meaningless.

CARC has outlined for us several ways in which DIAND bureaucracies make policy decisions and implement them without any real involvement from the people concerned or even from their democratically elected representatives. Policies about dams, river diversions, roads, and pipelines are made secretly and then the confused public is left to sort out the technical details. "The government informs people about pre-existing plans and then suggests ways in which they could adapt them," explains CARC. Public hearings, established by the cabinet, are set up *after* high-level policy decisions have been made. The Berger inquiry is classic. The decision on the pipeline has been made. It merely remains for Berger to inquire into the details, which no matter how important, are still details. The public will have its day in court but the real decisions are made where power resides — in the corridors of Ottawa's civil service.

CARC maintains that some senior civil servants clearly understand this dilemma and use it to protect their specialities and to get a strangle-hold on the entire system. Senior bureaucrats and the executive assistants of the Minister of DIAND, according to CARC, did everything possible to discredit people who attempted to ask high-priority or "first order" questions about Northern development. What follows is a short account of the way DIAND behaved when people and groups across Canada asked for more involvement in developing Northern policy (our italics).

> The first thing done was to firmly categorize a group or individual. The idea is to keep *Native groups, environmentalists, economic nationalists and lawyers* of all stripes from being concerned with areas other than their own; in other words, from forming an overview. Second, they took each group and grossly overstated its position. The end product is a fanatic.
>
> When elements of Canadian society first expressed concern over developments in the Mackenzie Valley, the tenor of their concern was usually, "What's the rush?" Instead of discussion the questions were discarded and the questioners were thrown into the trash can of fanaticism. If a conservationist asked, "What's the rush?" he was branded a card-carrying member of the *"Zoological Garden Society"* —an imaginary society whose members' only desire is to view nature in its pristine form. Those who voiced concern over the treatment of Native communities were turned into *absolutists who were against any development of the North.* Economists who wanted time to evaluate the economic benefits relative to economic costs were *isolated by a premise they never held*: that Canadian resources must lie in the ground until Canadians pay for every component of them. Everybody was isolated by premises they never held. The premises were always extreme and meant you were either right or wrong.
>
> This fallacy, commonplace in logic, is known as an *eristic discussion. Two sets of false abstractions are set up which do not exist in real life, and one party then sets out to prove that he is right and the other is wrong.* The senior civil servants in DIAND prefer discussion with imaginary entities like the Zoological Garden Society. The use of eristic argument has another purpose. It allows for one of the finest juggling acts in Canada. For between the straits of Scylla and Charybdis comes the dazzling Minister of Indian and Northern Affairs steering his craft through the treacherous waters of *"Indians"* *"eco-freaks"* and *"up and at'em rip out artists".* In more prosaic terms, it is known as option B and an integral part of decision-making in DIAND. Two phony and often ridiculous extremes, A and C, are posited allowing the decision maker to arrive at a solution to provide ultimate comfort for everyone, namely option B. Between the ex-

tremists of the Zoological Garden and the old-time developers stands the man who balances it all. It makes good theatre, but when Canada is about to embark on projects costing more than five billion dollars, we can only hope the show does not become a smash hit.

A further tactic to keep the public at bay is to *make an issue as complex and technical as possible.* Divide a problem into twenty-four committees, set up interagency groups and then leave the impression that only a massive bureaucracy or industry can coodinate and understand the detail. *The same procedure is used by the petroleum industry.* At a meeting with Imperial Oil some of our Committee members were treated to a slide show pointing out the complex interlocking committees set up by industry and government to deal with Northern development. *Such complexity* requiring thousands of people and millions of dollars *allowed no room for public involvement.* As the chairman told us at the meeting, "When there are two elephants involved there is no room for a mouse." He was carrying on in the best Cornelius Vanderbilt tradition, *"the public be damned".* When senior civil servants echo the good commodore's words, it becomes clear we have a problem on our hands.

A corollary of this technique is to convert all political and social questions into pseudo-technical ones. This has strong psychological appeal for administrators but obviously contains grave defects. Environmentalists usually are regarded as people who deal with highly technical pollution problems that can and will be solved. In the North, however, environmentalists are also concerned with the requirements of long-term land-use planning: how it is possible and how the various interests are to be weighed and valued in the process of planning. The use of land, in fact, lies at the heart of every environmental problem. Dealing with land use planning involves political and social judgment as well as the necessity of thinking holistically; therefore, the question is conveniently ignored by the civil servants. *Similarly when Native people talk about a land settlement they view land in a different perspective from that of southerners.* Because they themselves are an integral part of the land, they do not see a settlement only in terms of a cash exchange.

Another tactic is to divide the north from the south. DIAND officials in Ottawa have always demeaned the role of the southern Canadian. Yet very often in the North they speak of the national needs of the country. Much of the southern-northern hostility has been generated by this tactic to keep various groups apart. In the North some DIAND officials refer to pesky southerners. It soon became clear that they were only referring to *southern Canadians.* *Their friends with Georgia and Texas accents*—the real southerners —were quite welcome.

A further tactic to consolidate power is to exploit the constitutional ambiguity pertaining to Northern Canada. *Officials in DIAND can play the Territorial government off against the Federal government in such a way as to rationalize abdiction of responsibility.* When it suits their purpose, the Territorial government can have a great deal of autonomy. *A senior official in the Canadian Wildlife Service told me that if DIAND wants to stall an issue they refer it to the Territorial government. Whenever they are really concerned with an issue, they will make the decision without ever consulting the Territorial governments.*[16]

With such tactics, such cynical manipulation of the democratic process, how, it must be asked, can democracy survive? Are the rise of citizens' groups fighting to save a neighborhood or stop an airport sufficient to say that Canadians are becoming more enlightened? If comparatively sophisticated, comparatively well educated people, much wiser in the ways of white man's democracy, have little impact on Ottawa and provincial bureaucrats, what hope do the Native groups, unaccustomed to white man's ways, have? How can trust be rebuilt when we find a Prime Minister whose utter contempt for Parliament infects every level of bureaucracy, and whose ministers find public discussion and participation time consuming and wasteful?

But Native groups, underfinanced, threatened with loss of funds, dismissed as irrelevant, and accused of having no community support, may yet prove to Canadians the value of local involvement, for they are determined to hold DIAND to its promises and to negotiate their claims from the strength of the people in the communities. Perhaps government administrators may yet turn away from their present course of demanding ever more discretionary powers and turn to participation in decision-making, for the trust level, whose loss the Prime Minister so rightly laments, can only be found again through the untidy involvement of people.

Notes

1 The Progressive Conservative Programme for Native Peoples, Ottawa, 1974.

2 Flora MacDonald, MP, Kingston and the Islands, in a speech to the Educational Congress, Traffic Clubs International, Montreal, September 10, 1973.

3 Ed Ogle, *Annual Report of the Government of the Northwest Territories,* (Yellowknife, N.W.T., 1974), Page 9.

4 Ibid, pages 9 and 10.

5 The Honorable Jean Chrétien, Minister of Indian Affairs and Northern Development, statement of "Claims of Indian and Inuit People," Ottawa, April 8, 1973.

6 Ibid

7 Ibid.

8 Memorandum from George Manuel, President of the National Indian Brotherhood, to all Indian organizations regarding DIAND Policy Guidelines and Program Regulations, Ottawa, April 30, 1975.

9 A composite statement by the authors based on interviews with Indian, Metis and Inuit leaders in Whitehorse, Yukon and Yellowknife, Northwest Territories, during April, 1975.

10 *The Globe and Mail*, (Toronto), May 16, 1975.

11 Ibid.

12 Excerpts from two papers written by Kitson Vincent, executive secretary, Canadian Arctic Resources Committee: "Cornelius Vanderbilt is Alive and Well: DIAND and the Public Interest" and "The Citizen as an Obstacle to Efficiency", Ottawa, 1974.

13 Ibid.

14 Ibid.

15 Ibid.

16 Ibid.

There is a relationship with the land which is terribly difficult to understand. We westerners again battle land, develop it, clear it, bring it into production, fence it in, buy it up, sell it off, and even speculate in it.

That is completely foreign to the Indian. He does not see himself over against the land, as "having to do something with it," but he sees himself as on the land, in the land, of the land; a living part of a living land. You can't own it anymore than you can own the air you breathe, you live off it, you share of it, but you also give yourself to it—you can't fence it in any more than the air, you can't buy, sell or lease it, least of all speculate in it. . . .

This difference in views is why so many of the treaties, while perhaps duly signed, were never really understood. The idea of buying land was strange, they never had the faintest notion of our concept of land and what we were going to do with it.

This is how the Indians were done out of so much land. They simply did not understand what it was all about.

The Reverend Hugo Muller
in *Why Don't You?*
Noranda, 1974
page 82

4

Beads and Blankets

*A Look at Two Modern-Day Settlements
in James Bay and Alaska*

At four o'clock in the afternoon of July 27, 1871, negotiations got underway in earnest between the Indian people at Lower Fort Garry in southern Manitoba and the Indian commissioner and the lieutenant-governor and his staff. The negotiations, complete with Indians in ribbons, feathers, and paint and the representatives of Queen Victoria dressed in Windsor uniforms and accompanied by aides de camp, were to extinguish title to Indian land in the new province and to make a legal treaty to this effect.

> Your Great Mother wishes the good of all races under her sway. She wishes her Red Children as well as her white people to be happy and contented. She wishes them to live in comfort. She would like them to adopt the habits of the white man, to till land and raise food and store it up against a time of want.[1]

The treaty, duly signed under a canopy, in effect transformed the Indian from a hunter to a farmer and gave him 160 acres of land per family of 5 and a few farm implements. He was also to get treaty money of $5.00-a-head-per-year. The land was worthless for farming, but it was gathered together into a reserve, and to this day, for the extinguishment of title to vast tracts of land, Manitoba Indians have only this settlement. In other places the Great Mother was a little more generous and granted 1 square mile of rock or bush per family of 5 as a reserve and the munificent sum of $5.00-a-year. And there was no built-in-cost-of-living bonus. Treaty money is still $5.00-a-head. No wonder it was called beads and blankets. The paternalism, the total lack of understanding about what they were doing, the haste and the lies of Indian commissioners are history, and from 1871 to 1923 some 13 of these treaties were signed, mostly in the Prairies and Ontario.

Treaty-making came to an end in 1923, largely because it was thought that land in the rest of Canada was worthless, and the Native people were welcome to it. What sane white man would want to live in cold, harsh, isolated conditions when he could live in the comfort of big cities in southern Canada? The treaties were abominable instruments in every way. The Natives didn't understand them, because to them the land belonged to everyone and was for everyone's use, to be safeguarded for future generations. Reserves were, almost without exception, the worst possible land for farming, often too small for adequate hunting or trapping, and in many places Natives had to compete with the more avaricious white trappers who stripped the land of the fur-bearing animals and then left.

The treaties of 50 years ago were simply rip-offs. But they had one essential factor which must be remembered, because they were the cornerstone of Native relations then and they remain that cornerstone today. They were extinguishment treaties; they were reserve treaties; and their primary aim was to hasten assimilation of Natives into white society. In other words, for a sum of money, a guarantee of a certain tract of reserve land, some hunting, fishing, and trapping rights, Native people extinguished their rights to their aboriginal lands to the white governments and became wards of the Department of Indian Affairs, under whatever portfolio a capricious government might assign it.

Today we find federal and provincial governments again going about the business of signing extinguishment treaties which still are gigantic rip-offs, still predicated on assimilation, and still make Native people wards of the Crown. These treaties are now called settlements or agreements and involve larger sums of money, but they are still drawn up in haste and under pressure, and although the dishonesty is more sophisticated, it still leaves Natives uncertain and unhappy about what they've done. Eventually these treaties will be enshrined in legislation, which sounds great but really means that only the white man's government can break them.

One such settlement is nearing its final conclusion. In November 1974, the James Bay Cree and Inuit signed an agreement in principle with the province of Quebec, the James Bay Energy Corporation, and the Government of Canada, which extinguished their claim to 400,000 square miles of Northern Quebec. It was to have been a model for the Yukon (see Chapter 5), the Northwest Territories (Chapter 8), Northern British Columbia (Chapter 7), and anywhere else where unextinguished land claims were lying about ready for "development." The government reluctantly agreed that it need not necessarily be the only model, but at the same time Buchanan made it clear that his mandate from cabinet — the policy of the Liberal government in 1975 — was to extinguish all land claims and to negotiate settlements. Canada was clearly back in the treaty-making game.

One other modern-day version of the old treaties is the massive, multi-billion-dollar Alaska settlement. It is one of the most complicated pieces of legislation ever devised as a means of extinguishing aboriginal title, but for the United States, it ends forever the Native problem — they hope. It is their last treaty.

In order to lay the groundwork for an understanding of future negotiations and alternatives for Native people in Canada, it is necessary to examine in some detail these two modern treaties and their implied philosophy of assimilation and extinguishment. Beads and blankets — modern style.

The Alaska Settlement

Alaska's Indians, Eskimos, and Aleuts lived, until recently, pretty much in the old way. Many of them still do, despite the fact that they have become the recipients of a billion-dollar cash settlement and now, theoretically at least, run their own affairs. Until 1971, the 80,000 Natives living in tiny villages had a per capita income of about $1,000-a-year and little welfare. They trapped, hunted, and fished, and probably unknown to most of them, held aboriginal title to nine-tenths of Alaska's surface or about 500,000 square miles, a region just slightly bigger than the area claimed by the Native people of the Northwest Territories.

According to lawyer Eric Treisman of the Alaska Legal Services Corporation, aboriginal title means approximately the same thing the world over, and under United States law, prevents "the inconsistent use or occupancy [of land] by anyone but the aborigines" or original inhabitants. Unless it is completely abandoned, title cannot be extinguished except by the federal government —

similar to legal opinions existing in Canada today. "By fire and the sword" is the bloodthirsty description written into early American treaties where Natives lost title through war.

Until 1968, as in Canada, no one worried about Native people in the North or their aboriginal rights. The people came under a federal agency known as the Bureau of Indian Affairs. But it all changed when, in 45-below-zero weather an Atlantic-Richfield drilling crew brought in a gusher on Alaska's North Slope and the rush was on. Of course a pipeline had to be built and is now well under way, but plans showed the line crossing the Yukon River Valley in Central Alaska, and the Indians there rebelled. In 1970, a District of Columbia judge ruled that they did have aboriginal title and so did the rest of Alaska's Natives.

What to do? Alaska needs every cent it can get between now and 30 years—when the Prudhoe Bay fields are expected to be sucked dry. Natives must not be allowed to block such a project any more than environmentalists could. So on December 14, 1971, the United States Congress took note of the Alaska Natives' aboriginal title and extinguished it. In return for this aboriginal title, Congress set up an enormously complicated treaty which has been widely hailed across the length and breadth of North America as imaginative, generous, and a possible model for future claims in Canada.

It is also estimated, by some Alaskan Natives we talked to, that only about 100 of them understand the settlement, and each of these needs a lawyer at all times to interpret the clauses. It affects about 80,000 people, each of whom had to have at least one-quarter Native blood. Each of the 220 Native villages became a Native Corporation, to be managed with assistance from 12 larger regional corporations, covering the state of Alaska. They represent the 12 tribes or Native groupings, and all Natives became shareholders in their particular regional corporation.

The village corporations are the closest thing Alaska has to an Indian reserve. But the village lands are not protected from sale as are Canadian reserves. The land issue is the most complicated. The regional corporations have been given full title to 60,000 square miles with all subsurface rights, but there's a catch. The land can only be taken from certain areas, and these are not necessarily the best land. In most cases they cannot be side-by-side, because the Native Claims Settlement Act of 1971 does not favor the establishment of "Native enclaves" or reserves. The Native regional corporations made their selections along with the State government, which got 161,000 square miles, and the Federal Department of the Interior, which took about 125,000.

The enormous amount of money to be paid the 80,000 Natives is what caught the eye of many Canadians, but it is not quite as generous as one would think. One billion dollars is a lot of money, but when it's paid over 11 years spread among that many people, with half of it coming from royalty payments on North Shore land, it is something else. A lot of it is also locked up in regional and village corporations. In 1974 each Native got the enormous sum of $181.00 as his or her 1/80,000th share of village and regional dividends. Although most Alaska Natives traditionally live off the land, there are no special provisions for hunting, trapping, or fishing. In fact at the present time, there is a legal controversy going on as to whether a Native people has the special right to hunt and fish for food for themselves and their families. The whole agreement terminates in 1991, and after that there will be no special status and no special laws for Native people. It is a total integration-assimilation treaty. After that date, 20 years from the date congress took note of Alaskan Natives' aboriginal rights, the land can be sold by the corporations to non-Native people. At the same date, the Bureau of Indian Affairs will end all its programs.

Already regions are working against each other in an effort to make as much money as possible by 1991 and have been induced by those clever fellows in the oil business to grant some special deals on Native land. Because the regional corporations differ widely in stockholder population, they have been discouraged from coming to a common policy on mineral exploitation (the old familiar divide and conquer ploy). The Alaska Pipeline will be completed in two years. Alaska, with its newly won statehood, hopes to be solvent with royalties exceeding a billion dollars-a-year on oil alone. With the natural gas pipeline still to come, regardless of what route is taken, more money can be expected at state house in Fairbanks.

But many throughtful Native leaders are wondering what will happen to their children when the settlement terminates in less than 20 years. Some of their leaders are getting rich, some of the regional corporations are rolling in money, looking for schemes in which to invest their new-found wealth, but outside the Alaska Federation of Natives, in the villages, great fear is expressed. They don't agree that commercial development is the best for all of them.

Back in 1871, the Indian treaties in Canada, as explained by the white treaty commissioners, looked good at the time. But then, all Indian treaties look good on paper—especially if it's a billion dollars worth of beads and blankets in return for assimilation.

The James Bay Settlement

In November 1975, as this book was going to press, another "great landmark" in Native settlements was achieved when the James Bay agreement in principle between the 10,000 Cree and Inuit in Northern Quebec and the provincial and federal governments became a final and irrevocable settlement.

Recited quickly—like the Alaska settlement—it sounds as if the white man has again shown great generosity to the Red children.
—A cash payment of $75 million over 10 years;
—Royalties on the hydro development of $75 million over a longer period;
—25 percent of all royalties for 20 years on Northern timber and mineral developments begun within the next 50 years;
—5,250 square miles of their own;
—exclusive hunting and fishing rights on another 60,000 square miles of land;
—some modifications to the James Bay hydro development scheme.

So great was this settlement, in fact, that the Cree and Inuit leaders who hastily agreed to it called it a "great victory." DIAND officials saw it as a precedent for other settlements. But it wasn't long until the National Indian Brotherhood and the Indians of Quebec Association, along with other associations of Native people, were more skeptical.

By agreeing to allow the hydro project to proceed, by agreeing to drop all legal action and to surrender their aboriginal rights to 400,000-square miles of land, the Natives got something like $3.05-an-acre—a bargain similar to the purchase of Manhatten Island for $24.00. The Natives will also get up to $1,500 each for the next 10 years. But what about their children and future generations when most of the land is gone? More beads and blankets?

The basic principle behind the James Bay settlement is that land should be readily exchanged for money, with the province retaining the real wealth in surface and sub-surface rights. In other words, the Indians could keep the beaver, but the whites would keep the hydro, zinc, iron, and timber. Some bargain. As the land is flooded for one of the costliest, most ill-planned, most dubious projects in Canada's history, the culture of Indians and Inuit is sacrificed on the altar of progress by the unknown demands for more and cheaper energy in the south. The most disturbing aspect of this agreement in principle is the process involved in reaching it. And before examining the settlement in greater detail, it seems important to look at this process and the suddenness with which an agreement was announced.

For two years the negotiations dragged on. One totally irresponsible offer was rejected by the Natives. A court victory involving aboriginal rights was overturned by the Quebec Appeal Court. The federal government did everything possible to stay out of the controversy, and the Quebec government simply refused to negotiate seriously. Then the costs of the $2 million project skyrocketed (latest estimates show costs as high as $20 billion) and financing proved difficult. Further, because title to the land was so unclear, and because of all the publicity surrounding the Natives' case, markets to buy the potential power were drying up. Suddenly, negotiations began in earnest, then a settlement was reached, and presto— another Indian problem solved. If this is to be the pattern DIAND so eagerly wishes to follow elsewhere, then land claim settlements will only be bumped up the political priority ladder when some huge development project forces the issue.

The hydro project itself has been discussed elsewhere in this book. It relates to the settlement only as the cause for settling an aboriginal claim which was supposed to have been dealt with in 1912, when Northern Quebec was ceded to the province by Ottawa. The development called for diversion of rivers, construction of dams, and flooding of lands over which the James Bay Cree and Inuit had hunted, trapped, and fished for years with little interference from white society. Clearly, the project was going to destroy much of the land and life style of the Native people. The two Native groups began negotiating with Quebec to try and get the project changed to make it less destructive, although construction and surveying were well underway when negotiations started. They also wanted a land settlement.

The negotiation process quickly proved fruitless. Bourassa's government, still rocked by the FLQ crisis of October 1970, when it had been little more than a messenger boy to Ottawa, was desperate to polish up its image of a get-up-and-go government and said that no minority Native group could halt the "Project of the Century." The James Bay Cree and Inuit then went to court, and in the longest case of its kind ever in Canada, Mr. Justice Albert Malouf of the

Quebec Superior Court granted an injunction late in 1973, on the grounds that the Natives had aboriginal title to the land. It was a great day in Montreal, and the workers stayed in their bunk houses in the North. But the victory was shortlived. In eight days construction had resumed in the wilderness of James Bay, following an obviously political decision by the Quebec Appeal Court to allow work to proceed while appeals were heard from the James Bay Development Corporation.

It was during this period that the province made its first unacceptable offer of 1-square-mile-per-family-of-5, $100 million in cash and royalties over 10 years, hunting and fishing rights, and a guaranteed annual income for people who wanted to live off the land. The Natives rejected this offer, partially because it contained no alterations in the project and because they wanted more land. Their first choice, of course, was to end the project forever.

The Cree and Inuit were in a box. The court hearings were dragging on at terrific cost, estimated in excess of $1 million. Their chances in the Quebec Appeal Court were slim and the proceedings long. By the time they would get to the Supreme Court of Canada, where they felt they had a better chance of winning, the project, with construction going full blast, would be almost completed and the destruction to their land and way-of-life beyond repair. Their dilemma was whether to go for broke in the courts *or* to accept a less satisfactory settlement and get changes in the project itself that would be less destructive to their traditional life. They decided to try negotiating again, as long as significant changes were made by Quebec Hydro, and on November 15, 1974, an agreement in principle was signed—the final agreement to be signed one year later with certain details to be negotiated in the interim. Ironically, and as a sad blot on our judicial process, exactly one week later the Court of Appeal came down with a devastating decision in which the Cree and Inuit lost on every point.

Before looking at the implications of the process used in negotiating—a process some would call negotiating with a gun at your head—we should examine the essential terms of the agreement and their meaning. Those eligible are all status and non-status Cree and Inuit people in James Bay and Northern Quebec areas, roughly about 10,000 people. The non-status Cree are excluded from the reserves and from Indian Act protection. Two-thousand square miles of land for the exclusive use of the Cree, based on the old formula of 1-square-mile-per-family-of-5, of which 1,274 square miles of Cree lands will come under the Indian Act as reserves, were set aside. The remainder of the land, plus 3,250 square miles for the Inuit, will be under provincial jurisdiction "subject to adequate safeguards" but not the safeguards of the Indian Act. In return for this land, the Inuit and Cree surrender their aboriginal rights to the 400,000 square miles of land.

One of the best features of this agreement is the 60,000 square miles of Crown land set aside for the exclusive hunting, fishing, and trapping preserve of the Natives. While it is not protected in the same degree as the 2,000 square miles for the Cree and 3,250 square miles for the Inuit, it is still the best agreement in Canada in terms of living off the land. It should be reiterated that the Native people get no subsurface mineral rights at all.

Over 10 years, the Natives will get a total of $150 million tax exempt money, paid to some sort of corporation yet to be defined. There are to be "legal entities," perhaps like the Alaska regional corporations. There will be Native school boards, regional governments, and membership on an environmental committee of the James Bay Energy Corporation. Native people will also get 25 percent of mineral royalties in Northern Quebec for the next 50 years, but no particular firm will be required to pay for more than 20 years, during which, when you consider that the first years of any mining operation are the lean years, the royalties will be somewhat less than agreed.

It is not a termination plan such as Alaska, since the DIAND must continue to provide programs in the James Bay area on the same basis as the rest of Canada, and the 1,274 square miles of reserve are under the Indian Act and therefore beyond the power of the province. One of the major concessions wrung from Quebec were modifications to the project itself, minimizing some of the flooding and diversion damage.

Now back to the dynamics of the negotiating process which, because of the precedent—and we must be clear that it is a precedent —are crucial to further land claim settlement proceedings in Canada.

The James Bay negotiating team consisted of Indian and Inuit representatives along with their legal counsel, James O'Reilly, a Montreal lawyer who had successfully argued their case before Judge Malouf. The Inuit and Indian negotiators varied from time to time but included Billy Diamond, Robert Kinatewat, and Philip Awashish representing the North and Ted Moses representing the South. Charlie Watt from Fort Chimo was the chief Inuit negotiator. These people are important to remember, for they had at one time the complete backing of the Native people of Quebec. The Quebec government was represented by John Ciaccia, a special representative of Premier Bourassa and a former assistant deputy minister of Indian Affairs in DIAND. Representatives of DIAND, particularly Denis Chatain, were also involved. Funding was through grants and loans from DIAND and is estimated to have reached, by now, $2 million or more.

One of the major difficulties was geographical—keeping people in the North up-to-date on negotiations which were held in secret in the south. There are large white communities in the southern part of the area, but still largely traditional Native villages in the North. Race relations are not good, with language and religious factors increasing the tension. The incredible insensitivity of the Bourassa government, combined with the fact that no consultations were ever held prior to the arrival of construction gangs, forced the Natives to negotiate a project about which they knew nothing and to which most of them were totally opposed.

The Cree, in particular, did not want to see themselves confined on reserves and without rights to their whole territory. The Inuit, although less directly affected by construction, were even more committed to the land, and as negotiations progressed, this commitment to their traditional life grew. In fact there is no doubt that, following the Malouf decision, the people especially in the far North were ready to "go for broke." However, the lack of support from DIAND, which never went beyond the funding stage, and the subsequent action of the Quebec courts seemed to exhaust the leadership. They changed their minds, feeling they had done as much as could be done, and now would settle for the best deal possible. They became committed to a process which started in the villages and settlements of the Cree and Inuit. It was a mandate to get the best deal possible, and eventually they were forced to go back and say "here it is; it's the best we can do." At that point the people were forced to decide whether or not to accept, and the question must be asked. Did they really have any other choice but to accept?

There were many other factors in the decision still to settle. There were disputes between professional advisors, arguments between native groups, time pressures forcing corners to be cut and compromises to be made. All of these are common in any negotiating process and merely contributed to the general feeling of exhaustion. There was, however, a serious breakdown between the regional group—the Cree and Inuit of James Bay and Northern Quebec—and the parent groups, the Indians of Quebec Association almost entirely based along the St. Lawrence, and the Inuit Tapirisat of Canada, the national Eskimo group. One Eskimo village, Puvungnituk, has recently repudiated the agreement altogether, on the grounds it was never advised or consulted until six months after the agreement in principle was signed.

But these were only contributing factors, and the truth of the situation lies in the weakness of the judicial process and the impossible situation of negotiating while development is under way. We were told by one long-time, close observer of the James Bay situation that it was his impression that, although the Cree and Inuit were well organized and as deeply committed to their land as anyone, they had had enough; all they wanted to do was get it over with.

What These Settlements Mean

A comparison between the Alaska and James Bay settlements shows positive aspects in both; however, the one overriding feature from the Natives' point-of-view is that they are land extinguishment, colonially-oriented, assimilation agreements.

The Alaska agreement places almost no emphasis on the traditional way of life, whereas one of the best features of the James Bay are the hunting, fishing, and trapping rights. The James Bay agreement protects to some extent the traditional—if it still remains viable —and the Natives retain their special status, while the Alaska terminates after 20 years. The other big difference is that the Alaska structure is enormously complex from an institutional view, while the James Bay remains quite simple. Alaska got far more land for its communities and villages, but James Bay got the exclusive 60,000 square miles for hunting, fishing, and trapping purposes, which if interpreted as exclusive domain, means a very large land entitlement.

Compared with Alaska, the James Bay settlement is very small in terms of financial compensation—$150 million to $1 billion. Per capita, James Bay Natives get slightly more than Alaskans, but there are no mineral rights which are so important to the Alaska settlement. The main reason for this is that project changes will cost the James Bay Hydro Development Corporation as much as $300 million. There are also some hidden compensations like a guaranteed annual income for trappers, a Native Development Corporation, continuation of federal programs, and other benefits.

The Alaska settlement emphasizes termination, and therefore, puts the Native people under heavy pressure to abandon their traditional ways and embrace the wage economy, along with whatever economic benefits accrue to them from their investments. The James Bay agreement in principle allows for a choice in retaining the traditional, but the future looks bleak with little other choices than tourism, outfitting, or labor—all in the wage economy—along with whatever will come out of their investment.

Certainly British Columbia, the Yukon, and the Northwest Territories will be affected by James Bay and Alaska. There are some valuable lessons to be learned from both settlements and the processes leading up to them. The odds in James Bay were formidable. Time pressures, hostile courts, and insensitive governments worked against the Native people. Whether they should have gone all out or taken the best they could get remains a moot point. But clearly, it is imperative that land claim settlements should never again be negotiated under the threat of imminent development or with extinguishment and assimilation the basic philosophy.

Beads and blankets—or the right to survive?

Notes

Most of the material for this chapter results from research into the Alaska and James Bay agreements, interviews by the authors, and access to confidential documents prepared by various Native and government groups.

[1] *Treaty Days*, (Winnipeg; The Manitoba Indian Brotherhood, 1971), Page 8.

God made this land and now we are old and don't understand what is going on and who the strangers are. I was born, brought up on Crow Flats with the game. The fish go up Crow River to spawn and back down again. In the old days when the fish used to go up by Dave Lord's place we have fish traps. In fall we get caribou and ground squirrels because we didn't have no groceries like we have now. Only tea and bannock.

When I was kid, used to shoot caribou when father too old. In spring we run out of groceries and go to Herschel Island in June to get groceries. We get very hard time.

After that time, stayed home. Then get married. Then go up Porcupine River. Learn how animals act. Now, because of airstrip and drillers, they act funny. Different, I think. This is why I'm against the pipeline. I'm thinking of our grandchildren. I want to know if the caribou will cross the pipeline, or if they'll go away and never come back. I want caribou for my grandchildren and great-grandchildren.

Martha John Charlie
An elderly Loucheux woman
living at Old Crow in the
Yukon, north of the Arctic Circle
speaking April 8, 1975

5

The Yukon

Together Today for Our Children Tomorrow
and a
Growing White Backlash

Someone always seems to be trying to explain the plight of Canada's Indians, but no one ever does so with such eloquence or poetry as the Native people themselves. Early in 1973, a stumpy, bespectacled Indian patriarch from Whitehorse flew down to Ottawa and handed over an historic document to Prime Minister Trudeau and Indian Affairs Minister Jean Chrétien. It was beautifully entitled *Together Today for Our Children Tomorrow* and laid out in detail what it was the Yukon Indians felt was their due.

It was really the first definitive land claim ever presented by Native people to a Canadian government. In the past, the federal government had offered the Natives a treaty and then coerced them into signing it. From time-to-time other groups would ask for discussions or preliminary reactions to certain points, but never before had a group of people who had never been conquered, never ceded their aboriginal rights, never agreed to any treaty, come to Ottawa to tell it to them like it was. Furthermore, they made it clear how they wanted it to be.

The prime minister responded with some enthusiasm and told Chief Elijah Smith, then president of the Yukon Native Brotherhood, that the Yukon approach was "very welcome," and in an uncharacteristic burst of enthusiasm which may be regretted in the halls of bureaucracy today, told the Indians that there wasn't a great deal of difference between their position and that of the Department of Indian Affairs and Northern Development.

That was February, 1973 and negotiations were to start immediately. Now, more than two years later, the minor differences have blossomed into full-blown controversies. The Indians' position paper was countered this year with a "Federal Government Working Paper" presented to the Yukon Natives as a proposal, and only after Smith's insistence was it reduced to a working paper for discussion only. The negotiations have bogged down so seriously, and the question of adequate funding during the negotiation period has become such a major issue, that both sides accuse the other of not bargaining in good faith.

When Trudeau first got *Together Today for Our Children Tomorrow* he hailed it as a major breakthrough in federal–Indian relations and acknowledged publicly in Ottawa, when talking with Smith and his confreres, that his adamant ruling against the doctrine of aboriginal rights in 1969 was a mistake.

The Yukon was to be the first—and model—modern-day settlement of Indian land claims in an area where there had never been any treaties. Today there is still no settlement and no sign of one. But there is a mantle of secrecy over the whole process. As a result there is heightened frustration on the part of the Natives who claim the problem is a new and insensitive cabinet minister in the person of Judd Buchanan, who is a prisoner of DIAND bureaucrats and special assistants.

Compounding the problem is one of the most serious and open white backlashes in the country. Yukon Natives are in a distinct minority, even though they constitute nearly a third of the population. Whites, partly because they've always been in the driver's seat where Indians are concerned and partly because they don't know what's happening either, fear they are being sold down the river. So, neither side trusts DIAND or the federal government. Because there was no pressing development scheme on the horizon—like a pipeline or a hydro dam—it was thought negotiations could take place in a more open and relaxed fashion. Nothing could be further from the truth.

Yukon Indians, status and non-status alike, have combined in the Council for Yukon Indians (CYI) under Smith's presidency, to negotiate their claim to 90 percent of the Yukon's 200,000 square miles on behalf of about 7,000 Natives scattered across the territory in 12 small villages or bands.

To most Canadians the Yukon is a land of Midnight Sun, the Gold Rush of '98, and Pierre Berton's birthplace (not necessarily in that order if you asked Mr. Berton's mother). It was probably better known at the end of the 19th century, because of a freakish discovery of gold by two Indians—Skookum Jim and Tagish Charlie—and a white man, George Carmack. That find in 1896 on Bonanza Creek near where Dawson City (of Robert Service fame) now stands, brought by 1898, more than 80,000 whites from all over the world to the greatest gold rush in history. In 1899, the Yukon had a white population larger than any of the Prairie provinces at the time and boasted the largest city—Dawson—west of Winnipeg, with a population of some 25,000 people, more than the entire territory today. But by 1910, although more than $100 million in gold was taken out of the territory, there was nothing left of the dream but some clanking dredges and provision for an elected territorial council, as a prelude to a provincial status which has yet to become a reality.

Through all that boom and bust period the Native people were totally ignored, or worse, exploited. The two men who found the gold got little more than a hangover for their pains—whisky and a few dollars. Today the majority of those people, who never saw a white man until about 100 years ago, have no work, no hope, no future except in their land claim and the benefits they hope can come from it. Today the Yukon lives largely on tourism in its southwest corner around Whitehorse and eyes the future eagerly, as base metal mining brings in another influx of whites. Only far north of Dawson remains one tiny Loucheux village—Old Crow on the Porcupine River—where about 250 people still live much as they did.

But out on the muskeg of the Porcupine Plain, the drilling rigs are probing the earth for oil, and Old Crow recently acquired an airstrip for the drilling crews, but it doesn't make the people happy. They are frightened. Their men work seasonally with the oil and gas exploration crews and live on welfare the rest of the time. Few go out the 15 miles to Crow Flats where game abounds—which is the life blood for these people. The caribou still range there; so meat is plentiful, but now the people hear that one of Arctic Gas' alternative pipeline routes is to run through their beloved Crow Flats. They know that they may be forced further into the White man's economy—welfare and meaningless jobs that will disappear when the pipeline is finished or the drilling completed.

Prior to 1948, so the CYI claims, Yukon Indians were economically independent. Today more than 50 percent are permanent welfare recipients, and at times, as many as 80 percent receive some form of government assistance. Not a pretty picture.

Northerners are great romantics. They have their dreams and "tomorrow" is their favorite word. The key for "tomorrow," for white and Native, may well lie in *Together Today for Our Children Tomorrow*, if togetherness they can achieve. The problem for Native people and, we suggest, for whites as well, is whether "tomorrow" will be a continuation of the past and present—a "get rich quick" philosophy of despoiling some of the grandest country in Canada— or true development making it possible for the whites and Natives to live equally and side-by-side, sharing but not being assimilated by this magnificent land and its enormous potential.

Yukon Indians are part of the once-famous Athabaskan Indians who occupied the Northern half of the Prairie Provinces, the top of British Columbia, and the forest regions of the Yukon and North-west Territories. In the Yukon they were the Kutchin, Nahanni, and Loucheux and were uniquely adapted to the harsh land they inhabited. But what that harsh land was unable to subdue, the white man all too easily destroyed.

> We have watched the white man move onto our land without even asking our permission. We have watched the white man destroy parts of our land. We have watched the white man destroy our trap lines. We have watched the white man bring in alcoholism and prostitution. We have watched the white man take away our children and destroy our language and culture.[1]

It sounds like a war with the white man calling all the shots, trying to force the Indian to deal in the white man's society, using the white man's political and social system. The winners and the losers were never in doubt.

The Native people of Canada have never had a written history —their ways have been passed on by word of mouth. And this is important to them, because as *Together Today* puts it, "history is to be learned from not lived in." So, in their statement of grievances to the federal government, the Yukon Natives described more simply than historians ever do, how it was before the first white arrived. It is their tradition, and for those cynics who say Canadian Natives had no culture and were a dying race when the great saviors of the world —the whites—arrived, let the people of a small and scattered group of Yukon Indians speak.

> For many years before we heard about the white man, our people, who lived in what is now called the Yukon, lived in a different way. We lived in small groups and moved from one place to another at different times of the year. Certain families had boundaries which

they could not cross to hunt, because that area was used by other Indians. Sometimes we gathered together in larger groups to fish and relax after a hard winter.

We had our own God and our own religion that taught us to live in peace together. This religion also taught us how to live as part of the land. We learned how to practise what you people call multiple land use and conservation and resource management. We have something to teach white men if they will listen to us.

Our family was the centre of our Indian way. The man was the head of the family and was the provider of the food and clothing and housing and protection. The mother was the centre of the family and the children took her name. Marriage, adoption and care of people was arranged by custom.

Education was handled by our parents and was done by children, watching and copying what they saw. A child was considered an adult when he proved that he could handle adult responsibilities.

People were busy supplying the needs of the community. All possessions belonged to the group, and individuals did not suffer unless the whole group was in need. This required planning, organization and leadership, words you have taught us. But they were carried on without any formal organization, which is one of the reasons why we are finding it difficult to adopt to the white man's way.[2]

These scattered nomadic Natives probably first came in contact with whites just over a hundred years ago, when the first fur traders came into the North and trade with easterners was established. It was a one-way trade because the Indians had no idea of the cost of their furs and sold them for knives, trinkets, and finally, guns and powder. There are recorded incidents of more than 200 prime pelts being sold for a kettle or steel knife. The white man's free enterprise system even then saw exploitation as a matter of good business. Today the only thing that has been altered is the medium of exchange—kettles and knives for furs, to welfare cheques for oil, gas, and land.

But with this new commerce came problems. Outsiders wanted Indian women, children, furs, and souls. Also disruptive to the original ways was centralization of life. Whereas people had lived simply in small groups, they now had to come together in the same place to trade, and it wasn't long before the traders began to realize that alcohol at these meetings made it easier to part the Indians from their furs. Values began to change. Where property had always been communal, furs and trade goods became private property, and this was another breakdown in culture.

By 1885 there were probably about 15 whites in the Yukon, but the greatest disruption of all was just around the corner with the discovery of gold in 1896. For the next 10 years the Indians acted as menials to the "crazy white men" who "moiled" for gold. They were the guides, packers, and life savers to the uninitiated outsiders who flocked north for the brief decade of greed. By 1910 most of the whites had left, but many of the Natives had learned to speak English and had adopted the white man's Christianity, mainly Anglican and Roman Catholic. Looking back, most destructive of all perhaps was the acceptance of the white man's emphasis on personal possessions.

Many Indians left the bush to take jobs on the river boats or cut wood for their huge boilers, and as in many other primitive societies, the contact with the white man resulted in many Indian women bearing white men's children. Between 1900 and 1930, Indians estimate that more than half of their people died from white man's diseases—influenza, tuberculosis, venereal disease—so that by the time World War II arrived, the blood lines had been drastically altered and the population decimated. At the same time, fearing further assimilation by whites, many Indians returned to the land—hunting, trapping, and fishing. At least there was no welfare.

During the period up to the end of World War II or later, there was another constant threat—unwittingly perhaps, but nonetheless sinister—designed to break down the Indian way-of-life and the Indian family. This was the residential school system, run first by the churches and later by both church and government. Children were taken from their homes when they were six, and there are examples of many never returning home for 10 years. Others were away 10 months at a time.

> We were taught in such a way that we were forced to give up our language, our religion, our way of life, and because of this, we no longer identified with our parents. But what we were taught didn't make sense and it seemed wrong to us. Most of those people who went to the church schools gave up the Indian way but couldn't accept the white way. Only now are white men beginning to find out what was wrong with the residential school system. But we were caught in between the two and didn't know which way to go.[3]

In 1941 came the famous Alaska Highway, stretching some 1,500 miles across Alaska, the Yukon, and Northern British Columbia, with 30,000 American soldiers and the big money that lured Native people out of the bush and onto the United States payroll. Bloodlines were changed again, and when four years later most of the whites left, the traplines were overgrown, the cabins broken, and the traps rusted; and there were no jobs for the people who squatted on the edge of white towns like Whitehorse. Indian Affairs "helped out" with welfare cheques and gave Indian villages band lists for easy administration. Later came Indian housing which, Smith charges, is nothing more than bribery to get people to move in from the bush as the final step in the program of changing Natives from their economically independent way-of-life to a dependent hand-out.

The changes grew as the river boats were beached, the roads were improved, and the tourists flocked north, until by 1973 when *Together Today* was written, the Native picture was a decidedly unpleasant one. This picture differs little across Canada except in circumstances and dates: the residential schools, the well-meaning missionaries, the resource rape, and the endless pressures for the Natives to accept and become "white men."

In the Yukon as the time neared for land claims to be negotiated, the two races had become disgusted with each other—all the gaps from generation to communication to economic were almost unbridgable. Racism had become more blatant; there was little tolerance or understanding. Whites saw the Indians as sullen and uncommunicative, and seldom realized that words don't have the same meaning for Native people, who are uncomfortable in English and who "feel" more often than "talk" about their life. They are slower, more polite.

Indians are accused of having no concept of time or place. In a sense this is true. The eight-hour day is a white concept whereas the Native lives by the sun and moon and stars and the seasons. It will take more than money to change those concepts of time; it will take meaningful employment and purpose. The same with land. Traditionally the Indian went where the fish were, and then the caribou and then the fur-bearing animals. He was truly a man for all seasons and his home often moved. Today under welfare schemes, there is no opportunity to provide for the family as the Indian man always did, instead the woman calls the Indian agent when she wants food, clothes, or fuel, and the man's traditional role is gone, leaving him stereotyped as the lazy, drunken Indian, unwilling or unable to care for his children.

> What is happening to our children? We do not know because you are not telling us. We take them to your schools, they go to your movies and dances, they watch your television and hang around your poolrooms. You told us they had to learn to live like white man so we did not interfere. You said our way of life was dead and that

we had nothing to teach them. Please tell us what you are doing to our children, because they are breaking our hearts. If you would only give us back control of our own children, of our own lives, no Indian child would be in need of a home. Divorce, adoption, foster homes, and illegitimacy are white inventions, not Indian.[4]

As we have mentioned in previous chapters, the Indian Act and its paternalistic clauses comes in for special attack. The Yukon's non-status Indians, of whom there are about 3,000, are part of the situation today and must be part of the settlement. Natives claim that the right to be Indian is something only Indians can decide, and that the law, which coldly allows people to sign away their status—and their heritage—for some fleeting right, must be changed.

Indians lose their status in many ways. If an Indian woman marries a white man, she automatically becomes "white," but if a white woman marries an Indian man she automatically becomes "Indian." Simply by signing a paper called enfranchisement, an Indian loses his status forever. This might be in return for such generally accepted rights as Northern allowance, allowing children to attend public schools rather than residential schools, owning private property, drinking in a public place, or holding a business licence.

It is small wonder that, even though the law has recently been amended to end such discrimination, Natives feel they were bribed to give up status as Indians simply to achieve rights that whites take for granted. And even though the more discriminatory aspects have been eliminated from the Act, those who lost their status still cannot get it back. A settlement, therefore, will include anyone who has 25 percent or more Indian blood and can trace his or her ancestry to a Yukon Indian who was resident in the Yukon prior to January 1, 1941. So, with the 2,500 or so status Indians, the total Native population of the Yukon is in excess of 6,000, or about one-third the total territorial population.

Together Today for our Children Tomorrow is first of all a settlement for the future. It is a statement of grievances and a proposal for settling these grievances that will attempt to solve long-term problems without assimilation. The emphasis is on tomorrow. The underlying premise behind the Yukon Natives' proposal to DIAND and the Prime Minister was simply the opposite to the treaties Canada entered into on the Prairies. Those treaties were to "help" the Indians adjust to the white man's way-of-life, and the Indian Act was to "protect" the Indian from the white man. The objective of the Yukon Native people is to obtain a settlement in place of a treaty, that will protect their children from the mistakes and horrors of the past 100 years.

"If we are successful, the day will come when *all* Yukoners will be proud of our heritage and culture and will respect our Indian identity. Only then will we be equal Canadian brothers," is the way Elijah Smith expresses it.

And contrary to what fearful whites charge—along with greedy developers and their DIAND supporters—the Natives of the Yukon, and anywhere else we've been, don't want to stop development in the North. Rather, they clearly state they want to be part of it. "But we can only participate as Indians. We will not sell our heritage for a quick buck or a temporary job."[5]

The settlement proposal is a complicated one, but it is a start for negotiation. It is based on aboriginal title. They want land and they want cash and they want control over their own destiny. Negotiations are underway, and the individual proposals will no doubt be altered. The government's working paper (which we look at in detail later in this chapter) is a counter proposal. What the final outcome will be—or when—is still up for grabs, but the basics will remain or Elijah Smith and the CYI will not sign. The land claim of 1973 has eight basic components which we must understand before looking at details of land, cash, and structure, for it is these basics that attempt to meet the problems outlined earlier. Briefly these eight basic assumptions underlying the proposal are:

Programs: These are now planned and executed by DIAND and are usually white solutions to Indian problems. The Indians charge they never work and merely siphon funds away from the people who need them into the pay envelopes of DIAND employees. Eventually these would be phased out. But even now the settlement insists that planning, as well as administration, must be given to the Native people who could change, add, or eliminate programs in the light of what they see to be their cultural heritage. This sends bureaucrats into a frenzy of preoccupation with their own futures but obviously makes sense.

Old People: This is the first priority after a settlement is negotiated. Because they are the only living part of Native culture, the elderly have the right to live out their lives with their own people and not in white senior citizens' "twilight homes." Rather, there would be facilities in each village, along with adequate funds for the aged who, in Indian culture, enjoy so much respect. In the proposed administrative structure of the Indian society envisaged after the settlement, there would also be a "Senior Council."

Culture: One of the charges often levelled against Indians is that they want to return to a romantic version of the old days—a sort of Noble Savage living regally off the land. Some undoubtedly will return to the land and live as they did. Others will opt for the white man's world. It is here the Indian has trouble because he's been treated as an inferior in intelligence, industry, and opportunity. He's been the loser, a failure at being either white or Indian. So a settlement must take into consideration Indian religion, philosophy, history, and language, and for many Indians this will be a process of rediscovery. What, in effect, Yukon Indians are asking is to have their culture become a unique part of Canada's vaunted multi-culturalism. They pin a lot of hopes on a statement made by Jean Chrétien, then minister of DIAND, in the House of Commons in 1969.

> The Indian culture is worth preserving. These people were in Canada before we arrived here, they have contributed to making Canada the country it is. We must help them retain their traditions and their own culture, because in themselves they have good values. We can help them. There is no such thing in Canada as "assimilation". I do not want anyone in Canada to be assimilated.[6]

Community Development: Most of the 12 Yukon Indian communities—Burwash, Carcross, Carmacks, Haines Junction, Dawson, Mayo, Old Crow, Pelly Crossing, Ross River, Teslin, Upper Liard, and Whitehorse village—are sick. Alcoholism, welfare, unemployment, illness, and school dropouts cause incredibly low morale. The spiritual, economic, and social health of these communities is in desperate need of a cure emanating from leadership by Natives. Problems have to be identified, leaders brought forward, and programs and administration placed in the hands of the Native people in a kind of parallel administration to the white communities, rather than in a separate white-controlled municipality. As the CYI proposal so eloquently puts it, "We have lived too long with the police, the welfare worker, the Indian agent, the nurse, and the probation officer breathing down our necks. We lived without them once, we believe we can do so again."[7]

Education: There is an almost 100 percent dropout rate among Indian students in the Yukon—and similar statistics exist across most of Canada—despite considerable changes in the education system. Native leaders believe this is due to an almost total white orientation in the design of the curriculum, which puts the Indian student at a serious disadvantage in predominantly white classrooms. At this point, the Yukon Natives are asking that the curriculum be drastically revised to include history, language, culture, land, conservation. Otherwise, they say, they will be forced to look seriously at a separate school system, along with separate community development. More shudders from the civil service in Ottawa and Whitehorse!

Economy: Without a solid economic base, the hopes for the future of the Yukon's Natives will never reach beyond the rhetoric of their original claims. The one word that describes it best is "control"—control by and for natives—and it is a word that the federal government pays lip service to but never implements—the reason being, ostensibly, that Natives lack the expertise and management skills to plan and implement a way-of-life that makes sense to them. The land claim utterly rejects this in the harshest of terms—"We are fed up with all Indians being treated as employees and all employers in the Yukon being white. We are fed up with Indian money all going into white cash registers." Native people say, instead, that outside experts can be hired, and training can be made available. They have prepared more than 100 proposals for economic development as part of the settlement, ranging from the traditional fur market through outfitting, construction, tourism, logging, and mining. A fair settlement must allow for full participation in every aspect of the economic life of the Yukon. The white community finds this aspect of land claims enormously threatening and the basis for a most serious white backlash, far beyond mere racism.

Communication: Simply put, the Natives want to change a situation where the whites do all the talking and the Natives are forced to listen. The brotherhood knows that no one will take them seriously until they have an opportunity to talk and until white people are prepared to listen. Radio, television, videotapes, and newspapers prepared and presented by Natives is the goal. "We plan to teach the white man something about who we are and why we are different. Maybe then he will understand us better."[8]

Research: Only recently have native organizations felt the necessity of having research done on their behalf and for their own use in negotiations. Such research would be fed into the settlement details, the negotiating team, and the future development of an Indian way-of-life. The main areas of research are once again a threat to the status quo, and those Yukoners who insist that Indian people stay in their place. Examination of all DIAND programs is high on the list. All aspects of Northern-style colonial development would be examined, including royalties, taxes, conservation, and how Natives can be involved in, and benefit from, development. Immediate research is needed, and in fact is underway, on the social impact of the proposed gas pipeline at Old Crow. Perhaps, however, the most important aspect of research would go into the implementation of the land claims settlement. Organization, investment, programming, education, and myriad other details are presently beyond the full comprehension of those involved in negotiation.

We must now turn to the details of the land claim itself, bearing in mind that the whole idea is to achieve social and economic equality for the Native people of the Yukon, and until this is achieved, they will insist they be treated as people with a special status under section 92 of the British North America Act of 1867. The proposed settlement is essentially to enable the Indian people of the Yukon to live and work on equal terms with whites, and the method they propose is to provide an economic base from which Natives can compete. So, while the cornerstone of the settlement is land, money is also necessary to develop a solid economy from which the Indian people can develop.

The settlement claim envisages complete administrative control of their own affairs, which would eliminate DIAND in the Yukon. A central organization to handle land and funds received from the settlement would be established, as would local municipalities to administer the needs of the 12 bands. These central, local, and perhaps, urban corporations bear some similarity to the Alaska corporations, but the proposed settlement is not a termination one as Alaska clearly was. Critics call it a form of separate development which will emphasize the differences between races rather than resolve them. This criticism is usually from whites whose philosophy that "we're all Yukoners together regardless of our background" is scorned by the Natives.

The Natives of the Yukon propose to select certain areas of land in the Yukon that are not now under private ownership. These tracts of land would be held in perpetuity by the Crown for the use of present and future generations of Native people. The land could not be sold or traded except with permission of the central corporation and the Crown. The corporation would be free, under its local counterpart, to levy taxes and create other by-laws and rules within its own jurisdiction. The amount of land, its precise location, and what demands would be made on surface and sub-surface resources are not spelled out but are key subjects of negotiation, obviously.

Without land, Indian people have no soul—no life—no identity—no purpose. Control of our own land is necessary for our cultural and economic survival. For Yukon Indian people to join in the social and economic life of Yukon, we must have specific rights to lands and natural resources that will be enough for both our present and future needs.[9]

A temporary freeze on land transactions was requested in the 1973 claim presented to the government, because the Natives felt they needed time to select, survey, and transfer land to Indian control. The freeze was only to affect unalienated Crown land. However, it was rejected by Chrétien, who said that any freeze imposed on Crown land in the Yukon would have an adverse effect on economic development. This statement has annoyed both whites and Natives. Whites say the freeze is a fact of life, albeit unofficial, and the Indians maintain that the freeze is essential because already the most valuable land in the territory is in the hands of government or private development. Indians fear they will lose even more land before their settlement is finalized; so they are keeping their selections quiet. But such is the secrecy that shrouds the negotiation that no one is certain whether a land freeze exists officially or unofficially, and this is responsible for much of the suspicion that has made race relations in the Yukon so unpleasant.

Land must be set aside for Indian municipalities for each of the 12 bands, so that permanent homes may be established. A suggested formula is one square mile per family in a municipality, as part of the total land allotment to the Indian people. Rough estimates put this at somewhere in the vicinity 1,200 square miles. Indians claim use of more than 90 percent of the total land mass of the Yukon, which is 207,076 square miles. They say they are not asking for the return of their land, but only that they be allowed to keep and develop some of it, including sub-surface mineral, timber and forest, and water rights.

Land rights would be held in five different categories: Indian burial grounds and cemeteries, historical and traditional village sites, municipalities, economic development areas, and hunting, trapping, and fishing cabin sites.

The Natives want the right to hunt and fish for food on all land in the territory and the right to trap on all unoccupied land. They are asking for 15 percent of all revenue collected from the commercial hunting industry, as well as involvement in its management. The Yukon provides excellent big game hunting which Indians maintain they should have a part in. Indian lands must be preserved for exclusive hunting, fishing, and trapping by the Native people, and a complicated procedure for regulating trapping management, involving the two levels of government plus the Natives, is requested.

Moving into the area of reparations for past wrongs and for land that has already been taken away, the claim asks for royalty payments in perpetuity, and in return the Natives are prepared to extinguish aboriginal rights forever. The royalties on gas, oil, and mineral production along with wood and forest production are to be paid annually by both territorial and federal governments, the percentage to be worked out by the negotiating teams. The money would be used to finance Indian programs, research, economic development, and resource development.

The cash settlement is the most controversial area of any modern-day claim, and the Yukon Indians decline to spell it out to the last dollar and cent. For this reason whites in the Yukon look at the sample appendices to *Together Today for Our Children Tomorrow* with considerable apprehension, and charge they will be sold out. But to date, the Indians are only saying publicly that they want a fair cash settlement and that they will not squander it.

> We are saying that we deserve a cash settlement for all our past grievances and for the rights that have been taken away over the past 100 years. We are saying that we should be compensated for having been left out of the Yukon's prosperity, the highest in Canada. We will not accept promises because we have very little faith left in the white man's promises. There must be a generous cash settlement that will convince us that you practice what you preach about a Just Society. We will not waste this money. It will be invested in our children's future. It will not go to individuals but to organizations which we will set up for a program of human and community development. The purpose of this program will be to raise our standard of living and allow us to participate as equals in the development of Yukon and Canada.[10]

One unique feature is the method of payment proposed for the cash settlement. It is to be deposited with the Bank of Canada, and tax free payments are to be made quarterly, the unpaid balance to be used by the government, with tax-free interest paid to the Natives to cover inflation and rapid population growth. In their sample outline, the settlement schedule calls for $1 million the first year, $2 million the second, $5 million the third, $10 million the fourth, $15 million-a-year from the sixth to the tenth, and further cash funds for many more years to come. Additionally, of course, certain royalties and land would be held forever.

There are many more claims in *Together Today for Our Children Tomorrow*, but the details we have examined—the background and hopes—are important in any understanding of what Native peoples across Canada are seeking.

It is important to remember that this Yukon proposal is the first to come from a group of Native Canadians to the federal government in a comprehensive and detailed manner. It is imperative that Ottawa acknowledge this, in fact as well as in rhetoric, because Prime Minister Trudeau indicated his general support back in 1973. It is crucial to the Native people of the Yukon that the protracted, frustrating negotiations that have dragged on since then be speeded up to avoid prolonged court action or delays in Parliament. It is equally necessary that a settlement be reached before rumored massive development projects start. Finally, it could be to the distinct advantage of Northern whites, although few will admit it today, that a just settlement be achieved so that the Yukon can develop in a united way.

The Yukon settlement and the process used in achieving it is the key, if not the precedent, for all other unextinguished and disputed land claims across Canada. The slowness, the ponderous machinery, the lack of trust, the threats from DIAND, and the deteriorating race relations make the process even more urgent than in 1973. If the Yukon is to be a model settlement, then we face a choice: will it be the model for just and responsible settlements of unextinquished aboriginal rights, or will it represent the same acrimonious, protracted, and unsatisfactory dealings between Indians and Ottawa such as have marred Canada's dealings with its Native people since the white man first arrived in North America.

The beginnings in the Yukon were auspicious. First, Mr. Trudeau made his supportive statements and then his Indian Affairs' minister followed it up by appointing a negotiating team from various federal departments along with the federally-appointed Commissioner of Yukon territory, James Smith. R. B. Hutchison, a Victoria lawyer and son of a noted Canadian author and journalist, Bruce Hutchison, was named chief federal negotiator, and by August of 1973 two meetings between the Council for Yukons Indians and the federal team had been held.

While Hutchison's mandate was broad, he was at first hampered by the unwieldiness of the government team, which included representatives of DIAND, justice, and finance as well as two or three representatives of the colonial government of the Yukon, and by the middle of 1974, Chrétien could only say "some progress" had been made. The negotiations are conducted behind tightly closed doors, and both sides brush an inquirer off with a terse "no comment" or a defensive statement that no decisions will be made unilaterally. It is known however, that the federal negotiating team has been reconstituted, still under Hutchison's chairmanship, to make him the sole negotiator, with the other government representatives acting in an advisory capacity.

The CYI is also in a special position, since it is made up of the Yukon Native Brotherhood and the Yukon Association for Non-status Indians. Its chairman is still the patriarch of Yukon Indians, Elijah Smith. But he has recently resigned his presidency of the brotherhood to devote his full attention to the negotiations.

The federal election of 1974 did nothing to speed up the negotiations, but during a campaign speech in Whitehorse, June 6, 1974, Chrétien, who was soon to leave the portfolio with the victory of the Liberal party, tried to reassure both whites and Indians that negotiations would "produce satisfactory results for all Yukoners." The fact that Erik Nielsen was re-elected for the Tories may be seen as some indication where the Yukoners of both races place their trust.

That day, Chrétien told his predominantly white audience that negotiations were no threat to Yukon development, and reassured them that a land freeze was out of the question, even though Trudeau had agreed with the principle a year earlier when *Together Today* was presented to the then minority government.

Then in his speech, he moved to tackle what have become the sore points in all the negotiations—the secrecy and lack of understanding, what it is that Natives want, and how it will affect the white population.

> I know that negotiations behind closed doors are cause for some concern, but in a process of negotiation as complicated and sensitive as this, the bargaining process cannot be carried out in public. . . . No deal will be struck behind closed doors. Whatever is agreed must be approved by Parliament. There will be ample opportunity for all Yukoners, Indian and non-Indian—indeed all Canadians—to study the proposals and make their views known. . . . You may rest assured that in the process of negotiation the Government team is not going to give away the Yukon or mortgage its future. The Indian people certainly do not want this, because they expect to be part of that future. What they are looking for is sufficient land under their own

control to ensure their cultural identity, a place in Yukon society, and, combined with cash compensation, an adequate base for their role and contribution in that society.[11]

It was—in line with the Liberal campaign strategy for 1974—a something-for-everyone speech. There were a few subtle warnings too for both sides, since after all, the Yukon only sends one MP to Ottawa and it has been "Yukon Erik" for years.

The election came and went. Trudeau got his majority. Chrétien got out of DIAND, and his former parliamentary assistant, Judd Buchanan inherited "the Indian problem" and with it the desultory Yukon negotiations. Furthermore, despite the fact that Chrétien adamantly insisted during election campaigns that the Yukon was not a "guinea pig for the rest of Canada on Indian land claims," most people, including Buchanan, saw the neat package that could come out of the Yukon as a precedent for British Columbia and the Northwest Territories.

By the time Buchanan took over, towards the end of 1974, the only marks of progress that could be reported were vague references to eligibility under the claim—that is, a determination as to who would benefit from a settlement—and a Native census must be approved before this is finalized. On March 3, 1975, Buchanan and a group of aides flew into Whitehorse with a proposal for the CYI. It was the government's answer to *Together Today for Our Children Tomorrow* and was to serve as the basis for "meaningful negotiations" between the two parties. It took two years, almost to the day, for the federal government to respond in any concrete manner, and the method with which it was done brought scorn and contempt on the DIAND and its neophyte minister, forcing him to return to Ottawa with his vaunted proposal reduced, at CYI insistence, to the status of a "working paper".

The gist of Buchanan's working paper is that status and non-status Indians can participate; that 1,200 square miles of land (1 square mile per family of 5) will be set aside; that 15,000 square miles will be a hunting, fishing, and trapping area for Natives; and that the plan will not terminate but continue in perpetuity. The original proposal also included a cash compensation of $50 million, half of which would come from land royalties. The CYI insisted this monetary figure be removed from the working paper, and it does not appear in later documents. The CYI found the paper "so bad we couldn't even look at it" and began preparing a counter-proposal to the government's counter-proposal.

The 1,200 square miles of Indian land does not include legal protection. This must be negotiated. It does not give Natives any subsurface rights. But they would get 50 percent of all government revenues from resource development in those Indian lands. The hunting preserve is not exclusively for Natives and is severely limited in comparison to the James Bay settlement. It also appears that Natives could not hunt for food outside this area unless their hunting was demonstrated as need, rather than use.

Shortly after presentation of the working paper, we had a series of long interviews with members of the CYI and with members of Buchanan's personal staff on the situation in the Yukon, where despite optimistic statements, negotiations are dragging on longer than ever. In between (as we shall demonstrate at the end of this chapter) are the Yukoners both Native and white, who feel they are caught by intransigent and ambitious politicians and self-serving Indian leaders.

The Yukon Indian Centre is a large frame building in Whitehorse that used to be one of the hated hostels, where Indian children lived far from home in a vain attempt to get them a white man's education. It now houses offices and other Native facilities including the brotherhood, the non-status association, and the CYI. One of the people who works there is a white lawyer who sold his private law practice to work full-time on a fee-for-service basis for Indian Yukoners. Early in 1975, Allen R. Lueck moved from his big downtown practice in Whitehorse to the Indian centre, and it was there one day in the spring of 1975 that he told us a story, that differed only in degree and detail from one heard across the North, of relations with the federal DIAND.

There are two essential problems in the Yukon negotiations, and they must be solved, according to Lueck, before any real negotiating can take place.

The first is the cumbersome wheels of government, its negotiating process which makes it hard to do anything creative or to come to any conclusion. They wanted, Lueck told us, specific terms like a labor contract or an industrial "buy-sell" agreement, and they wanted it to be final, and then the Indian "problem" would disappear. With this inflexible cast of mind, nothing will happen "and they know it and we know it". The government would like to announce that the Indians got so much land and so much money, and now the land claim is settled—aren't we great guys to solve this wretched problem for the people of Canada?

The Indians are saying that they would like to sit down with the Minister of Indian Affairs as a partner in the British North America Act and discuss their mutual problems. The Indians have some prior rights, their land was taken away from them, and compensation is needed. They want legal title to the land that is left. They want some regularity to their lives and to the lives of their children, and they don't want to be the wards of the federal government, thank you very much. This partnership concept between the minister of Indian Affairs and the Native people is important to the CYI, and it will be important in other land settlements.

"The constitution sets out a trust of the highest order on the Minister of Indian Affairs to be fair and just and also to take care of the interests of the Indian people," Lueck stated in carefully legal language, but his frustration was close to the surface. It is this question of trusteeship or partnership that poses the second problem and made the CYI insist the federal proposal be reduced to a working paper. How can the minister seriously sit on the opposite side of the table and ask us to accept the working paper? the CYI asks. In all seriousness, the Yukon Indians insist that Buchanan should be on their side in the negotiating process and should be prepared to throw the not inconsiderable resources of his department behind the Natives' attempts to achieve a just settlement. It is precisely this adversary role that people like Lueck reject so completely.

"When you think of it, the deck is badly stacked against us. We have one minister, and the rest of the people of Canada have 263 MP's, yet he sees himself as the opponent. How can we win? There's a real constitutional bind shaping up for the minister," Lueck insisted.

At this point in history, with Indian land claims confronting Northern development, there has to be something more than DIAND to adjudicate land claims. The CYI and other Native groups are looking to some kind of quasi-judicial commission to rule on Indian land claims, because Indian Affairs can no longer, in the opinion of Native people, be both judge and adversary.

Another bone of contention in the Yukon is provincial status for the territory. The territorial administration, which is a semi-independent arm of DIAND, with an elected council and an appointed administrator in the person of James Smith, is concerned that under any settlement of land claims, a parallel administration for the Natives would be established before provincial status is achieved. The CYI believes that the three territorial representatives

on the negotiating committee will hold out as long as possible against
a settlement in hopes that the question of provincial status can be
dealt with first.

The ever-present bogey of inadequate funding for the research
and negotiating process also hangs over the CYI. It operates on a
monthly budget of just $25,000, which has been coming to them in
bits and pieces on an ad hoc basis from DIAND, with the ever-
present and implied threat that it could be cut off if negotiations get
sticky. "We're negotiating with a gun to our head," Lueck said.

This modest budget pays for four negotiators, three enrolment
officers doing the eligibility census, one research consultant, and one
lawyer—Lueck. Shaking his head in some admiration, but also some
bewilderment, Lueck explained that "Elijah won't let us spend a
cent we haven't got" and won't hire research staff until their salary
can be guaranteed for at least a year. While the government demands
a further proposal in one breath, it threatens to reduce funding in
the next.

Lueck and the CYI admit there's been little activity in terms of
negotiating since the fall of 1974 because of preoccupation with
funding. The possibility of a loan from Ottawa, using an eventual
settlement as collateral, is one alternative method of funding, but
even that will be viewed with suspicion unless the DIAND is prepared to make it substantial, perhaps $2 million on a possible $100
million settlement. Ottawa is known to oppose a massive loan, pre-
ferring to dole it out from year-to-year. The CYI sees this as another
blatant attempt to have negotiations go the way Buchanan wants or
the money gets cut off. "Judd's the savior of the DIAND bureaucracy.
At least Chrétien fought them off. We'll never get a settlement as
long as he's the minister," one CYI negotiator complained to us.

We took these negative reactions to DIAND strategy to one of
Buchanan's special assistants who, along with two or three other
special and executive assistants, a deputy and four assistant deputy
ministers, and all their aides, takes part in the brain trust on the 15th
floor of Centennial Towers which houses Ottawa's DIAND staff.

Mike Robinson is a young, politically aware westerner who,
like a lot of ministerial aides, works at the political rather than
strictly bureaucratic level of government. These young men and
women come and go, owing their allegiance to their minister and to
the Liberal party, rather than to the public service commission. They
usually move on—or out—with their minister and are really his personal staff. This is an accepted political reality in Ottawa, and many

special, personal, or executive assistants wield considerable power. They travel with the minister, have ready access to him, and keep him briefed on an almost hourly basis. They can block or assist people in trying to reach the man himself.

Robinson spends a lot of time in the North with Buchanan, and his version of the situation in the Yukon differs markedly from the CYI, and like Buchanan, he is optimistic that a settlement will be reached soon. In fact he told us, there is a veiled suggestion that there had better be a settlement fairly soon or . . . "The ball is in the CYI's court, and they should realize that the general mood for settlements won't get any better as time goes on, because money is getting tighter all the time."

Robinson claims the proposal-that-became-a-working-paper was prompted by the very slowness of negotiations in the previous two years, but because of an undefined communications problem, the CYI wouldn't accept it and reduced its status, so that they could come back with a similar paper that would be more specific and less philosophical than the 1973 land claim.

Being white and tuned into current realities, DIAND wants to have a cut-and-dried proposal that puts in dollar figures, land acreage, and locations, and then an agreement in principle can be negotiated, which hopefully will be acceptable at the community level. Robinson, quite naturally, insists that the federal government is negotiating in good faith and counters the trustee argument of the CYI with the claim that DIAND—through its Northern development —must also be cognizant of the interests of white Yukoners.

"We must reach an agreement on some form of aboriginal title, but the lack of communication and fear of the unknown makes the whites extremely apprehensive. Until the process can develop, there's not much we can do," Robinson insisted.

White Yukoners will find little reassurance in Robinson's denial that blanket equality is the solution. Like the Indians, he believes that this is an unrealistic position for whites to take, until some economic base is established for Natives. The territorial council, while lacking financial and administrative clout, gets some blame from Robinson. Somehow, he told us, the elected councillors, all of whom are white even though about one-third of Yukon's population is Native, have to convince the Indians that they are working for them as well as for the whites.

"The fear of separate development at the municipal level is not a problem for the federal government," Robinson said. "Rather, it is up to the territorial administration and the Native organizations to convince each other that they can work together."

This ignores the fact that Ottawa is perfectly within its rights to become fully involved with any territorial decision if it should choose to make its influence felt. The Yukon does not now have, nor is it likely to attain in the immediate future, provincial status which, of course, is the number one priority of many whites. As so often is the case, the federal government is in middle, mistrusted by the Natives and feared by the whites who have had things pretty much their own way for the past 100 years. Their main fear is that the Indians and federal bureaucrats are ganging up to sell out all Yukoners at a staggering price.

In the North, as in the West, any tendency to look for special status is seen as a separatist plot which must have its origins in Quebec, and it requires only a simple extension of this logic to blame the former minister, Jean Chrétien, for all their woes, simply because "he couldn't even speak English when he first came up here." Buchanan, born in the West and representing a staunchly Anglo-Saxon riding in Ontario, was the hope of the future to most white Northerners who like to assert "that we're all just Yukoners together and if you just work hard you can carve out your own destiny."

Now, with Indians claiming a special position in the Yukon, the flames of discord that have been smoldering for generations are beginning to burn brightly. For years, most non-Indians in the Yukon would seldom speak up in public about the Natives for fear of being branded rednecked bigots. But now there's a whole organized white backlash expressing outrage at what they claim is an atempt to "select one segment of the population for preferential treatment at the expense of the remainder of the Yukon people."

We spent some time around Whitehorse and had little difficulty talking with three whites who, because of their positions and convictions, represent one of the most serious threats to a peaceful and just settlement of Indian land claims, and these whites have their counterparts in other parts of Northern Canada, who at this point are simply less vocal.

Danny Lang is a young—mid-twenties—machine operator, married to an Alaska Eskimo woman. They live in the area outside Whitehorse, called Porter Creek. When the first sketchy details of the negotiations and Native demands were made public, his anger knew no bounds. He immediately gathered together a band of like-minded people and launched an organization called the Society for Northern Land Research. What started as a white backlash movement soon found broad backing, and within a few months, more than a thousand Yukoners including, Lang says, a handful of Indians, paid their one dollar to join, and today the organization claims 3,000 adherents.

"The people are very bitter in the outside communities," Lang told us. He had proved something of this when he led all the polls during the last territorial election in his first-ever bid to sit on the 12-member Yukon Council.

He insisted his organization was not out to incite people against the Indians and their land claim but rather to inform them about the "federal government's sellout. We're promoting integration, not segregation. It's ironic that we even have to form a group. The government should be standing up for the majority as well as the minority."

Lang made no bones about his position. He would get rid of the Indian Affairs department, refuse to recognize aboriginal rights, and give Indians only minimal land around their villages so they can "make it just as I have to." He claimed Indians could have the same rights as whites but nothing more and certainly no compensation.

"Why the hell do you people in the south want to pit Indians against whites? We're all Yukoners together and for years we got along fine side-by-side. Now Indians want special status, and that's only "an idea sold to them by some radicals in the brotherhood."

The "radicals in the brotherhood" are the same people that whites claim spend thousands of dollars on luxury travel, rented cars, wild parties, and lining their own pockets. While no one put Elijah Smith in with this group, Indians themselves admit the brotherhood has a radical element, as do other institutions in society. By keeping these red power individuals where he can watch them, Smith's method is to defuse some of the rhetoric, but this doesn't appease the Lang group.

"The government appears to have accepted the Yukon Native Brotherhood's assertion that it represents all Natives. For an organization that is supposedly so concerned with their Native brethren, how come they're getting ripped off almost as badly as we whites?" Lang asked and then answered his own question.

"We believe that any harm done to any minority group in history, such as the Indians of Canada, has been amply repaid by the advances in technology introduced to them. For example, if you have ever tried to light a fire with two sticks of wood, you can't help but think that it's a lot easier with Eddy matches. Take a look around you at the rental cars these professional Indians drive instead of dog teams, using oil furnaces, electricity, plumbing, and other modern conveniences, and ask them if they want to go back to living the old way."

Lang's anger borders on the extreme, and although he denies he's a racist and claims to have many Native friends, his position is not always seen as rational. But others—far more a part of the Yukon "establishment"—share it, even if they express their views more moderately.

We interviewed Hilda Watson in McAuley Lodge, a senior citizens' home in a Whitehorse suburb. But this attractive, alert middle-aged white woman is no retired senior citizen. She was there attending a meeting about the Yukon's aging people, in her capacity as a member of the territorial executive. She's "minister" of health and social welfare and is implacable in her opposition to anything that smacks of special status or privilege. She's the epitome of the "we're all Yukoners together philosophy."

Her first problem, as an elected representative on the council, is the lack of input into the land claim negotiations by white Yukon residents. The secrecy of the talks means there's no way to allow the three Yukon members of the federal team to report back to the people. So no one knows what's going on. Like Lang, Mrs. Watson maintained that the brotherhood is not in any way representative of the Indians in the local communities. Elijah Smith totally rejects this charge, answering that he spends almost half his time at the community level, that all decisions are ratified there, and that the brotherhood and CYI are democratically elected.

"This is nothing but an outright separatist movement. There are dark political forces behind the Indian movement that recognize the clout they have lies in keeping them together, and what is so distressing to us all is that it is supported by the federal government," Mrs. Watson said.

She would like Indian Affairs abolished and Indians treated the same as every other person in the Yukon—with no more and no less than white people. The land should only belong to individuals, not local or central committees, and if they—the Indians—have any culture left, they'll fight for it the way Scottish Canadians or German Canadians have to.

"Granted, they lost their culture under that dreadful Indian Act

but society isn't going to wait for them to regain it. If culture means
anything like self pride then the government doesn't need to pay you
to keep it alive."

Mrs. Watson has lived in the Yukon 27 years and represented
Kluane riding for five. She knows her way around, she's self-possessed
and confident. Her concern for the Yukon is evident. She worries
about the backlash but insists it wasn't caused by bigots.

"Initially, most of us supported the formation of the brotherhood six years ago, because the bands had all fallen apart due to the
ridiculous welfare system and the terrible drinking."

Mrs. Watson's idea for a settlement, which seems widely supported by whites, is to set small plots of land aside for individual
Natives, and some kind of small business or industrial loans. There
should be no lump sum cash settlement and no special hunting,
fishing, or trapping rights. She insisted that integration and assimilation are not the same, because Indians only live separately from
the white communities now, since Indian Affairs built Native housing on the edge of existing communities. The racism, according to
Mrs. Watson, exists at present only among Indian leaders, not
whites, but "I'm afraid it could come."

Flo Whyard epitomizes all that is beautiful about Northerners.
She's open and friendly, kind to everyone, talkative and knowledge-
able, a stalwart church person and an active member of the community, a friend to white and Indian alike. She's also scared and
worried, because she's bewildered at what is happening to her beloved Yukon, and as a third-generation Northerner, she wonders
what's going to happen. Mrs. Whyard is a white-haired grand-
mother, former editor of the *Whitehorse Star,* and presently a member of the territorial council for suburban Whitehorse West. Indian
people, she told us, have always been her friends, but lately they
won't speak to her. They don't understand what's going on, and
they're only talking through their advisors, not for themselves.

"This thing hits you right in your guts. We're all Northerners;
we're all friends. Why do they want segregation? All they're going to
get is this backlash that's ripe and ready to go."

And for Flo Whyard, it's against her grain to be forced to take
sides against people that have always been her friends. She told us
that Yukoners got over prejudice and segregation years ago, when
Indians used to sit at the back of the churches. "But we worked with
them and played with them and there was no racial discrimination.
Now, whammo, we're back where we started."

And that's where it is in the Yukon. No one trusts Ottawa, both sides eye each other with suspicion, and it would seem that a long period of tension, distrust, and perhaps even violence, graces the land of the Midnight Sun.

Notes

1 *Together Today for Our Children Tomorrow,* The Yukon Territory Land Claim of 1973, (Whitehorse; The Yukon Native Brotherhood and The Yukon Association of Non-Status Indians, February, 1973).

2 Ibid.

3 Ibid.

4 Ibid.

5 Ibid.

6 *Hansard Debates,* House of Commons, Ottawa, July 11, 1969.

7 *Together Today for Our Children Tomorrow.*

8 Ibid.

9 Ibid.

10 Ibid.

11 The Honorable Jean Chrétien in a public speech at Whitehorse, Yukon, June 6, 1974.

We feel strongly that our Treaty Rights are being jeopardized by the Manitoba Government. We feel the Manitoba Government is attempting to narrow our options to simple compensation. Mr. Minister, how can we discuss compensation without knowing how or to what extent we are going to be affected? We feel strongly that this unilateral action on the part of the Province of Manitoba is completely unacceptable and unconscionable. We are extremely pleased that you take the position that you have and will maintain your "special responsibility to the Indian people of Manitoba, particularly with respect to their lands."

Henry Spence
Chairman of the
Northern Flood Committee to the
Honorable Jean Chrétien
at Cross Lake, Manitoba
June 25, 1974

6

Northern Manitoba

*The Saga of How the Manitoba Government
and its Crown Corporation
Betrayed the Native People*

The mighty Churchill River rises in Methy Lake, Saskatchewan, near the Alberta border. There the river flows north-eastward through a magnificant chain of lakes, crosses the Manitoba border, and empties into Hudson Bay. The Nelson River, lying several hundred miles south of the Churchill and running slightly parallel to it, receives its flow from waters beginning their journey on the eastern slope of the Rockies. These waters drain into Lake Winnipeg via the Saskatchewan River; here they join the Nelson which flows out the north end of the lake, on its way to Hudson Bay.

In their search for more and cheaper electricity, Manitoba's hydro power planners dreamed up an awesome plan to divert that province's last great river, the Churchill, into the Nelson River, providing additional water flow and producing enormous amounts of hydro-electric energy. Hydro planners had known about the potential of the Nelson for more than half a century. The Kelsey generating station had already been built on the river to service the International Nickel plant at Thompson; but it was not until the Winnipeg engineering firm of Gibb, Underwood and McLellan did some studies in 1964, that the "engineer's dream" began to take shape and form. The scheme, conceived in secrecy, executed with little advance planning, and destined to affect the rights and lives of Manitoba's Native people, has caused the fall of one government and seriously questioned the integrity of another.

In 1966, Manitoba Hydro, the federal government, and the Conservative government of Premier Duff Roblin entered into an agreement to proceed with the multi-billion-dollar project. Manitoba undertook, under the terms of the agreement and at its own expense, "to design, construct, and place in service the electricity generating facilities according to a schedule which calls for the Station to be placed in initial service on or before the 30th day of November 1972." Electricity generating facilities include:

(i) The Station; (Hydro-electric generating station at Kettle Rapids)

(ii) A control dam on the Churchill River at the outlet of Southern Indian Lake, a diversion structure for releasing water into the Rat River, a tributary of the Burntwood River which flows into the Nelson River, and certain other ancillary works for the purpose of making available considerable water storage on Southern Indian Lake and to increase the power production of the lower Nelson River and to increase the potential capacity of the hydro-electric sites along the route of the Churchill River Diversion; and

(iii) A control dam, spillway, and flood control works to be in the vicinity of the outlet of Lake Winnipeg, which works will be designed to permit the levels of the water of Lake Winnipeg and the outflow of the Nelson River to be regulated and controlled.[2]

Since that agreement the generating station, Kettle Rapids, has been completed and other projects are in various stages of construction.

When the Manitoba Conservatives first made their public announcement on the project, they were filled with optimistic enthusiasm. But they did not talk much about the Cree community that lived on the shores of Southern Indian Lake or the other Indian communities that would be affected. There was no discussion of how the "high-level" diversion and fluctuating water levels would cause flooding of Indian land. They did not seem to care much about the fragile balance of nature in the North or the easily disrupted permafrost or the unpredictability of a land that reacts violently to the "rape" of its resources and whose wrath is felt for generations to come. The "far-sighted" politicians of that day did not mention the floating debris or the beautiful beaches and river banks that would be lined with dead vegetation. What was to happen to the livelihood of Native people, their lost traplines, the retreating animals, or dead fish, was never the subject of thorough study. But there was a good deal of talk about more and cheaper power and the "greater good of the people." To most Manitobans the huge expanse of empty territory at the top half of the province was as remote and unfamiliar as a foreign country. Most of them would accept the plan at face value.

The Churchill diversion plan is typical of the short-sighted approach perpetrated all over the North by power hungry developers—cheap power for interests in the south and the United States. (Manitoba plans to sell its excess summer power to the American midwest), and environmental and social disruption in the North. The need for these enormous amounts of hydro-electric power lay in the visions of the Crown-owned Manitoba Hydro. It predicted that the province's hydro needs would continue to grow at seven per cent a year, and its sole responsibility was to fill that need using the cheapest power resources available. But Dr. Robert Newbury, Professor of Civil Engineering at the University of Manitoba, a former employee of the Manitoba Water Commission and outspoken critic of the diversion scheme, challenged these assumptions.

> For almost two decades there is sufficient Hydro-electric power ready to be developed on the already-committed Nelson River without touching the Churchill. The Nelson River power potential can meet Manitoba's needs until 1991.
>
> The addition of Churchill water to the Nelson via the diversion will only add four years to the period for which Manitoba's power needs can be supplied by this river.
>
> But Manitobans can safely wait for another 17 years before being forced to decide whether four additional years of power is worth the loss of the Churchill River.
>
> And this is under the Manitoba Hydro assumption that Manitoba's hydro needs will continue to grow unchecked at seven percent forever into the future. If we assume, more sanely, that more efficient and moderate energy use will be encouraged, then the safe period becomes still longer.
>
> The Churchill is presently the last large river in the province still in its natural state. A 17-year period of grace would give Manitobans time to better measure the true value of the last great river and its communities for habitation, fishing, wildlife, recreation, tourism and conservation.
>
> Nowhere is the cost of the loss of the Churchill River calculated. Its existence, aesthetics, native community options, ecology, and unique role of creating a liveable environment in an otherwise harsh land are considered to be worthless in the energy budget.
>
> Not diverting the Churchill River does not affect the use of the Nelson River plants or transmission facilities. Nor does it significantly affect the cost of power, economic development, or employment for 17 years.[3]

Early questioners of the scheme were frustrated and baffled by the insensitivity and secretiveness of the Conservative government. The University of Manitoba, after a preliminary study of the plan, recommended in-depth sociological, biological, and environmental studies. But the government refused to fund the studies. In December, 1968, an open letter was presented to the Hon. Harry Enns, then Minister of Mines and Resources, by a group of University of Manitoba professors expressing their very real concern about the high-level diversion plan at Southern Indian Lake. The published letter was instrumental in bringing to the public the first awareness that the Cree people would lose their community through flooding—forcing them to relocate—and would suffer widespread social and environmental damage as well.

The news of the proposed flooding brought first shock and surprise and then hopelessness to the Indian and Metis people of South Indian Lake. Many of the 700 residents there had originally belonged to the reserve at Nelson House which is federal treaty land, but being aggressive hunters, they moved on to better hunting grounds. Most are status Indians, although they now live on non-treaty Manitoba Crown land.

In the North, where many Native communities suffer from an inadequate economic base, South Indian Lake was unique. It was an independent, yet cohesive community that had used all its talents in creating a flourishing commercial fishing business. When the lake —spawning grounds of the whitefish—was opened to commercial fishing in 1942, the community invited a few experienced fishermen in to train the local people in this type of fishing to help develop and maintain a stable economic situation. The Indians then restricted commercial fishing to members of the community.

The South Indian Lake fishing industry represented approximately 40 percent of the community's income, and they were justly proud, because they were producing some of the best pickerel and whitefish found anywhere.[4] This would seem like pretty small potatoes to a big operation like Hydro, who claimed that major social disruption was inevitable even if there were no plans for a diversion, but to the people of South Indian Lake, who had preserved and were now developing their own resources, it was a way of maintaining their independence and their traditional way-of-life.

When the New Democratic Party, then the Opposition, received the news of the possible effects of the flooding, they recoiled in horror, as the Loyal Opposition is wont to do. But having recoiled, they let the matter drop. After all, it was not a political issue! But by 1969 it became an issue, and a hot one, when Manitoba Hydro applied for a licence to proceed, and public hearings under the Water Powers Act (Manitoba) began.

Opponents of the plan were vigorous and vocal, centering their objections on the callous and cruel disruption of the South Indian Lake community, the lack of impact studies, and the refusal of government to make public all existing information. Manitoba Hydro, exercising the primary law of big corporations everywhere, insisted that its sole responsibility was to provide "adequate power at the lowest possible cost." Earlier, in a fine show of generosity, the provincial government had secured lawyers to work out "terms of compensation" with the residents of South Indian Lake. In February, 1969, those lawyers also challenged the lack of information and the nature of the project, and they, along with the community, became determined to fight at a legal level unless the licensing hearings were properly concluded.

In the ensuing legislative session the government introduced Bill 15, which if passed, would have been an act superceding and having preference over any other act or hearing, thus effectively circumventing any injunction which might have been imposed. And then the NDP, political axe in hand, joined the fray, decrying the lack of information and the government's refusal to release reports. Bill 15 did not pass second reading in the House, and a snap election was called in the spring of 1969. The Conservatives lost—enter the People-Matter-More-Party.

In his first press conference following the 1969 election, Premier Ed Schreyer reassured opponents of the Southern Indian Lake scheme when he said:

> Manitoba Hydro surely cannot proceed without reference to all the human factors, and if the human, the sociological, and the natural resource conservation factors weigh more heavily in the minds of my cabinet colleagues than the mill rate Hydro will have to charge, well then we'll have to reverse the present course Hydro is embarked on.

As good as his word, Schreyer announced in September of 1969, that the high level flooding of Southern Indian Lake would be abandoned. But like any good politician, he left himself an out. That "out" was an old plan in a new disguise. His first move was to bring in David Cass-Beggs, former General Manager of the Saskatchewan Power Corporation, to conduct another study. Predictably he concluded, as the result of further "study," that there were certain "alternatives" to high-level-diversion—"*low*" level diversion.

To further convince opponents of the plan that their fears were groundless, the government appointed two of Hydro's most outspoken critics, Professor Cass Booy and Dr. Robert Newbury, to the

Water Commission, a body which had the power to review any hydro plans and if necessary hold public hearings. In January 1970, David Cass-Beggs was named General Manager of Manitoba Hydro. These three appointments, at least for the time being, convinced many people that Schreyer meant it when he said, in 1969:

> Can we face up to the prospect of disrupting two communities of 750 people, completely upsetting the lake on which they depend for their livelihood, making it quite impossible for at least some of them to continue to live independently?

But it soon became obvious that Schreyer's speeches weren't worth the paper someone else had written them on. Manitoba Hydro was anxious to get on with the plans, and it was charged with the responsibility of reviewing the old flooding plans and coming up with some new ones. Gibb, Underwood, and McLellan, the consultants who devised the original plans, now came up with a brand new, shiny alternative—regulate Lake Winnipeg,[5] divert the Churchill by a "low level" dam, thus adding only 10 feet to the level of Southern Indian Lake. In other words, "we won't flood you a lot; we'll just flood you a little."

In addition to this, the government proudly claimed, their new plan would not force the people at South Indian Lake to relocate, because most of the buildings would remain intact. As usual, in imposing development plans on Native people, the government—stupidly or deliberately—missed the point. The main issue was not moving to higher grounds to save houses, although this worried some of the residents. The issue was the destruction of the environment, particularly the fish and wild life, and the loss of an economic base for the community.

It didn't matter much to the government that the Indians would wake up some morning to find debris instead of fish in their nets, and their boats and equipment damaged. They could always be compensated with dollars—which pretty much amounts to welfare, no matter how nicely you say it. It didn't seem to matter much to the government or Hydro that the viability of an economically independent Indian settlement would be lost, the wild life habitat along hundreds of miles of wonderful shorelines, and archeological and grave sites would all disappear under the relentless flooding—perhaps forever.

A statement by Sidney Green, the minister of Mines, Resources and Environmental Management, reflects the arrogant and autocratic approach of his government.

The Nelson River Development program is like many other programs that have been undertaken and will be undertaken by the Canadian people in keeping pace with the material progress throughout the world. While there are some who are bluntly opposed to the concept of so-called modern civilization and materialism, the Government of Manitoba feels it owes a responsibility to its citizens to proceed with intelligent development of our natural resources for the material benefit of our citizens. In our view the Nelson River Development is a program comparable with the Tennessee Valley Development, the St. Lawrence Seaway, the Trans-Canada Highway, the utilization of our mining potential, the cultivation of the prairies, and other such activities. In each case society had to consider a trade-off between maintenance of the ecology in its existing form and developing to the fullest the potential of our natural resource in accordance with value standards adopted by society. There is no question that the Nelson River Development will result in ecological changes. In our judgement the values to be obtained greatly overshadow the problems which will arise.[6]

In September, 1971 the then Federal Minister of the Environment, Jack Davis, and Sid Green signed an agreement for a $2 million study to determine the effects of the Churchill Diversion and Lake Winnipeg Regulation on Manitoba's natural resources and the environment. Reports of the study were to be due at least once a year; the final report was to be completed by the end of 1974.[7] The study involved experts from universities and federal and provincial agencies, and hopes were once more raised that this study might come up with some viable alternatives to the massive hydro development plans. But the government was secure, and it had handily won two by-elections in April 1971, obtaining a safe majority in the Legislature. All they had to worry about was a few Indians and some noisy cottagers up on Lake Winnipeg who were worried their land would be affected if the regulation plans were carried out, and some bitter Conservatives and ex-Hydro types who were hollering about the sanity of the whole thing. But the decision had long ago been made, although not publicly, and the next series of events indicates that the arrogance of the Manitoba NDP government matches any in Canada.

In October of 1971 Cass Booy, chairman of the Water Commission, received a memo from Sid Green saying, in effect, that the government was determined not to hold public hearings on the Lake Winnipeg Regulation. After a few weeks of being leaned on by Green, the commission gave in. Because the independence and integrity of the commission was sabotaged, Bob Newbury, the Churchill

Diversion critic, resigned. (It is interesting to note that Cass Booy failed to have his appointment renewed the following August).

In May of 1972, the NDP government solemnly announced its intention to proceed with the gravity diversion of the Churchill via Southern Indian Lake raising it to a maximum of ten feet. Desperate, the South Indian residents appealed to their lawyers to do something. The government refused to fund them, and the lawyers, donating their services to the community, attempted to get another action going against Hydro. Because of delaying tactics on the part of Hydro, the case has never been brought to a conclusion.

It also became apparent, in May of 1972, that Hydro was not about to wait for the results of the federal-provincial impact study. They selected their own advisory group under the leadership of Dr. P. D. McTaggart-Cowan to examine what land-clearing should take place on Southern Indian Lake and what resource loss might occur. The committee spent a few days around the area, talked with a few interested parties at Hydro and people from government, and four weeks later came up with a report that went against Hydro, claiming that a rush job was required of them and no firm decisions should be made until the federal-provincial study was completed.

By December 1972, nothing could stop the government. Earlier on in November, a group called the Friends of the Churchill was formed to attempt to publicize the issue, but by an Order-in-Council, the cabinet eliminated the need to advertise Hydro's application for a licence to proceed. The government then changed the Water Power Act so that Green could issue the licence for the diversion by Order-In-Council (effectively sidestepping legislative review and cancelling the requirement that notices of the licence must be published), and on December 22, 1972, Manitoba Hydro got the best Christmas present ever, an Interim Licence to go ahead and raise the level of Southern Indian Lake to the maximum 10 feet.

Public opposition to the diversion was now in its death throes. The Manitoba Environmental Council, which Sid Green had created and which was warned that he did not want any advice from them, held an all day meeting January 19, 1973. After hearing statements and receiving a number of written briefs, the council voted 26–1 in favor of a resolution which urged postponement of the project, so that alternative means of meeting Manitoba's hydro electric needs could be studied. But nobody would listen. In the spring of 1973, Bob Newbury, then a member of the federal-provincial study group, was fired by Green who said that Newbury would likely present "biased" information.

And so, despite valiant efforts of a few concerned citizens, the great diversion scheme had become a *fait accompli*. In the elections of 1973, the diversion was a dead issue. Construction began in earnest in the summer of 1973, and by 1974 considerable damage to the environment was already visible. (The diversion is expected to be finished by the end of 1976.)

Up until this time most of the publicity was centered around South Indian Lake (some say this was a ploy on the part of the government to distract opponents of the diversion away from the thousands of acres of federal treaty land that were likely to be affected). In February of 1974, a DIAND Regional Office Representative complained in an internal report:

> The Regional Office (Winnipeg) has not been involved by the province or Hydro in any of the local consultations. Also the Regional Office would have been reluctant to be involved in explaining a provincial project on which there was often a lack of even rudimentary information.

The lack of provincial consultation with Native people is evident.

> If the department is to discharge its responsibility to the Indian people in this area, it is essential that they be provided with accurate information as well as the resources to substantiate any legitimate claims they may have for loss of livelihood or dislocation.[8]

Now that the massive project was rushing to its conclusion, and decisions were made and carried out without any in-put by the Native people, Manitoba Hydro and the provincial government began to make overtures to the eight widely scattered communities living adjacent to the Nelson River system. They were saying in effect, "We think this project is for the greater good of Manitoba people; so we will have to go ahead and flood your lands. Since we plan to ruin those lands and mess up your lives, we would like to know what you want in the way of compensation." But this time the flood gates would be opened on federal treaty land, land the province clearly had no jurisdiction to encroach upon, flood, or destroy.[9]

In 1875 a treaty was executed by the ancestors of the band members of the communities of Nelson House, Split Lake, York Landing, Norway House, and Cross Lake, giving up their aboriginal rights to a huge tract of land in Northern Manitoba. They did not give up, however, the rights that include water, fishing, trapping, and hunting in any occupied lands in the province. In return for signing Treaty 5 they were given reserve lands which are guaranteed against exploitation under the BNA Act and the Indian Act.[10] The scene was now shifting toward the federal arena.

In April, 1974 a meeting was held at Nelson House with representatives from these other communities, Manitoba Hydro officials, and provincial government representatives. The reason for the meeting was to discuss "compensation." Hydro would determine the damage caused by the diversion; they would pay out some dollars and everything would be settled. But the people instinctively recognized the pay-off game, and they knew, if they allowed themselves to become divided, that the government and Hydro would move in and attempt to settle with individuals. Moving quickly, each band represented at the meeting prepared a Band Council Resolution in which the new-born Northern Flood Committee (NFC) was appointed to be their agents in any and all matters having to do with the diversion plans.

At the same time Manitoba Hydro offered to build a mitigation structure at Nelson House[11] to offset some of the effects of the flooding. The Band Council of Nelson House politely suggested Hydro surveyors leave the reserve and told Hydro to come back when it was ready to fully disclose all the available information pertaining to the flooding plans. Hydro was so incensed with this "childish" treatment that it refused to send representatives to a meeting previously scheduled between Hydro and the Northern Flood Committee in Thompson.

In May, 1974, a very angry Jean Chrétien, then the legal guardian of all Native rights, got involved on behalf of Ottawa. In a strongly worded letter to Schreyer, he attributed the apprehension of the Native people to the lack of information from the province and stated categorically that the federal government would not give Manitoba the Indians' land without agreement from the bands. In another letter he blasted Leonard Bateman, who was the new chairman of Manitoba Hydro, for not having sent a representative to the Thompson meeting. What he really did was place the buck squarely in Schreyer's lap.

In June 1974, the Northern Flood Committee was formally constituted with chiefs representing the various communities on its Board. Henry Spence of Thompson was named chairman and offices were set up in Winnipeg and Thompson. The committee was funded by DIAND, with a non-interest bearing loan to be repaid out of any settlement received and to cover the cost of communication, negotiations, expert advisors, and legal counsel. Its first strategy would be directed towards the whole question of the legality of Manitoba (through Hydro) encroaching upon—by flooding—Indian reserve land.

Up until the time of the formation of the Northern Flood Committee, the provincial government had continued to sit on most of the information compiled by the federal-provincial Study Board, although it was known that many of the studies were already completed. The NFC immediately set about trying to obtain the all-important information. It wasn't easy. Three months of pleasant correspondence passed between provincial government officials and the NFC. Often the committee was sent on wild-goose chases to other departments, or given phony reassurances that the Study Board reports, construction schedules, and technical information were being prepared and would be forthcoming shortly. Finally the matter was settled in a trade. The Nelson House band rescinded the ban placed on Hydro officials visiting their reserve in return for the Study Board reports. "But not all of them," Ken Young, the volatile young Indian lawyer for the committee said. "Our engineering consultants were unable to complete an affidavit based on the reports. There always seemed to be information missing."

On July 5, 1974, Premier Schreyer received a letter from the NFC that must have made his day. The committee informed him that they intended to file an injunction in the courts to force him to stop the diversion plans, on the basis that it was illegal to flood Indian lands protected by a federal treaty, and asked that Hydro stop all its work at once, until a court decision had been handed down. This strategy was later changed by the NFC—they decided to try to obtain a "Declaratory Judgement," stating that by flooding Indian lands Hydro was performing an illegal act. They were attempting to strengthen their bargaining position for a settlement, rather than asking for a halt to the project which was now certainly a *fait accompli*.

Three weeks later Schreyer wrote to Prime Minister Trudeau, telling him in no uncertain terms just where the federal government's responsibilities lay in this whole affair.

> I believe that it should be of some concern to the federal government that the province of Manitoba has recently been informed by the solicitor representing a group designated as the Northern Flood Committee, that this group intends to seek an injunction restraining the province of Manitoba from continuing to proceed with its Hydro development program. We are also informed through statements made in the media that funding of the activities of this group, which include political mobilization of northern communities in Manitoba and legal costs relative to such procedures, is undertaken by the federal government.

In view of the federal government's relationship to this process I believe it becomes necessary that there is a meeting just as
soon as possible at the First Ministers level to discuss the implications
of these events. I would see value in the attendance of the Honour-
able Messers. Jean Chrétien and Sidney Green along with whomever
else you may suggest.

After briefly outlining the history of the development Schreyer got
down to business.

The government of Manitoba takes the position that the federal
government in signing the agreement, obligated itself to do all those
things that were necessary in its jurisdiction to facilitate the program being proceeded with. As a corollary the federal government
also undertook not to take any action which would hinder the development.

The Manitoba government recognizes its responsibility to
satisfy any and all claims of a private or community nature which
may arise as a result of the program being proceeded with. In this
connection the Manitoba government has already indicated its will-
ingness to compensate persons adversely affected and to permit such
compensation to be established by an independent tribunal.

Schreyer went on to discuss how this tribunal could be set up between both governments and to defend his government against suggestions that it was withholding information. The letter continued,
and Schreyer made two very significant and clear threats.

The Manitoba government is willing and ready to discuss any and
all of the heretofore mentioned principles and is prepared to modify such principles upon reasonable suggestions being received from
the federal government in connection with the same. The only
qualification is that the Manitoba government will not negotiate as
to whether it has the right to proceed with the Churchill River
Diversion. We consider that right to have been established eight
years ago and we consider that the two governments who were signa-
tors of the agreements have all legislative and executive powers necessary to complete the program.

Although it has not been specifically stated, it would appear
that certain of Mr. Chrétien's statements imply that an Indian band
in northern Manitoba has a veto power over this program if reserve
lands are affected. It is also the case that the federal government is
financing a legal position which implies such veto power.

I believe that it is important that the government of Manitoba point out to the federal government that all the funds thus far
expended and the potential loss in benefits which would result from
such veto power are directly in conflict with the federal government's
obligations under the 1966 agreement. It will therefore be our
legal position to hold the federal government responsible for any

damages suffered by the people of Manitoba as a result of a federal actions inconsistent with their contractual obligations . . .[12]

In other words, Ed Schreyer, in this not-so-subtle letter, told Pierre Trudeau that if the federal government continued to support Native groups financially on land affected by the diversion, thus giving them a legal position from which they could veto the development project, then Trudeau had better be prepared to be held responsible for the "potential loss in benefits" i.e. dollars and "damage suffered by the people of Manitoba."[13]

We can only speculate as to what Trudeau's reply was (we all know how he hates to be reminded of promises), but Thanksgiving Day 1974 found the new Indian Affairs Minister, Judd Buchanan, his wife, and small son, making a whirlwind tour of Manitoba's Northern communities. In a meeting held at Nelson House, he pledged his support to the Native people, but he avoided meeting with the NFC, saying he thought it was a bit too soon, and besides he had already written them a letter which said in part:

> I will continue to support the Committee in all reasonable efforts to reach a settlement with the province and I believe the time is opportune for the parties to enter into direct negotiations. I am not prepared therefore to support any type of court action until there has been an honest attempt by both parties to reach a settlement through negotiation.[14]

And he turned "thumbs down" to the Committee's proposed court action for "60 to 90" days so everyone could cool off. And yes, the NFC could have additional funding—$168,000 worth—but it would be doled out every few months and subject to review.

On that same trip Buchanan expounded on his interests - of - the - smaller - group - must - be - subordinated - to - the - interests - of - the - larger - group theory, and gave his now-famous example of how in his home town of London, Ontario, residents of the street where he lived gave up 20 feet of frontage to make way for a wider street. But the Native people weren't impressed, and they didn't buy the ridiculous comparison; and they began, along with many other Natives in Canada, to wonder which hat Buchanan really wore. It seemed that Buchanan was keeping his options open. Meanwhile the project construction moved inexorably to its conclusion.

And so the next few months was a time for restructuring and reassessment in the NFC and perhaps some indecision too. But there was unanimous agreement on some important points: the provincial government must recognize the NFC as the sole bargaining agent for the Native people; the Native people had rights and they must speak with one voice; and the time to speak with that voice, and to assert those rights was fast approaching.

In February of 1975, Premier Schreyer, government and Hydro officials met with the Northern Flood Committee to begin negotiations. Schreyer said he would be happy to negotiate with the NFC. He was not sure, however, that he recognized the idea of exclusive bargaining, and he did not want to give up the government's right to deal with private citizens—he was sure that the problem ought not to interfere with the negotiations.

By April it was clear, as indicated in letters between the NFC and the government, that Schreyer had changed his mind and was not prepared to grant the committee a mandate concerning the protection and rights of "Northern citizens." "It is important to realize," government lawyers said, "that sometimes there is great urgency in negotiating interim settlements with concerned citizens."[15]

In May the letters were more strident, "The Advisory Committee to Cabinet is led to the conclusion that the Northern Flood Committee is attempting to usurp the role of government for the Native people of Northern Manitoba. The Northern Flood Committee appears to conceive itself as a sovereign power having jurisdictional rights over a certain segment of the people of Manitoba."[16]

Clearly Schreyer's brand of colonialism is as onerous as can be found anywhere. By insisting on dealing with individuals he was sowing the seeds of division among the Native people. He was denying them the right to bargain collectively against the financial strength and expertise of a government and unaccountable Crown Corporation by deliberately undermining the role of the Northern Flood Committee. And he was narrowing the options of the people by offering them compensation, when they did not even know what the damages would be.

The provincial government was determined to relegate the role of the NFC to that of a watchdog, making comments and suggestions from time to time, while the government—through Hydro—went about its divide-and-conquer game. By the middle of 1974 negotiations had seriously broken down.[17] To reassure the people in the remote communities that the government had their best interests at heart, form letters were sent out to "Residents of Northern Manitoba."

We attach for your information a copy of a letter which our solicitor has received from Mr. D'Arcy McCaffrey, who is the lawyer for the group calling themselves the Northern Flood Committee.

Mr. McCaffrey says that, with regard to the hydro-electric development in northern Manitoba, "Meaningful negotiations cannot, and will not, occur until there is an express recognition by the Government of Manitoba that the Northern Flood Committee is the sole negotiating agent for the constituent communities.

We understand that the Northern Flood Committee purports to represent virtually all communities in northern Manitoba, including Norway House, Ilford, Nelson House, South Indian Lake, Churchill and others.

The Northern Flood Committee's lawyer, in his letter, by implication indicates that it is his contention that the Manitoba Government has no right to proceed with the hydro-electric program in the Province of Manitoba unless it first obtains the approval of the Northern Flood Committee and unless and until the province negotiates the political, economic and social rights of the citizens in northern Manitoba.

No doubt the position put by Mr. McCaffrey will be of some concern to you, since you live in a democratic country and your representation is established by virtue of the democratic process through your elected representative in government. You no doubt have been of the opinion that you are entitled to settle your own damage claims, without preclearance from the Northern Flood Committee. You also have the option of appointing the Flood Committee to represent you and this right is recognized.

Lest there be any misunderstanding of the provincial position in this connection, we wish to advise you as follows:

1. The Government of Manitoba believes that it is and has been proceeding legally in connection with the Nelson River development, pursuant to an agreement entered into between the provincial and federal governments in 1966, and that work on this project has been in progress since that date.
2. The Government of Manitoba has no intention whatsoever of abdicating its responsibility for social and economic programs respecting northern Manitoba to the Northern Flood Committee, or anyone else.
3. The Government of Manitoba has no intention of proceeding illegally with the construction of the Nelson River power development and rejects any contention that it is doing so.
4. Manitoba Hydro will not proceed with any portion of the program held by the Courts to be illegal and will not bargain for the right to so proceed.
5. Manitoba Hydro will proceed with northern power development in such a way as to not violate any legal rights. With the concurrence of the Government of Manitoba, Manitoba Hydro has already undertaken to compensate persons who can establish material damage by virtue of power development in the north.

6. As had already been indicated, in the case of any dispute as to whether a person has or has not suffered damage, the province is willing to submit such dispute to third party arbitration, with the arbitrators being named by persons independent of the Government of Manitoba.

This letter is being sent to you in order that you be aware that the Government of Manitoba intends to represent the interest of the people of northern Manitoba and has no intention of transferring this responsibility to the Northern Flood Committee.[18]

The platitudes about "your elected representative" must have amused as much as angered the Natives, whose only representative is a white member of the NDP.

Nelson House is one of those communities that the Manitoba government "intends to represent in the interests of," and to get there from Winnipeg you catch the 8 A.M. Trans Air flight up to Thompson, population 22,000 and site of a huge mine and smelter —the International Nickel Company. If you can't hitch a ride, you have to rent a car—they won't insure the undercarriage, and as you grind over the 40 odd miles of gravel road to Nelson House you know why. Nelson House is situated on Footprint Lake, designated to rise about 17 feet after the diversion (perhaps even 30 feet when the ice-jams start in winter), and up to 4,000 acres of treaty land may be covered in water.

The day we arrived was one of those unpredictably beautiful days you often get in the North. One minute the sun shines brightly, the next great splatterings of raindrops send you running for shelter. We talked to many of the 1,250 Cree who live in the community, the old and not-so-old, those who had opted for the wage earning way of life and those who stayed with the more traditional hunting, trapping, and fishing. And everyone, without exception, expressed the fear, uncertainty, and sense of betrayal they felt because of the impending flooding, and because they had never received any open and honest information.

"When Hydro first came in 1973 and offered compensation, we did not know we would be flooded, so how could we discuss compensation?" the shy, kind, Chief of Nelson House, Peter Spence, told us. "I would like a community settlement but others want to settle individually. One man got over $1,000 for his trapping cabin, and then Hydro came and knocked it over with a bulldozer."

"I am going to move and take my grandchildren with me," one woman said. "I don't want a wall of water coming down on me."

Others told us the animals were retreating already, and people are worrying about their livelihood and about going on welfare.

The first hard news received from the government by Nelson House and other communities came in the form of "Lime Green Brochures," (named after the hideous color of their covers) giving the Native people the bad news and the good news about the diversion plans. (The bad news—your houses and docks will be flooded, the animals will disappear and the fish will die. The good news— you'll get color T.V.) Along with this came another fancy form letter straight from the Premier's office, outlining the compensating technological "benefits" of the diversion scheme, in exchange for which the Natives would have to surrender their homes, their means of livelihood, their culture, and their human dignity.

> The attached brochure was prepared by the Government of Manitoba and is being sent to your community as a summary of what might occur when the regulation and diversion plans are in operation. I wish to emphasize that the study group has generally proceeded on the basis of making its predictions in such a way as to prepare for every conceivable change. Actual changes are not entirely predictable and will have to await the operation of the program itself. However, it would generally be fair to say that the conditions which will actually occur will be at least as favourable, or more favourable than those predicted because the predictions are based on the worst possible consequences being foreseen in order to prepare for, or guard against, them.
>
> There is no doubt that the hydro development will have some negative effects on your community, as outlined in the information bulletin, but it is also true that Manitoba Hydro's activities have created a number of benefits. For example, because of Manitoba Hydro's microwave system between Winnipeg and Northern Manitoba, your community can now receive, or will soon be able to receive, direct colour TV broadcasts of improved quality, and has or soon will have direct dial telephone service. Similarly the power projects in Northern Manitoba have made it possible for your community to be connected to the provincial electrical grid, so that there is now no limit to the power available to residents of your community. This means that residents can now use many electrical appliances, such as stoves, refrigerators and TV's, which were not possible when the community was dependent upon limited diesel generated power.[19]

But it is the "Notice for claim for compensation" on the back page of the brochures that confuses many Native people.

> What was your loss?
> When did you suffer loss?

Where did you suffer loss?
Why do you think Manitoba Hydro caused your loss?

"How can I ever explain it to them?" one old man said sadly. "I can tell them where and when I lost my trapline. But how can I explain the loss, when the land is damaged and the fish and animals are gone. And what can I tell my grandchildren?"

Ironically, that day we visited, most people were preoccupied with the drop in the lake level that was only one foot above the all-time low caused by diversion structures. Water normally is taken from the lake in buckets, and now they have to go several hundred feet from shore to get good drinking water.

"The water is so bad not even a dog would drink it," Nelson Linklater, former chief told us. "One man almost died from hepatitis, and many of our people have diarrhea," he said.

There were other stories of children with open running sores on their mouths. Brenda Badger, nurse-in-charge at the federal government nursing station, claimed the bacteria count of the lake had not changed much, and if there were outbreaks of illness people were not coming to the nurses for treatment. There were other bizarre stories, some true, some born out of the fear of not knowing. The fact remains that, due to construction, lake levels rise and fall, making the water foul and the fish taste terrible.

Dick Swaren, the young, soft-spoken United Church minister at Nelson House, talked about the people who are under his pastoral care. "When we first came here in 1972, we found a friendly, happy-go-lucky community that had been here for a hundred years. We thought we had found paradise. Then the road [Hydro] opened up and booze came in, and you could feel the whole community tighten up. Church attendance dropped. There is family breakdown, and the whole social structure of the community has badly deteriorated."

Later, as we sat in his small boat chugging across Footprint Lake, Swaren reflected on the community's dilemma. By the marks on the rocks, we could see the lake was down about six feet. It is one of the most beautiful lakes we have seen anywhere. Now and then whole familes drifted by in canoes and waved silently. Some others had built a little fire near rows and rows of small white crosses, the graves of their ancestors.

"The people have been betrayed," Swaren said. If they [Hydro] had sat down at the beginning and said 'let us bargain now,' it would have been a whole new story. There is an old Indian legend," he went on softly, "that Wesakachak walked here—the First Indian, man yet spirit, messenger, teacher. You can see his footprints on a sheer rock face down the shore a little way. And if you look carefully you can see a large indentation in the rocks that the Indians say is Wesakachak's chair. Maybe all we can do now is pray that Wesakachak will watch over his children."

Notes

The information in this chapter has been obtained from many sources— from the research departments of the Northern Flood Committee and the Manitoba Indian Brotherhood, from confidential government documents and letters, interviews with many people, both white and Native, and DIAND officials.

1 Agreement between the Government of Canada and the Government of Manitoba in which both parties agreed "to early development of some of the power resources of that river [Nelson] for use in the Province of Manitoba and if feasible for exports to markets outside the province." The agreement was signed in Winnipeg, February 15, 1966.

2 Ibid.

3 R. W. Newbury, "The Churchill River Diversion Controversy", an illustrated examination of the rationale, plan and environmental implications (St. Adolphe, Manitoba, December, 1972).

4 According to the *Summary Report*, Lake Winnipeg, Churchill and Nelson Rivers Study Board, Canada-Manitoba, April, 1975:

The most significant effect of the Churchill River Diversion project on the South Indian Lake community has been the creation of new jobs. As at Cross Lake and Nelson House, few residents have acquired skills along with their new prosperity and their higher hopes will go unfulfilled when projects in the area are completed. The attraction of better paying jobs has added to problems in the local fishing industry. South Indian Co-op Fisheries Ltd. was forced to pay higher wages to compete with wages on construction projects, but despite the higher wages the co-op continued to lose members and employees. The result was the decline in fish catch.

5 The control structure and channel works at the north end of Lake Winnipeg will be able to hold, or release, the waters of the lake into the Nelson River. This is intended to keep the level of the lake more constant and increase the power capacity of the Nelson plants. The control structure designed to regulate the flow is the Notigi dam.

6 Statement by the Honorable Sidney Green, Minister of Mines, Resources and Environmental Management, Winnipeg, Manitoba, in response to a special issue of *Bulletin*, Vol. 15 No. 3 (Ottawa: Canadian Association in Support of Native Peoples), Dec. 1975.

7 The Summary Report, Lake Winnipeg, Churchill and Nelson River Study Board Canada, Manitoba/April, 1975, is seen by the Northern Flood Committee as both "good" and "bad".

"It is a mixed bag of forthright disclosures and vague assertions.

All in all the report reveals an incredible tangle of loose ends and uncertainties.

"Nevertheless on the positive side, the Summary Report can be seen as a considerable improvement in disclosure, over the Impact Statements circulated last January by the Premier's office. By this comparison, the report represents a substantial, and in many respects satisfactory acknowledgement of changes in the magnitude and timing of future water levels and flows. (Except for Nelson House).

"As well, in many instances, the Summary Report gives a much more honest account of adverse effects and irreparable damages, than did the earlier Impact Statements, which didn't have a forthright declaration among them. And too, the Summary Report clearly establishes what the Provincial government has consistently denied, namely that the project has already affected the rights, lands, lifestyle and economic pursuits of the native people of the north."

Press Release, Northern Flood Committee, Winnipeg, Manitoba, June 6, 1975.

8 DIAND discussion paper, "Churchill-Nelson Development Impact", Manitoba Regional Office, Winnipeg, Manitoba, February 5, 1974.

Confidential reports done for, and by, the DIAND recommended again and again the need to keep the people of the communities informed and the need for time to digest the information. They stress the need for Native people to be advised of their rights. The author of some of these reports continually reminded the DIAND of their responsibility to the Native People and the treaty land they hold in trust.

9 Concern has been voiced by the Manitoba Indian Brotherhood that as many as 14 other reserves adjacent to Lake Winnipeg may be affected by the flooding.

10 The Manitoba Indian Brotherhood, under the presidency of Dr. Ahab Spence of Winnipeg, Manitoba, has been involved in a five-year program of research into land claims, aboriginal rights, and hunting and trapping rights. The program is funded by DIAND and includes research into Treaties 1, 2 and 5 whose conditions may never have been fulfilled.

11 Manitoba Hydro had proposed a dam to be constructed between Footprint Lake and Three Point Lake to offset the flooding at Nelson House. Without the dam, water levels could rise to approximately 30 feet above historical levels. Hydro officials agreed in principle that the dam should be built but later backed off saying the structure would be too expensive.

12 Letter to Prime Minister Pierre Trudeau, Ottawa, from Premier Ed Schreyer, Winnipeg, July 31, 1974.

13 Ibid.

14 *The Manitoban*, special supplement on the Churchill River Diversion, Winnipeg, Manitoba, November, 1974.

15 Letter to the Northern Flood Committee, Winnipeg, Manitoba, from lawyers acting for the Manitoba Government, April 14, 1975.

16 Letter to the Northern Flood Committee, Winnipeg, Manitoba, from lawyers acting for the Manitoba Government, May 12, 1975.

17 At a meeting in Ottawa, June 2, 1975, the Honorable Judd Buchanan, minister of Indian Affairs and Northern Development, told the Northern Flood Committee that he would obtain a legal opinion from the Department of Justice to establish whether or not there was cause for court action against Manitoba Hydro and the provincial government for the encroachment by flooding of treaty land. Later that summer, Buchanan gave the Manitoba Government until August 6, 1975, to provide information regarding the impact the diversion would have on Indian treaty land, or legal action would be instituted against the province by the federal government.

18 Letter addressed to "Residents of Northern Manitoba" from the premier of Manitoba and signed "Edward Schreyer", May 13, 1975.

19 Lime Green brochures put out by the Manitoba government; (so-named because of the color of the covers) were sent to the various communities affected by the diversion project, January, 1975.

The Indians of British Columbia, as the original inhabitants of the country, claim they have certain rights to the land, and before the government can sell or dispose of the land, these claims should be considered.

The Government of the Province, on the other hand, takes the position that the Indians have no rights, and though they have never given any reason for their position, they positively refuse to modify it.

From the common sense point-of-view, it would seem to appeal to all unprejudiced and disinterested people that men who have inhabited a country from time immemorial and have made their living there must have certain rights which no newcomer should altogether overlook and override.

The Reverend Canon Tucker
of Vancouver in a
statement to the
Canadian Minister of Indian Affairs
November, 1912

7

Northwest British Columbia

*Where Violence may be the Only Way
to Make Things Change*

During the long hot summer of 1973, a newspaper reporter asked George Manuel, president of the National Indian Brotherhood, if he thought violence could break out in Canada. Will there be a Wounded Knee here? Is Kenora about to be repeated? Manuel thought for a minute and replied that if Canadians were prepared to negotiate with the Native people in good faith, it was unlikely.

"But if not, the young Indians will certainly take matters into their own hands."

Nowhere in Canada is this violence more likely to occur than in "Beautiful British Columbia," where a socialist, populist government still perpetuates the policies of 50 years ago, declaring as in 1912, that Natives have no rights and are not really citizens of the province but a federal responsibility. And Premier Dave Barrett who, prior to his election three years ago, was trumpeting support for Natives, has now indicated his unwillingness to sit down with the various Indian groups in British Columbia and the federal government to negotiate the rights that have been denied to them since 1871 when the province joined Canada.

Treaties extinguished title to land across most of Canada as the various provinces joined Confederation, and while the signing of these treaties constituted little more than "legalized theft," they were official Canadian policy. Enter British Columbia in 1871, and despite clause 13 of the Terms of Union, there has been a stubborn refusal to even discuss Indian lands with Ottawa ever since. After 100 years of arguing over the mechanics of transferring provincial Crown lands to the federal government for the purpose of establishing reserves, the province is more worried about who's going to pay than the rights of its 100,000 Natives.

At one point the federal government came close to taking the province to court, and only a change in administrations aborted that plan. During the period 1871 to 1924 the Indians were tossed from one level of government to the other as reserve commissions were established and disbanded, reserves were surveyed but never transferred, Indian agencies were refused, indigenous culture was suppressed by the infamous Potlatch Law (1885 to 1951),[1] and established reserves were sold for urban expansion or industrial development. But through all this, the question of Indian aboriginal title was never resolved; so treaties were never signed, and hence, what reserves were set aside had no protection.

After 1924 and the ratification by both governments of the McKenna-McBride commission, the "Indian question" in British Columbia was said to have been settled, at least to the satisfaction of the various levels of government. What that commission did was to confirm the existence of reserves laid out in the period 1876 to 1908, refuse to deal with Northwestern coast Indians who wanted title settled, cut off 47,000 acres from old reserves, and add 87,000 acres of new land.

And this to date is the situation—signed, sealed, and delivered —but no one ever asked the Indians how they felt. Only in 1973 when the Nishga Nation of Northwest British Columbia won its moral victory (described in Chapter 1), did the governments realize that the "Indian problem" still hadn't been resolved and wouldn't go away, because "those pesky Natives" didn't know their place.

For a change, Ottawa was prepared to start settlement proceedings in 1973 but, quite rightly, insisted the province be part of the negotiations, since by the Terms of Union (1871), they controlled all the land and the natural resources. But Barrett refused to deal, and there exists today the same impasse that frustrated the Natives in 1912. Some things never seem to change in the lotus land of the Pacific.

There are two issues in British Columbia. One is the whole question of aboriginal title. The Union of B.C. Chiefs has claimed almost all the province for their own, asking that this be the basis for a final settlement of land claims. The second is the question of cutoff lands. Under the Indian Act, no land can be taken from existing reserves without the consent of the Crown and the consent of the Indians—in other words, expropriation does not exist, legally, at any rate. This was ignored by the McKenna-McBride commission which took 47,000 acres of land away from 23 bands in 1919-1920. This issue has never died and has been the focus of much of the squabbling, blockading, and open violence of the last couple of years. While it is important to the bands, it is not the central issue —that of settling aboriginal rights. This issue then, the claim that "B.C. is Indian Land"—a slogan which, incidentally, is calculated to send the white denizens of that province into an uncontrollable rage—focuses on a legal and political settlement of land claims. Nowhere is this focus more obvious than in Northwest British Columbia.

The $500 million industrial development scheme there is in jeopardy until the Nishga (in the Nass Valley), Haida (Queen Charlotte Islands), and other land claims are resolved. It was the Nishga court case in 1973 that redefined the whole question of aboriginal rights for the federal government. Furthermore, a major alliance—and an unusual one—between organized labor and the several Native groups has pledged itself to halt, by any means, the Northwest project until land claims are settled. Given the buck-passing of Ottawa, the intransigence of Victoria, and the determination of the Natives with their new-found allies in the labor movement, a major confrontation is predictable.

The Nishga fight for a land claim settlement is, perhaps, the most unusual in Canada. Certainly it is the most individualistic and has been going on the longest. As far back as 1883, the Nishga expelled from their homeland, the Nass Valley, provincial government surveyors who had been sent to give the people small parcels of reserve lands. This action by the government was incomprehensible to the Nishga. "How" they asked, "can you possibly give us land that is already ours, has always been ours, and always will be ours?" They told the surveyors, as they escorted them from the valley at gunpoint, politely but firmly, that Nishga land extends "from mountaintop to mountaintop and from the source to the mouth of the Nass River."

That little vignette is recorded in Nishga history—none of which is written but passed on from generation to generation in Indian fashion—and it illustrated to the proud and self-sufficient people of the Nass the unbridled arrogance of the British Columbia government, an arrogance that neither time nor history has done anything to temper. From that time in 1883, the Nishgas, through their leaders in the tribal council, have fought, often alone, for their land and for a just settlement of their claims.

According to anthropologists, the Nishga have occupied their land for about 10,000 years, as have other Northwest British Columbia coastal tribes. They have fared well with their fishing and hunting. Their culture is complex and sophisticated, exemplified even today after years of suppression, in superb art work in wood, cloth, and metal, a strong sense of cultural identity and community cohesiveness, and a genuine religious expression which melds their traditional religion with deep expressions of Anglican Christianity. While they live in four distinct villages strung along the Nass Valley, the nearly 3,000 Nishgas have one of the most organized and socially integrated Indian nations in Canada.

The Nass Valley (a simple description of their geographical land claim) extends from the Pacific coast east to Meziadan Lake, including the Nass River Valley where their communities are located, and takes in about 4,400 square miles. It includes Kincolith on the coast with 750 people; Greenville, 750; Canyon City, 130; and New Aiyansh, 865. They are small in number to take on the might of Ottawa and Victoria. Their land has valuable timber rights and mineral deposits and is the home of many successful commercial fishermen, with the Nass being the spawning grounds for British Columbia salmon.

Always self-sufficient and independent, the Nishga have a traditional tribal system of clans, known as houses or families, with a matrilineal way of passing on family names. Their chiefs have always been elected, and together with councillors chosen from the four villages, comprise the Nishga Tribal Council. The four bands act in close concert with each other and make, with one voice, all decisions which would affect the lives of the whole nation.

These people are industrious and skilled. Their intense ability to conduct business and to negotiate has proven invaluable in pressing their land claims, although their fierce independence of thought and action has often put them at odds with the rest of the Native people in the province. Fishing and the Nass River are the focal point of their life style and livelihood. They not only fish commercially but harvest annually in the spring, the tiny oil-rich oolichan, partly for its rich yellow grease but also for the social value they attach to this traditional activity which is linked to freedom from want and hunger.

The three key components of Nishga life are their river, their church, and their language. Their clergy, although often white and

Eastern in origin, are truly adopted into the tribe and take on a Nishga presence. They thus become part of the land claims' team. The river, with its fish, transport and communications, is their life line. Recently they took over their own school system, in a determined bid to increase the value of their culture and to ensure that it should not be watered down, now that contact with the outside world is permanent.

From the time 100 years ago when the white man became a fixture around Nishga land, the ancestral leaders began a struggle, using their own funds and taking their own directions, to maintain their hold on the land which had been theirs from time immemorial. Bill McKay of Greenville, one of their vice-presidents, told us that the Nishga had spent more than $600,000 of their own money since the battle began. Where other Indian organizations did nothing or used federal funds, the Nishga fought their weary and lonely battle.

In 1887 their leaders went to Victoria, surely a terrifying trip in itself, and told the frock-coated, stern legislators of the day (referred to by one deputy commissioner for Indian Affairs as the "superior race") that they had always exercised the privileges of free men in the tribal territory.

> We hunted in its woods, fished in its waters, streams and rivers. Roamed, hunted and pitched our tents in the valleys, shores and hillsides. Buried our dead in their homeland territory. From time immemorial, the Nass River Nishga Indians possessed, occupied and used the Nass River Valley and we have never ceded or extinguished our aboriginal title.[2]

In 1909 the Nishga took another unheard-of step and actually paid a Vancouver lawyer $500 for a legal opinion of aboriginal title. It was enough to convince them that British justice would prevail if only they could get their grievances to the monarch of the day, King George V, and his Privy Council. So on January 22, 1913, at a meeting in Kincolith, the Nishga decided to go to London for their day in court, and it is recorded in the files of the British Privy Council of that day. After outlining the extent of their land, their grievances against the British Columbia Government and their belief in the monarch's supreme wisdom and authority, the Nishga, through Messers Fox & Preece of 15, the Dean's Yard, Westminster S.W., London, England, "humbly prayed" that "your majesty in council may be pleased:"

> To adjudge and determine the nature and extent of the rights of the said Nishga nation or tribe in respect of their said territory.

To adjudge and determine whether, as your petitioners humbly submit, the Land Act of British Columbia now in force and any previous Land Act of that Province, in so far as the same purport to deal with lands thereby assumed to be the absolute property of the said province and to confer title in such lands free from the right, title and interest of the Indian tribes, notwithstanding the fact that such right, title or interest has not been in any way extinguished, are ultra vires of the Legislature of the said province.[3]

The Nishga were asking for their land claims to be settled, as they are now; and in 1913, as now, the Crown decided it would do nothing.

One of the magnificent characteristics of the Nishga is their tenacity and undiminished faith in the legal system to bring about justice. After one defeat after another, after one evasive, dishonest action after another, they kept coming back. Other tribes drifted into apathy or assimilation, some tried violence, but the Nishga kept raising money from white friends and through their commerce in the fishing industry, and appeared before commissions and hearings at all levels of government.

In 1969, they took the province to court and lost. They went on, convinced their cause was a "righteous and holy struggle,"[4] to the British Columbia Court of Appeal, and in 1970, lost again. From 1971, though to the historic split decision of the Supreme Court of Canada in 1973, which forced the Canadian Government to change its stance on aboriginal rights, they fought on, even when the Union of B.C. Chiefs, the umbrella native organization in British Columbia, urged them not to and refused them any support.

This was a most historic moment for the people of the Nass. The delegates who attended [the Supreme Court of Canada hearings] were overwhelmed by the memory of the great men of the past who had struggled and died before seeing even this much recognition.[5]

The struggle continues, for now a political settlement must be reached and land claims settled in the face of industrial development which is more threatening to the Nishga than anything thus far in their history. The Nishga's traditional land lies directly in the path of the proposed Canadian National Railways route from Terrace, north to Dease Lake to join with British Columbia Rail. The railway line is crucial to the Northwest British Columbia development scheme. The surveying of the right-of-way has been completely stopped at mile 35 where the line would enter Nishga land. It has halted for more than a year. It will stay halted until Nishga land claims are settled, or until governments move, as they usually do, with total disregard for the legal rights of the Original People of this nation. But the Nishga now have powerful allies, and what the future holds can be characterized in one word—CONFRONTATION.

The essential message of the Nishga story to date is that the white governments of Pierre Trudeau and David Barrett must come to terms with history. The Indian view, we contend, has consistently been a more historical one than the European view. The overwhelming success of Europeans in colonizing this country—to the point that it was long expected the Indians would all die out—has obscured the issues for non-Indians. How could anyone argue with colonial success? Well, people are arguing. The Nishga argued and won; and others, concerned with the future of our life style in this nation and the future of our children in this nation, are arguing on their side and questioning whether the values of such people as the Nishga are not perhaps more valid than those of the colonists.

The Church is very much a part of Nishga life, and one Sunday we went to a couple of Church services at Greenville, deep in the Nass Valley, at the end of the logging road that connects Terrace, 90 miles away,with Nishga country.

One of the services was called Church Army. It was in St. Andrew's, a traditionally Anglican building dedicated to the patron saint of Scotland. But when we walked in, the pews were pushed around in a square and the men sat on one side and the women and children opposite them. The priest, the Rev. David Retter from Toronto, was there, but he did not preach.

The drums boomed rhythmically all through the service; the sing-song voices were raised in praise; there were testimonials to Jesus' love; and one sister who was ill and going off to hospital collapsed with emotion and was supported by other women from the village. It stirred the blood like old-time evangelism. The hymn tunes, pulsating to the beat of tambourines, took over the senses. It was indefinable, emotional, very religious. For a long time it went on, washing over our jaded urban feelings, and gradually, as Indian things do, it became more definable.

It was a real and unique blend of traditional Christianity and ancient Indian religion, and it was exactly right. Outside it was damp and the mountaintops were shrouded in mist. On lines stretched between the frame houses, the oolichan were drying—the smelt-like fish of life that have saved the Nishga people from starvation so many times. The service is a survival of the potlatch and other significant ceremonials of the Nishga, which had been so long suppressed by law. You couldn't find this weekly event in the pages of *Beautiful British Columbia*, and there were no tourists. Across the chancel a beautiful, shy-eyed, black haired girl sang softly to herself. Soon she'll be older and involved, perhaps, in the violence and agony that must surely come to Northwestern British Columbia, if the two governments continue to play their game of "it's-your-Indian-problem."

To get there, we dodged logging trucks over the pitted gravel roads, inching our way around deep lakes and speeding across 10 miles of lava plain between the 5,000-foot mountains. The logging truck, lurching and jolting over the uneven ground, seemed to epitomize the struggle going on in this rugged wilderness of the Northwest. Along both sides of the Nass Valley, the bases of the mountains bear the scars of clear-cut logging. The corporations get millions from cutting the huge fir trees along the Nass; the Indians who claim the land get nothing but some piece work in the bush.

Earlier in the day we had listened to Retter preach a gentle sermon to his brothers and sisters in Greenville, for although born and educated in Toronto, he has been adopted by the Nishga, and he takes it seriously. The land claim is never far from Nishga hearts and minds, and when he speaks, he speaks for them.

"The land is ours. There's no question of it, but many people are in ignorance of our claim. In Terrace there's a lot of tension that could easily cause white people to take wrong actions and take out their frustrations about unemployment and inflation on us Indian people."

"Ignorance of our land claim causes some of them to think that they will lose jobs if a settlement is signed. We must guard against losing our tempers, and we must pass on to the young men of our villages the message that they must walk calmly, so that they will not discredit our leaders who are working for a settlement."

"Right now is a critical time for our Nishga Tribal Council. We must not give the government or the RCMP any reason to point accusing fingers at us. We must walk with dignity, like Nishga have always walked."

Afterwards, we walked through the village with its Chief Councillor, Bill McKay, and he told Retter, "You're right on, Father." But he shook his head and wondered out loud how long they could keep the lid on.

The flames of discord are being fanned in Northwest British

Columbia by an enormous $500 million secretly planned agreement between the federal and provincial governments, announced in 1973 and 1974, that would create more than 20,000 new jobs for the economically unstable North—railways, highways, instant towns, mines, hydro schemes, super sawmills, increased logging, and even a steel mill poured out of the febrile imaginations of the federal and provincial civil service. The secrecy was beyond belief. The agreements were never officially made public, although they were leaked all over the place. There were no impact studies on the environment, the social structure, the economic benefits, or how the residents of the Northwest quarter felt about this massive influx of capital.

The local chambers of commerce were quick to praise the federal Department of Regional and Economic Expansion (DREE) and the various provincial departments for such a "farsighted" approach to financial needs in the North. But most other Northerners looked askance at the boom mentality that the "planners" in Ottawa and Victoria were exhibiting. Since the major announcements were made with great fanfare, consulting firms across the province have been getting rich preparing the studies that should have been done before the development was initiated. Most of their reports remain locked away in government filing cabinets.

Federal and provincial politicians crisscross the North contradicting each other, telling pro-development people that nothing can halt the scheme, not even Indian land claims. At the same time they reassure those "do-gooder" environmentalists, labor unions, and Native organizations that the agreements signed in 1973 and 1974 were only agreements in principle, and nothing sinister or secret is in the offing. In fact, Alf Nunweiller, the NDP minister of Northern Affairs (although he's really only a minister without portfolio), insists there's not even a development plan, just a lot of studying.

The extent of the project, its objectives and implementation, can only be pieced together from leaked documents and a series of statements, many of which are contradictory and vague, by a variety of federal and provincial officials. The project looks something like this; but when or even if it will ever be developed is another thing. It involves about 100,000 square miles of the Northwest quadrant of British Columbia from a point just south of the Terrace, Kitimat, and Prince Rupert triangle, north along the Alaska panhandle to the 60th parallel, and east about half way across the province to Fort St. John. There are perhaps 75,000 people in the sparsely populated region which is also the home of several thousand Native people.

In July, 1973, Federal Cabinet Ministers Jean Marchand, Jack Davis, and Ron Basford flew to British Columbia to sign, and jointly announce with Provincial Cabinet Ministers Dave Barrett and Bob Williams, a $325 million federal-provincial rail, road, and port development to upgrade the province's economy, then in a weakened state due to declining timber prices and higher costs of production. The price of timber and transportation was a major aspect of the project which, with the later inclusion in 1974 of resource development plans, has now reached something in the neighborhood of $500 million. It was also hoped that, with improved rail, road, and port facilities, private capital would pump in even more money for smelters, pulp and paper mills, and mining, making the whole gigantic industrial complex a multi-billion dollar investment. More than 20,000 new jobs were expected, along with new urban centres in Terrace, Kitimat, and Prince Rupert. A program of half a dozen instant towns, which was originally proposed, seems to have been abandoned, because even to planners in the south they are a social disaster.

The project was originally considered when the American owned Columbia Cellulose pulp mill in Prince Rupert was going to close, due to the increased costs brought on when the new NDP government forced them to start more selective cutting measures to conserve timber. The clear-cut logging, which has almost ruined the area around Prince Rupert, Terrace, and Kitimat, would have stopped. The logging industry itself would have been ruined, leaving only fishing at Prince Rupert and the Aluminum company's gigantic operations at Kitimat. Already under economic pressures, Barrett moved in and created the Crown-owned CanCel to buy out Columbia Cellulose and made a hefty profit the first year but was faced with huge costs the next years, because of the distance needed to transport plup chips. A railroad was needed for the Crown corporation, and with known copper deposits in three different areas (Stikine-Iskut, Northeast Babine, and Whitesale-Ootsa) of more than a billion tons, it was thought that a copper smelter would help utilize the railroad.

There were many other aspects to the grand scheme, all of which were predicated on the stability of the world economy which fell apart shortly after the federal-provincial 50-50 cost-sharing agreement was signed. Since then everything has been slowed down and the secrecy lid clamped on tight. In fact, to mention copper is to receive blank looks from Alf Nunweiller who, at a public meeting in Terrace in April 1975, could only sputter that current world copper prices are so bad that "it will be sometime in the unforeseen future before the Stikine deposits become feasible."

The steel mill, originally to have been heavily backed by Japanese interests and located at Kitimat, has been relegated to the study stage again for possible "alternatives combining the four western provinces." One super sawmill has been completed at Burns Lake, but this is a far cry from the expansion of nearly 200 million board feet of processed timber, creating 4,500 new jobs that were first promoted. These new mills were to provide wood chips to feed the Prince Rupert (CanCel) and Kitimat (Eurocan) pulp plants. Thus, the original purpose behind Northwest development was to get cheap by-product chips from the Nass and Skeena areas and to build up Prince Rupert as a super-port to ship lumber to foreign markets.

The development project then, once announced with such fanfare, has gone underground, which scares the Natives and permanent residents in the North perhaps more than the grandiose plans. Accustomed, as many of them are, to boom-and-bust dreams, they took the instant town and super sawmills with a grain of salt, but the planning behind closed doors and the known road and rail surveying before land claims were settled, leaves all Northerners uneasy.

Seven Northern highways, covering more than 2,100 miles and costing some $325 million are projected as part of the initial plan to open the North, and no one has denied the plan's existence. A report, prepared by the University of British Columbia, predicts "no significant social problems" as a result of improved access to the North but does warn that extensive contact with white society has always had a demoralizing effect on Native peoples.

> Indian social systems depend on their isolation from rapid and massive contacts with the white society. While the industrial society may look upon highways as an opportunity to develop land and resources, the Native peoples do not necessarily regard them in this fashion.[6]

The study warns the government to go slow on the Northern highway program because of a shortage of labor in the North and the disruption to existing society. It suggests 10 to 15 years for upgrading. Unfortunately, the study also predicts little economic advantage to the Indians, because white southern construction workers with more skills than the Natives would be brought in. The railroad plans are almost as staggering. A 410-mile British Columbia

Rail extension from Fort St. James to Dease Lake was completed this year. Two other government-owned British Columbia Rail projects of 120 miles and 74 miles are on the drawing board. The heart of the entire Northwest development is the CNR line, 245 miles from Terrace through the Nishga land to Dease Lake, which will provide the cheap transportation needed for logs and the optimistic copper development.

A number of hydro projects, none of which is in the immediate future, are shown on the maps of the development plan, but with the dependence of many Northerners, Indian and white alike, on fishing, the projected damage to the spawning grounds is predicted by fishery biologists to be as high as 75 percent.

If the project, now called a long-range program and "more of a concept than a concrete plan," goes ahead, community and social development will also be of major concern to the residents. A report, prepared for the CNR by sociologist William Horswill, states that Terrace is already "a chaotic concentration of people,"[7] and if it is to become the new urban centre of the North as the development scheme suggests, its 12,000 people would double or more when the construction of the CNR line starts. Already the town's tax structure, services, and schools are seriously overcrowded. But no concern or knowledge of this problem, which is expected to be repeated in towns like Chetwynd, Fort Nelson, Smithers, Prince Rupert, Prince George, and Fort St. John, was expressed by the promoters of Northwest development in Victoria and Ottawa. Horswill's report, which has never been officially released by the CNR, predicts inadequate housing, poor health, and increasing rates of alcoholism and mental illness in Terrace if it experiences the type of rapid growth that is envisaged by the developers of the Northwest.

In the Northwest quarter of British Columbia exists some of the last remaining wilderness in Canada. The area abounds in fish and wildlife. Wildlife biologists claim the grizzlies are "the best in the world" and the mountain goats are "fantastic." Dave Hatler, Dave Bustard, and Les Cox are based at Smithers, British Columbia, and their description of their jobs with the provincial Fish and Wildlife Branch sounds idyllic, and the project to develop the North frightens them.

With developers "breathing down our necks with bulldozers" the three men need time to develop an inventory before the roads and railways drive the game away and before the influx of hunters makes it impossible to pinpoint vulnerable areas.

"There are sheep, moose, caribou, and bears. We have, in the Northwest, some of the finest spawning grounds for sockeye salmon known to man. For uncharted wilderness, this area is about the best you are going to find anywhere in North America for diversity of habitat and variety of wildlife," Hatler claims.

The railway lines and highways are a particularly sore point, emphasizing again the total lack of integrated planning that took place before July 1973 and the launching of the initial Northwest development scheme. The lines are scheduled to go, or are already under construction, in the case of British Columbia Rail—through some of the best game country in the province—without any concern or knowledge of the effects it will have on the wildlife and on the traditional lifestyles of the Natives who live off the land. Hatler believes the railways could have been better routed and better built. The culverts are in a bad place, the contractors fill the rivers with rubbish, and there are bad slides caused through carelessness.

People who live in the Northwest do so from choice. They are usually conservationists. They like wide open spaces and good hunting and fishing. They don't want hordes of tourists pouring into their land. "Animals always have to go when they occupy the same land as a white man. Right now the moose are big and fat and live to a great old age. They are having calves when they are 10 and 12 years old and are just in beautiful shape," Cox extolled. But for how long?

Les Watmough writes one of the few good columns in the weekly *Terrace Herald*. He's an outdoorsman, folksy, and by any stretch of the imagination no "bleeding-heart liberal," but his reaction to the development of the North exemplifies best how the people feel.

> We hold at our doorstep the last great undeveloped region of North America. As Bobbie Williams (B.C. Resources Minister Robert Williams) said, in the light of world problems and population, it would be immoral not to develop it, but sure as sin is sick it would be fourfold more immoral to develop it without sufficient and proper planning.
>
> There is time to do this right, and make it a place to be proud of but it must not be a series of shots in the arm all strung together on the wires of waste and short term gain.
>
> One politician of my acquaintance claims the project is planned to accommodate only normal growth. Mister, when you announce a multi-million dollar scheme, nothin' ain't normal no more.[8]

With this kind of growth facing the Natives and Northern people of British Columbia, it wasn't long until opposition groups sprang up across the area. The very labor groups which had worked so hard to elect Dave Barrett turned on his development scheme. Indian leaders, long favorable to the NDP, demanded the project be halted until Barrett would sit down with Ottawa to negotiate land claim settlements. Environmentalists, conservationists, church groups, and ordinary towns people expressed growing concern.

As always in the North, it was secrecy and secrecy's hand-maiden, rumor, that caused the most problems. To this day, a plan that may never go beyond the planning stage or, at best, will be delayed for many years arouses opposition. But the fear, tension, and acrimony it has fostered may well prove to be what one labor leader pictured as, "the albatross around Barrett's neck that will bring down the NDP government."

Iona Campagnolo is a pretty, vivacious woman, active in community affairs in Prince Rupert, a broadcaster, and more recently an ambitious federal Liberal. Last year she took on long-time Member of Parliament for Skeena, Frank Howard who had held the seat for many years for the NDP. To almost no one but Howard's surprise she was elected, and during her freshman year in Ottawa, distinguished herself for hard work, political astuteness, and utter dedication to her riding. She was rewarded by becoming Judd Buchanan's parliamentary assistant. She calls the Northwest development scheme "The myth of the great Northwest" and is not at all abashed by the fact that originally it was her federal party and British Columbia's senior cabinet minister, Ron Basford, among others, who signed the first agreement.

On March 8, 1975, she told the Smithers and District Chamber of Commerce—about the only organization outside the association of mayors that still supports the development plan—that she would try to unravel the "so-called Northwest development package" for them. But all she could find in the package were "some verbal lies" which made people in the Northwest afraid of a development scheme that "to my point of view simply doesn't exist." She said it was a "hoax" and a "con game" which had failed miserably to pacify the Northerners who had to endure a 15 percent unemployment rate.

> Are they mythological developments? Let's hope they are, or we'd be living in a nightmare. However, it is clear we also need development in order to broaden our tax base. But I'm sick and tired of federal civil servants rushing about playing Russian roulette with our futures.[9]

Iona, as everyone calls her, has enormous energy, and she flies back to her huge constituency, often with a cabinet minister or two in tow, ready to do battle with the NDP in Victoria and to try and keep some cohesiveness in her own sprawling constituency. In her capacity as an assistant to Judd Buchanan, she is also genuinely concerned about race relations in Skeena and elsewhere in Canada. Her attitude to the Northwest development is to take it all back to the drawing board and start anew, continuing only perhaps with the transportation projects and the super port. With all the authority of parliamentary assistant she spoke to a policy conference of the Liberals in her riding on April 19, 1975 in Terrace.

> Northwest development, as we have heard of it, has a place in the future of our area as long as it is done on a rational basis, with appropriate input from the residents of the area, and with environmental and social safeguards. We need the permanent jobs it will provide and we need the transportation infrastructure, as well as the tax assessment base for our small towns to support new residents in the long run and present residents now.[10]

But in line with the realities of the political system, including the threats of violence in her area, Iona places the blame squarely on the shoulders of the provincial administration of David Barrett. In an interview with one of us after her speech in Terrace, she said that Skeena riding, which covers much of the Northwest, was known for years as a racially tolerant region. "I had hopes for the NDP, but they're as bad as the old Social Credit any day when it comes to dealing with the Natives. There's a real backlash here because people think the land claims are holding everything back. That's not true, of course, but given the fact that Barrett won't even talk to either of us [Indians or federal government], what can we do?"

Answering her own question, she insisted that, when the Nishga land claim was settled, the Northwest development scheme would not go through and allow the CNR to continue planning and building that key line north from Terrace.

"The development scheme cannot begin because of the NDP; they don't know what they want; they won't settle land claims; and now they realize their original scheme was ridiculous, and they want to change that. There's the reason for the fear and tension through this riding. It's not the Indians' fault and its not the whites'; it's the fear generated by a provincial government that doesn't treat the North any differently than did its predecessors."

The man who has to live with charges like this on a daily basis is Alf Nunweiler, a Northerner, an NDP cabinet minister who spent much of the spring of 1975 touring the Northwest trying, on one hand, to allay fears about the project, and on the other, to assure the municipalities and chambers of commerce that it hadn't completely died. He also had to contend with Native groups about their land claims, which was difficult, because to satisfy them he had to disagree publicly with cabinet colleagues. On April 16, 1975, he brought his road show to Terrace where 60 people heard contradictory statements about the state of the Northwest plans.

"To date they consist of nothing more than an agreement in principle between the federal and provincial governments to develop port facilties in Prince Rupert and a railway system to the Northern reaches. Everything else is in the study stage and in due course these studies will be released," he told his restive audience, most of whom wanted to hear about steel mills, hydro projects, and super saw mills.

He gave two answers to the suggestion that Indian land claims were holding up the railway projects: first, that the CNR's railway location survey was halted by the Nishga land claim, and second, that Nishga people had granted permission to the CNR to undertake preliminary survey work on the route. Both these were repeated in writing for the Northwest Study Conference '75 in a buff study paper, "compliments of Alf Nunweiler, minister for Northern Affairs." The Nishga may be pardoned if they are as confused as the rest of the populace.

At the Terrace meeting, Nunweiler further compounded the confusion by contradicting his cabinet colleague, Human Resources Minister Norman Levi, by saying the province was now meeting with the federal government to solve the "Indian issue."

> Extensive discussions between the federal government and the province have been initiated [on land claims]. The province reiterates that the primary responsibility for aboriginal land claims rests with the federal government under the terms of B.C.'s entry into Confederation.[11]

Straight out of 1912!

Nunweiler concludes all interviews by stating that Northwest development "has occurred"—which astonishes the Chamber of Commerce—"and will continue to occur"—which terrifies the rest of the people in the Northwest—"in a series of rationally timed programs in keeping with broad objectives."[12] These objectives, he reminds anyone who will listen, are "economic development, preservation of environmental quality, and stabilization and enhancement of living."

Given the vagueness of the above "objectives" and the broadness of the "rational timing," coupled with the secrecy to date, it should have come as no surprise to Nunweiler and the cabinet he reported to, that enormous opposition would coalesce and come to a head at a study conference in Terrace at the end of May, 1975. Whether the development scheme exists now or ever goes ahead is no longer the issue to Natives, workers, environmentalists, farmers, even small industrialists. The issue is clearly land claims, environmental protection, open planning, multi-national corporations, and preservation of the Northwest for its people and its way-of-life. Any government, at whatever level, who tries to block it may find itself facing the wrath of people, both Native and white who, for entirely different reasons, are ready to bury the hatchet and unite to combat big, insensitive governments and big, insensitive corporations, be they Crown or multi-national.

Early in 1975, the Terrace, Kitimat, and District Labor Council, concerned that the whole project was forging ahead with no involvement from the people of the Northwest, formed an organization called VOICE (Victims of Industry Changing Environment), funded it with help from the British Columbia Federation of Labor and the federal Secretary of State's department, and hired Bill Horswill away from the CNR, where his controversial report on the effects of the Terrace-Meziadin line was being suppressed.

The purpose of VOICE was to involve the people of the Northwest in all aspects of development and to try and ensure that proper planning went into the project. John Jensen, the bearded Scandinavian logger who runs the local labor council, shook his head in bewilderment when asked how labor could so quickly turn on its old allies, the NDP it had worked so hard to elect just a year earlier. He blames it on the bureaucrats, as a good socialist must, when the government turns against the policies of the party. The party had, along with the labor movement, pledged itself to no major industrial development schemes until land claims were settled by the Native people. But then the NDP came into power and found itself, so Jensen says, saddled with a bureaucracy inherited from the former Social Credit days, a bureaucracy unaccountable to anyone, especially the people of the Northwest.

So Jensen and some others formed VOICE to try and put the brakes on the project and to try and find out what the people in Victoria had in mind for the area some 700 miles north of the British Columbia capital. The other bogeys to the labor movement are the private enterprise corporations who want to move in after the railways and highways are completed and reap a profit regardless of the Natives or the environment.

"We're different up here," Jensen explained. "We live here because we like it. We like the fresh air and the open spaces, and we want to keep it as much that way as possible; and if it has to change we want to have a say in it."

"Maybe it is only a myth now," he said, referring to Iona Campagnolo's statements, "and maybe the government would like it to be a myth, but let housing starts increase and the lumber market go up and the copper industry revive, and you'll see how much of a myth it is. The place'll be crawling with speculators again who owe no allegience to the country or the people, only to their head offices in New York or Toronto." So VOICE was formed to try and influence a slower, more planned kind of development.

At the same time that labor was showing its concern for southern press reports about the North, the Nishga Tribal Council became uneasy about being caught in the middle, with a railway through their lands and, if rumor were right, a sawmill, and perhaps, a mine. As devout Anglicans, it seemed logical for them to turn to their hishop, who lived in Prince Rupert, and ask for help. Bishop Douglas Hambidge, an Englishman who years ago was adopted by the Nishga, moved quickly. He got some money from the Anglican Church of Canada and appointed one of his priests, the Rev. John Stokes of Terrace, to leave parish work and become a full-time liaison officer on behalf of the Nishga and other concerned groups, to try and find out what was in the scheme of things for the Northwest.

Stokes, a marine biologist before he became a priest, knew the country and the people well. He knew that most people had no idea what the plans that were rumored across the North really meant. He saw a need for information, now that all the fronts were trying to turn the British Columbia Government in another direction. He told us, following his appointment in July, 1974, that he was sure information on the scheme could be sought out and explained, as the first two points of his terms of reference—information and education —indicated. But the secrecy was so great, and information was so contradictory, that it became clear the second two points of his terms of reference—co-ordination and collaboration—were vital. His role became one of trying to bring together the labor and environmental people with the Natives to initiate the fifth point in his program— confrontation.

A more unlikely confrontation expert than John Stokes doesn't exist—tall, earnest, and slightly bemused by it all. He decided that all these groups and all their research and briefs and concerns had to be made clearly available to government. And then the government had to know that the people of the North, particularily the Native people, were saying "no development until land claims are settled" and then only slow, planned, participatory development after that.

Out of these concerns—VOICE, the Nishga, the Anglican Church, the environmental and outdoors groups, the homesteaders —the decision slowly grew to hold a major conference right in the middle of the Northwest development project, to see where people were really going and to tell Alf Nunweiler, Iona Campagnolo, Dave Barrett, Ron Basford, the mayors of the towns, and the chambers of commerce where the people were really at. It took a lot of planning and they hadn't much money, and less expertise. But the Anglican Church came through with $5,000, and Iona, rightly sensing that power was forming in her constituency, got another $7,500 from the Liberal Government in Ottawa; and then Alf Nunweiler, not to be outdone by other opponents, produced $6,000 to help travel costs, and pretty soon the Northwest Study Conference '75, a dream of John Stokes, John Jensen, and others, was a reality.

It wasn't your usual convention with hospitality suites and delegates arriving in new suits ready for a big bash. Many of the participants wore jeans and bush shirts. Some were young and eager and bearded, others were mature and seasoned members of the labor movement. The clergy were there with their people, and mingling all through the 400 registered delegates were the coppery-colored Nishgas, Tsimpseans, Haidas, and Kitsum Kalums—quiet, dignified people until they started to explain about their land. Then they became articulate as only Native people can, and for three days an uneasy alliance of left-wing labor, starry-eyed youth, earnest environmentalists, dedicated clergy, and just plain scared folks grappled with multi-national corporations and political realities, hydro development and socio-economic disruption.

The jargon was appalling and the mistrust was deep, but by the end of the weekend of May 23–25, 1975, a solid, united front had been forged that brought these diverse groups together, committed to fighting for Native land claims before anything else. These groups are not traditional allies, and the violence that threatens much of the rest of British Columbia can come from many of the same kind of people and could well have engulfed the Northwest except

for this incredible meeting, where tensions, mistrust, and old stero-
types got laid to rest.

The first commitment, and perhaps the symbol for the conference, was a decision by the loggers' union to honor all Indian picket
lines across logging roads, in particular, the Nishga blockade of the
CanCel and Twin Rivers' logging road.

Mel Watkins, a University of Toronto economist and one-time
Walter Gordon whiz-kid, who was last heard of talking the Waffle
Group out of the NDP, is a leading Canadian nationalist. He took
a couple of years out of teaching to work as an economic consultant
with the Northwest Territories Indian Brotherhood. In his keynote
address, he told the conference that it was in the selfish interests of
Northern whites to support Indian land claims against the encroachment of multi-national corporations who have no community involvement, and who prefer to work through a computer located in
some office on Bay Street.

But it was resource developers who exploit the North and then
leave who came in for the wrath of the conference, and Watkins insisted that whites who live in the North should form an alliance with
all sorts of local groups to fight off the multi-nationals and obtain
development that would be best for all. As keynote speaker, he set
the stage for the direction the conference was to take. Certainly it
looked to the left and to Canadian nationalism for its political
orientation and zeroed in on the bureaucracies that serve the foreign-
dominated resource developers, as the particular devil. But if Watkins set the tone, it was Bill McKay and Rod Robinson of the
Nishgas and Philip Paul of the Union of B.C. Chiefs who provided
the inspiration that broke down the traditional suspicion many
Northern whites have for Indians who, in 1975, are rejecting paternalism and welfarism and returning to the proud days of their
ancestors.

The outcome was often in doubt, for at first the labor-domin-
ated conference seemed to shut the Natives out with rigid rules of
order, while in issue groups many whites were more dismayed at
thoughts of losing their cottages or the right to hunt and fish. But
by the last morning, the conference agreed that Indian land claims
were legitimate and that white residents of the area must demand
a settlement of Native grievances. The whites and Natives "agreed
to stand together against the efforts of companies, governments, and
other selfish groups who seek to divide us."

The whites were reassured by the Indians over and over. Paul told them not to be afraid of being kicked out of their homes or their lands. "Maybe we should have done that when you first arrived, but even then we Indians weren't hostile."

Paul said it was no secret that the real enemy were the multinationals who controlled all governments, and that unless a coalition was forged to fight them off, everyone was doomed. By putting the emphasis on selfish survival and impressing delegates with the urgency of the issue, perhaps Paul encouraged the uneasy whites to join the Natives.

After the labor-native alliance was announced near the end of Northwest Study '75, Robinson, the most articulate spokesman for the Nishga, expressed his gratitude. He told the people bluntly that a first trial picket line would be set up immediately, and the loggers agreed to honor it. He threatened to proceed with further action if the province dragged its feet and refused to negotiate the Nishga claim. While loggers and others at the conference might honor the picket line, some fear was expressed that over-zealous RCMP, local police, or companies who saw profits dwindling because of blockades being honored might instigate violence which would appear to be deliberate.

One of the Indian leaders made it clear that violence is often precipitated as an excuse for the government to step in and settle a situation that is going badly for big business, even if the wishes of the people involved are violated. Answering charges by some whites, that the Canadian Indians, and particularly those in British Columbia, are dominated by the militant American Indian Movement (AIM), Robinson and others maintained that the decisions to take action all over the province originated in local bands and not through outside trouble makers.

Bill McKay, a portly bachelor whose off-the-cuff remarks helped to ease the tension, told one earnest woman who questioned road closures and blockades, that all the Nishga were asking was for whites to pay the back rent, "You won't have to move out tomorrow if you do." Sitting in a back row, very much out of the conference, was the British Columbia highways minister, successor to Flying Phil Gagliardi, who expressed concern that business and government representatives were not present. "How can you form an alliance with them?" McKay growled in response.

Highways Minister Graham Lea, whose department will be upgrading many miles of highway in the area, said the delegates were all worked up over nothing, because the development plans were the figment of someone's imagination. Imagination or not, the agreements were signed in 1973 and 1974. The surveys and studies are underway. The railways are being built. The highways are under construction. The people are afraid.

The Northwest development scheme may be Iona's myth, Nunweiler's rational plan, or Lea's imagination, and where it goes is still, like most Northern development schemes, at the mercy of foreign markets and multi-national corporations. But the result may well have been just to bring whites and Natives together to force land claim settlements, and no where else in Canada has this happened as yet! A development scheme secretly planned and then announced, that no one in the North wants, did more to break down Native-white hostilities in Northwest British Columbia than all the reconciliation schemes in 100 years. The decision to bring justice to the Natives took a mighty step forward at the Terrace Conference in May, 1975, and other Native groups would do well to emulate that alliance.

When churches, workers, environmentalists, and the middle class join hands with the Indians, perhaps the Just Society can reappear.

Notes

1 A statute of the British Columbia legislature, passed largely on the urging of the Anglican Church, forbidding the construction of totems, holding of Native religious ceremonials, particularly the potlatch feast and other aspects of Indian coastal culture. The law was repealed recently and the ceremonies are slowly being revived.

2 Frank Calder, MLA, then chief of the Nishga Tribal Council, before the Supreme Court of Canada, Ottawa, January, 1973, explaining what his predecessors had said in 1887.

3 Petition of the Nishga Nation to the Privy Council of Great Britain, London, England, 1913.

4 *Caledonia Times*, (Prince Rupert, British Columbia), February, 1972.

5 Ibid.

6 University of British Columbia, "Transportation Studies", Vancouver, British Columbia, 1974.

7 W. J. Horswill, "The Meziadin Environmental Study", Aspect Consultants Inc., Winlaw, British Columbia, July 10, 1974.

8 *Terrace Herald*, (Terrace, British Columbia), September 18, 1974.

9 Iona Campagnola, MP, Skeena, "The Myth of the Great Northwest", Smithers, British Columbia, March 8, 1975.

[10] Iona Campagnola, MP, Skeena, Northwest Regional Study Conference, Terrace, British Columbia, April 19, 1975.

[11] "Questions and Answers on Development in Northwest British Columbia, . . . updated to May, 1975", the Honorable Alf Nunweiler, British Columbia minister without portfolio responsible for Northern Affairs, Victoria, British Columbia.

[12] Ibid.

We are Indians and we live off the land. We are not used to the White Man's food and this year there are no rabbits. It's very hard. Everybody is talking about this pipeline and we hope you will do the best for us. Not so much for us but for our grandchildren. The oil companies have ruined everything and it's very bad for us. We are always in the hands of the government but why do they give everything away to the oil companies who ruin our land.

Caroline Carmichael

We didn't know the gas companies were going to make all those trails [seismic lines] on the [Mackenzie] Delta and no one ever told us what was going on. Now that we're starting to talk about it, I can see what's going on. I can see that for the future of my grandchildren and their grandchildren that everything is getting spoiled and I don't like that.

Lazarus Sittichinli

I'm very much against the pipeline. They should have told us about it, those government men and those pipeline people, instead of sneaking around. Now maybe when it's too late we can see what's happening. The game is gone mostly and we don't hear the ducks singing any more. And it makes us feel bad. The fish have changed too, they're not as fat. We don't want them to take our land. Once when the treaty men came, our chief spoke strong against it. He didn't want their money. He just wanted our land for us and that's all we want.

Mary Husky

Statements given to
Mr. Justice Thomas Berger at the
Aklavik community hearings, Moose Kerr School
April 2, 3, and 4, 1975
The people spoke in their Native tongue
about the Mackenzie Valley pipeline

8

The Northwest Territories

*Where Land is
More Important than Money*

The people who want to build a natural gas pipeline down the Mackenzie Valley are armed with all the facilities and expertise of our technological society. They're slick and they know what they want. They've got lots of money and the avowed support of the Government of Canada.

Canadian Arctic Gas Pipelines Limited launched its campaign to build the $10 billion, 2,625-mile conduit in March, 1974 with a barrage of documentation, a media blitz in five cities, and a $100 million budget just to get the show on the road. The bulky presentation, their public relations department said, cost $40 million, it weighed 50 pounds and contained 7,000 pages of reports, maps, and studies. It had taken five years to prepare. The press conferences in Whitehorse, Washington, Anchorage, Toronto, and Yellowknife told anyone who would listen that the 4.5 billion-cubic-feet-a-day of Arctic natural gas from Alaska and Canada was something of the same order as the Canadian Pacific Railway's scheme to bridge Canada more than 100 years ago.

The statistics were merely mind-boggling—7,000 construction workers, more than a million tons of pipe, 300 rivers and lakes to bridge, 27 companies in a pre-construction consortium called Canadian Arctic Gas Study Limited, chilled gas, buried pipelines, alternate routes across the Yukon and down the Mackenzie, economic forecasts, threads across football fields—utterly appealing to a society that measures everything in bigness and betterness, cost and technical know-how.

The fact that Arctic Gas faced two hearings—the National Energy Board to determine whether the pipeline was needed, and Thomas Berger's commission of inquiry to see what the consequences might be—seemed not to phase the army of engineers, economists, public relations men and women, stockbrokers, and above all, oil and pipeline company managers. To even question, let alone oppose, such a mammoth army of expertise was to suffer delusions of grandeur, unless one had all the resources of big government at one's disposal. And that was not to be the case, since the government, prejudging its two inquries, had clearly declared that "it was in the public interest to facilitate early construction of the pipeline."[1]

But the likes of Lazarus Sittichinli, Mary Husky, Freddie Greenland, and a few thousand like them were providing opposition with not much money—far less than one percent of Canadian Arctic Gas Study's budget—and less expertise and no public relations. They decided to take on Arctic Gas in drafty school halls, Legion auditoriums, and in the outdoors. There are fewer than 30,000 of these people spread across nearly 2 million miles of the Yukon and Northwest Territories, and all they've got going for them is Mr. Justice Tom Berger's promise that his inquiry "is not just about a pipeline. It relates to the whole future of the North."[2]

But Tom Berger keeps his promises, and when he went into Aklavik, he told the people of the tiny settlement hugging the banks of the Mackenzie that they were to tell him exactly what they would say to the government if they could have the chance to tell the government what was in their hearts. And they came to him there and in Hay River and Fort Good Hope, in Old Crow and in dozens of other settlements up and down the Mackenzie, and they told him how it was with them. They told it with poetry and in their own language, and how it was their children and grandchildren they worried about. They told him with legends and stories and passed on the wisdom of their ancestors about the muskeg and perma-frost, the caribou migration and climate. There were no maps and flow charts. The graphs and jargon of the slickly mounted presentation from Arctic Gas had little impact on these people, the Indians, Inuit, and Metis of the Northwest Territories, because many couldn't read it, and even the educated whites had trouble wading through its tedious verbiage.

Arctic Gas seemed to have everything on its side, but no one counted on the integrity of the judge appointed by the federal government, in the days when the NDP held the balance of power (back in March of 1974), or on the determination of a small band of five Native organizations in the Yukon and Northwest Territories. David and Goliath? perhaps—no one's predicting the outcome yet—but Arctic Gas now knows it's in a battle that has more to it than profit and loss; it's a battle for the survival of a race of people and for the survival of the North.

"My inquiry is a study whose magnitude is without precedent in this country. I have been guided by the conviction that this inquiry must be fair and it must be complete. We have to do it right."[3] That's how Tom Berger saw it on March 3, 1975 when he gavelled open the hearing into the Mackenzie Valley gas pipeline at the Explorer Hotel in Yellowknife. His mandate, under an Order-in-Council of the federal government, was to conduct a searching inquiry into the probable social, economic, and environmental consequences of the pipeline and to recommend conditions should the line be built. The NEB will decide *if* a pipeline; Berger will decide *how*.

He saw it as an inquiry into the future of "a great river valley and its people," but the people he was answerable to in Ottawa, DIAND and the federal cabinet, saw it as a nuisance and perhaps even a disaster, since as the commission continued, Arctic Gas began to look like a huge ill planned, unnecessary, and unwanted gamble. This is probably the reason the government refused to postpone any decision on granting a conveyance to Arctic Gas until Berger's report is written, most likely about the middle of 1976. The NEB hearings into the need for a pipeline got underway in the fall of 1975. It's probably also the reason that then Energy Minister Donald MacDonald threatened to curtail the inquiry's wide terms of reference, which Berger interpreted as broadly as possible when he ordered the Energy Department to produce all reports and studies in their possession. But Berger isn't intimidated easily, not by big corporations and not by big government. In his preliminary rulings, he refused to hasten the hearings so Arctic Gas could get the jump on the El Paso line (see Chapter 2).

"I will not diminish anyone's right to be heard, nor will I curtail this inquiry so as to improve Arctic Gas's position in relation to the El Paso proposals in the United States."[4]

A close associate of Mr. Justice Berger can't figure out why the Liberals appointed him, because there's no doubt they've unleashed a tiger, albeit an unruffled tiger, who wears horn-rimmed glasses and works well under pressure. But then Thomas Rodney Berger, born March 23, 1933, was surprised when former Justice Minister John Turner named him to the British Columbia Supreme Court, just one day after he had won a moral victory for the Nishga Indians in the Supreme Court of Canada.

"I suppose every lawyer's ambition is to be judge, but I didn't think about it, because I never thought it was an appointment that would be offered me. My work as lawyer meant I was an antagonist of the federal government in the courts, and my political background would not have endeared me to the government."

It could only have been the balance-of-power held by the NDP in those heady days of 1973-74, the cynics charged, because Berger had been a federal NDP Member of Parliament (1962-63), NDP Member of the British Columbia legislature (1966-69), and leader of the British Columbia NDP in 1969. Most of his life a lawyer, he took cases that legal aid today would have handled. He had always been a Native rights lawyer, and following his appointment to head the Mackenzie Valley inquiry with its $1 million-a-year budget, he and his wife Beverley spent two months travelling the North to meet the people that were going to be most affected by the pipeline, "because to most people," Berger observed, "it isn't just the pipeline but what will come with the pipeline that is so devastatingly apparent." After the gas line comes the oil line and then a highway—parts of which are already under construction—followed by a railroad, hydro transmission lines, and likely, a telecommunications system. Are they to be built piecemeal or as part of an integrated approach to a Mackenzie Valley transportation corridor? No one seems to know, but Tom Berger will have a go at it, never fear. Certainly it's more than a mere thread across a football field, as Arctic Gas is fond of describing the pipeline.

Formally opposing the pipeline are two Yukon Native groups, the Indian Brotherhood of the Northwest Territories and the Metis Association along with the Committee for Original Peoples' Entitlement (COPE), an Inuit organization from the Delta. They represent the Natives of the region and their traditional ways. Environmentalist groups are also among the 10 "intervenors" who oppose or demand serious modification to Arctic Gas plans.

The inquiry has two basic components—formal hearings, held largely in Yellowknife, with some evidence to be presented in Ottawa and other Southern centres, and informal or community hearings to be conducted in each of the 26 communities likely to be affected by a gas pipeline. The formal hearings, complete with rules of evidence, expert testimony, and cross examination, are divided into four phases: the engineering and construction of the proposed pipeline, the impact of the pipeline on the physical environment, on the living environment (fish, game, and birds), and on the human environment.

It wasn't long after the inquiry opened that the government made it clear that they would listen to Berger and give him time to hold the inquiry but would make no commitment to act on his report. Tommy Douglas, the NDP energy critic in the House of Commons, has bluntly accused the DIAND, whose minister, Judd Buchanan, will ultimately grant the right-of-way across the Yukon and the Northwest Territories under the Territorial Lands Act, giving "a sop to the general public in order to pacify the opposition."

Hansard, on March 4, 1975, the day after the formal hearings started, revealed some incredible manouvering by that old master of politics, Acting Prime Minister Mitchell Sharp. First, he declined to commit the government "categorically" to waiting for the results of Berger's inquiry before making a decision on the pipeline.

> In order, of course, to protect the position of the Government, in circumstances that one cannot foresee at the present time . . . I cannot give a categorical answer, but we fully expect that Mr. Justice Berger will be able to complete all his hearings in time for us to take action.[5]

To some, but not to Berger, this equals a time pressure threat. "My mandate is to conduct a fair and thorough inquiry. That must come first. I will not diminish anyone's right to be heard. But there will not be any undue delay."[6]

When pressed by Joe Clark, PC for Rocky Mountain, to say whether there would be any conditions under which the government would proceed with the pipeline before the receipt of Tom Berger's report, Sharp replied that any conditions "are uncertain and unforeseeable."

And it went on like that all during the question period. No one knows what the government will do with Berger's report or whether it will even show an honest, hard-working, dedicated man the courtesy of waiting till his task is over, to move on a proposal he is supposed to be inquiring into. Certainly the government is not doing any more than necessary to co-operate in the formal hearings.

At one point early on in the inquiry, the colonial administration in Yellowknife telexed all its employees that they were "not to make statements or testify as witnesses before Berger unless receiving instructions" from Ewan Cotterill, assistant commissioner of the Northwest Territories. Berger quickly blasted the Northwest Territories for attempting "to impose conditions" on the participation of government employees, and the territory backed down. It took heavy pressure from Berger and counsel Ian Scott to get assurances from the Energy, Environment, and Indian Affairs departments to allow their employees to give expert witness, if called, at government expense. Accusations that energy and environmental reports were being withheld were also made by Canadian Arctic Resources Committee (CARC) as the only environmental intervenor.

"The government has been evasive and unco-operative" Russell Anthony, CARC's lawyer, told Berger, who had ruled that "all documents requested by parties in the inquiry and not presented to this commission can be ordered to be produced if the judge believes it to be in the public interest.

The formal hearings in Phase 1 dragged on with complicated technical and engineering reports from Canadian Arctic Gas Pipeline Limited, through the summer of 1975, well behind schedule, with alternate routes still to be examined. Serious questions have been raised about the efficiency and thoroughness of Arctic Gas studies of the environment, and it is felt by many observers that the pro-development federal government is worried about the way the hearings are going.

The Goliath was finding David more than a nuisance; so it was no surprise when, on April 23, just seven weeks after the hearings opened, Berger was informed by Native and public interest groups that their funding had been curtailed by Indian Affairs Minister Judd Buchanan, the legal guardian of Native rights. According to assistant commission counsel Stephen Goudge, it was a "crippling blow" to the commission's ability to conduct a "full and fair" inquiry. Berger promptly adjourned the hearing for three weeks to help the voluntary organizations to recoup.

What it all boiled down to was that Arctic Gas and its $100 million budget just weren't holding up at the hearings. The Native organizations, with a budget in 1974 totalling $400,000, had asked for increases for their 1975 participation in the Berger inquiry because of added costs of research and presentation of their case. Instead they were advised they'd get $300,000 of an $800,000 request for the five groups. Further, the major environmental group, which had been working on a $200,000 budget the first year, was cut off completely.

"The effect of this was to make CARC's participation impossible," Glen Bell, the Native's lawyer, told Berger, explaining that the technical expertise of this Northern Assessment Group was being used by CARC and all the native organizations as well.

Berger kept his cool and said little, pending a decision on his own $1 million budget which was never tampered with. "Buchanan wouldn't dare," a commission lawyer muttered. But the Native groups in particular were demoralized. James Wah-Shee, the young president of the Indian Brotherhood, made a dramatic appearance before Berger, saying all Native groups would have to re-evaluate their participation.

> It is impossible for us to see what the government is now doing as anything other than a deliberate attempt to cripple us in our participation before your inquiry. We were never advised that our past funding was excessive and I can assure you that it was, in fact, needed in full to permit our effective participation before this inquiry, both at the formal hearings and the community hearings. The right of freedom of speech is surely the most elementary of human rights. The right of Native people to speak effectively before this inquiry has now been seriously curtailed.
>
> As you know the government has not seen fit to guarantee unambiguously that they will let this inquiry finish its full and fair consideration before the government makes a decision regarding the right-of-way. Now, they add insult to injury by denying to those participants, who just happen to have doubts about a pipeline, the right of effective participation.[7]

For a couple of tense weeks negotiations went on behind the scenes, and Buchanan was subjected to some tough questioning in the House of Commons. Finally, a face-saving compromise was worked out whereby the Natives got another $100,000 and DIAND picked up $100,000 of Berger's expenses, thereby allowing the inquiry to pay the Northern Assessment Group half the money they had asked for to continue environmental work.

According to Ian Hunter in the *Ottawa Journal* of May 14, 1975, the whole scheme was cooked up in DIAND, but Buchanan was ill-informed about the negotiations and the directions they were taking. While none of the budgets for the Native and public sector was met as requested, they continued to participate in the inquiry. It has to be asked, however, what is the commitment of Buchanan, as trustee of Indian rights? What does the federal government really think about the Berger inquiry? and when has anyone ever seriously compared the mammoth budgets of Arctic Gas with the puny amount of money allotted the Native people and

environmentalists to oppose, alter, or even participate in the pipeline that will slash across their land.

But looming over all the hearings and the major worry of
government and pipeline interests are the Native land claims that
encompass nearly all the route of the proposed pipeline. Berger
sharply rejected the Arctic Gas suggestion that the Native people
should not be allowed to argue, before the commission, their principle that no right-of-way be granted until Native land claims in
the Yukon and the Northwest Territories had been settled. With the
Indian Brotherhood already holding caveat on 450,000 square miles
of land across which the pipeline would stretch, and in the process of
consulting with its people about the kind of land settlement they
would like from Ottawa, the commission could not easily ignore this
aspect of the impact a pipeline would have on the lives of the
majority of people in the Northwest Territories.

Wah-Shee made a major presentation to Berger in which he
said that it was impossible to negotiate land claims fairly while a
pipeline was being built over the very land that was in question.
"We believe that extraction of our mineral resources is perhaps in
the best interests of the Native people," he told us, "but only if there
are reassurances that our share of the wealth will allow our people
to compete as equals with the rest of society."

Berger declined to state whether the Native's position was
well-founded or not, but went on to say:

> It seems to me that it provides an essential focus for the Natives'
> case regarding the impact of the pipeline on their communities and
> their way-of-life. Indeed I would go further. The case Arctic Gas
> intends to make is that the pipeline can be built without prejudice
> to the settlement of the Native land claims. The position taken by
> the Natives offers a focus for the consideration of those terms and
> conditions—not only those which emerge from the Pipeline Guide-
> lines, but also any others which Arctic Gas is ready to propose—
> which may enable a pipeline to be built without prejudice to Native
> claims.[8]

Even a full settlement of their land claims would not necessarily remove fears that the pipeline would disrupt the ancestral
patterns of Native life. The sudden influx of more than 7,000 construction workers will confront all Northerners with what CARC
called "all the worst things in our society. Native people will be taken
away from their traditional pursuits. They'll find it difficult to re-
equip themselves and go back. They'll be left in a social vacuum."[9]
Another fear is that wildlife mating and migratory patterns will be

inhibited or permanently damaged so as to ruin the Natives' relationship with the land forever, despite Arctic Gas assurances that the buried chilled gas pipeline will avoid wildfowl habitats, animal denning areas, and the spawning grounds of fish.

The unity of the Native organizations and their close relationship with the people in the villages and settlements along the Mackenzie are coming to the attention of the Berger commission as it moves out into the second part of its process, the community hearings, which are informal and generally do not involve the rules of procedure or cross-examination that the formal hearings require.

From the beginning of the inquiry the three Native leaders in the Northwest Territories—James Wah-Shee, president of the Indian Brotherhood; Rick Hardy, president of the Metis Association; and Sam Raddi, president of COPE—have made it clear that where the pipeline inquiry is concerned they speak with one voice. Wah-Shee, 29, knows of what he speaks. He's headed the brotherhood since its inception in 1970, and in 1974 helped bring the Indians and Metis into their first joint General Assembly. He came to the inquiry its opening day and described this unity to Berger.

> Native organizations got started and will continue to exist because they are the only means by which our people can survive and live well. Since its formation in 1970, the brotherhood has forced the government to recognize the rights of Treaty Indians. Now, in alliance with the Metis Association and COPE we are fighting for the rights of all Native people. From our unity grows our strength.[10]

The idea of taking the inquiry into 26 Mackenzie Valley and Yukon communities was Berger's own. It meant long, hard travel, and there were no precedents for procedure and testimony. The people were to come and tell him their story. He was to listen. It confounded the sophisticated city lawyers who were representing the multi-national interests. But the story being told—of broken promises and exploitation, of the debilitating effect of southern technology, and of skepticism about government—is the same one being told in formal hearings by Native organizations. The story is often pooh-poohed by Northern whites who insist that Wah-Shee, Raddi, and Hardy don't know their people, that they are professional Indians.

Just to make sure he's getting the whole story, Berger travelled by canoe, small plane, and helicopter to Fort Franklin, Fort Norman, and Fort Good Hope, to Inuvik and a host of other villages. It's out there where the real drama and pathos of the Native people comes across. Gone is the polite jargon of the formal hearings. There, they respect Berger as an individual, even if they are pretty cynical about the government that appointed him and fear that he's mere window-dressing for the white establishment. Out there, he finds a noticeable anti-white sentiment because it's a white government, a pro-development government, one that, Natives feel, relies on royalties from gas and oil companies.

> Mr. Berger, I am Charlie Furlong, and I would like to speak to you today on behalf of my people. The people are not ready for land development. By people, I mean the Indians, the Eskimo and the Metis. The oil companies want to build a pipeline down the Northwest Territories. They want to take our gas and our oil. We will not even be able to use our gas in our own homes. It will go past our communities to heat southern Canada and our big brother, the United States of America . . .
> Native people themselves are not qualified for decent jobs during the construction. White men will come from the south to build the pipeline; and again white men will come into our communities and take away our daughters and our wives. Even our mothers and children will be left homeless . . .
> I would like to see a land settlement between the government and the people of the Northwest Territories, a land settlement where the Native people will control their land and their development. You know, Mr. Berger, we are not against a pipeline or any other development, but we want to control it. We look at movies and in every movie the Indian always loses the war. I want to ask the government, the southern people, to let us win this one.[11]

Berger heard this statement in Aklavik and in many communities like it. His energy and interest when he's in the settlements is prodigious. He listens patiently and endlessly to long stories, seemingly irrelevant to the pipeline inquiry. But he promised to listen to the people, and the story that is coming through is about one of the most dramatic struggles in the history of Canada; and he's hearing it from the people and not just from the well-written sociological studies prepared by well-meaning southern liberals. It's the story of Natives and white settlers confronting this most enormous, rich, insensitive private enterprise job ever. How can they fight it? It seems so futile. Perhaps it is the "last frontier's" last stand.

Peter Usher, a social scientist based in Inuvik, said the people in the North see the Berger Commission as their last resort. He worries that positions may harden if nothing comes of it and Northerners are ignored. "I know of no race of people who have acquiesced gracefully to their own extinction." Some whites claim the real reason the pipeline is to be buried is to save it from angry Natives who want to blow it up. A buried pipeline is less vulnerable to sabotage.

The halls where Berger holds the informal hearings are often crowded, hot, and riddled with mosquitoes. The hearings have been known to go on until two in the morning, and the tales about the residential schools, fishing grounds, and caribou are endless. The judge's patience is awesome. Through the translations from Slavey to English and back again, he trades quips, encourages the shy ones, and listens, always listens.

Dolphus Shea, the 35-year-old foreman at the tiny hamlet of Fort Franklin told of how, when he was eight-years-old, he and a couple of friends were invited to go for a ride to a fish camp. Instead they ended up at a residential school in Aklavik.

> Before I went to that school, the only word of English I knew was "hello". But when we got there we were told if we spoke one word of Slavey we'd be whipped. I'd never been whipped before in my life. We were told all our religion was superstition. I whispered something to my friend in Slavey and they hit my hands until they bled.
>
> On the first day of school all our clothes were taken away and we were given a hair cut—a bald hair cut because they said we were dirty.
>
> I wanted to go home and I cried for weeks and weeks. I remember an Eskimo boy who cried all year long under his blankets because he was afraid the sisters would come and spank him.

Fort Franklin is up on the shores of Great Bear Lake and Chief George Kodakin told the judge that the lake was like a deep freeze to his people.

> How would you like it if someone came and took your deep freeze away? What are you people going to do if the animals get poisoned by an oil spill or the land gets wrecked when gas blows over it? Are you going to give them blood transfusions and put them back? Is the gas company going to collect the fish that are damaged and replace them?

And so, on their own ground, the native people told Judge Berger about their relationship to the land and how different it is from the white man's concept.

There are more Natives than whites in the Northwest Territories right now, and the membership of the first fully elected territorial council, which met for the first time in May of 1975, reflects this. The council doesn't mean much to the people Judge Berger met during his community hearing, but the fear of what will happen to them when the whites outnumber the Natives, as they inevitably must, was always present. These Natives are anxious to avoid the plight of those in the south, and among the young people there's a strong nationalistic sentiment growing, as the brotherhood makes its influence felt.

Steve Iveson at Fort Franklin is a brotherhood field worker, and he expresses skepticism and cynicism towards DIAND and its kept woman, the territorial government. "The key thing to remember," he told us, "is that we Natives here in the North consider ourselves to be a sovereign nation, and we must be as one government dealing with another. I expect there will be trouble, and the leaders won't be able to stop it, if there's any sign that his report is going to be shelved," he said nodding at Berger as he walked over to the community hall for another round of hearings.

It will be some time before Berger's report is handed to Judd Buchanan, and what it will recommend or what the federal government will do with it remains in the realm of speculation. But it is a fact that the Natives see it as their one last hope, and it is a fact that Berger is conducting his inquiry with integrity, thoroughness, and the conviction that it is more than window-dressing. The federal government, and it alone, has the responsibility for seeing that the North does not become the sole preserve of resource developers whose commitment to the people who own the land is non-existent. We contend that Canada's future reputation as a nation of justice will rest on how it implements and responds to Mr. Justice Thomas Berger's report of the Commission of Inquiry into the proposed Mackenzie Valley Pipeline.

The reason the Berger inquiry is of supreme importance to the Natives of the Northwest Territories, an area one-third of Canada's land mass, is that, because of their majority position— 31,000 Natives to just over 10,000 whites—and because they have developed a unique concept of a land settlement, they need the time and the freedom to negotiate their claims with Ottawa. Wah-Shee explains it with the slogan "land not money" and insists that no James Bay style settlement will be acceptable to the Northwest Territories. It is such a unique concept that Buchanan, who insists he can only extinguish title, has threatened to cancel all grants to the brotherhood if they continue on this "unrealistic" course.

In June of 1974, the brotherhood and the Metis association held a joint General Assembly at Fort Good Hope on the Mackenzie River, where more than 250 delegates hammered out a series of resolutions based on the premise that the 400,000-plus square miles of land covered by the spurious Treaties 8 and 11 and presently under caveat, belonged to Native people. It was at this assembly that "land, not money" became the key slogan and the long, arduous process of negotiation was authorized, including research into the land, using community involvement at every step. The government's response was to question the seriousness of the claim, even though it was a formal statement of deeply held feelings by the Indians and Metis in the settlements of the Western Arctic.

James Wah-Shee and Rick Hardy presented Judge Berger with a statement of what their claim really is all about. More clearly than any other argument we have heard, this alternative model of development could work for both Natives and whites in the North and for the greater justice of all Canadians. It does not deny development or even the construction of a gas pipeline or Mackenzie Valley transportation corridor. It was this argument that Berger insisted the Natives had the right to present for serious consideration.

Thesis—"no pipeline before a land claims settlement"—is more than just a request designed to protect a bargaining position. It is the formal expression of a more fundamental issue, one which involves the struggle between two opposing concepts of economic development for the North. The pipeline proposal, according to the Natives, represents the "colonial" philosophy of development. Opposed to this notion of Northern development is the "community" philosophy of development as exemplified by the Native land claim.

The "colonial" school of economic development is the one which is promoted by the American multi-national corporations and their Canadian subsidiaries. They see the North as the storehouse of resources for the industrial centres of the south—Chicago, New York, Pittsburgh, Montreal, and Toronto. Oil, gas, and minerals move south to these centres. The profits which they generate move south along with them. The North becomes a hinterland dependent on the south; it loses its resources and gets welfare in return. It is never permitted to develop an economic base which allows its people, and particularly its Native people, to enjoy the benefits of equality with the residents of the industrial south.

For the Native people of the North, the injustices of the "colonial" philosophy of development are cruelly multiplied and rubbed in. In the process of building a pipeline, Native society would be dragged from a land-based economy—hunting, fishing, and trapping—into a wage economy, a wage economy which would be the poor Northern cousin of the southern economy. The big petroleum companies would move in and suck dry the reserves of gas and oil from the North. After they have gone, what happens to the Native people who remain? What will be left for the owners of the land after Canadian Arctic Gas and its pipeline are just a memory? The "colonial" philosophy of development leaves them nothing except the desolation of a ghost town, the Berger inquiry was told. The "colonial" philosophy of Northern development means prosperity for the multi-national corporations. But for the North it means a weak, distorted economic existence and cultural and political retardation.

What are the alternatives? The "community" philosophy of development expressed by the Dene of the Mackenzie District bears repeating.

> As much as possible we want to be able to control our own destiny. We want to be the ones who decide what directions our society should take. We also want to participate in Canadian society, but we want to participate as equals. It is impossible to be equal if our economic development is subordinated to the profit-oriented priorities of the American multi-nationals.
>
> Therefore, the Native people are saying, we must have a large degree of control over our own economic development. Without that control we will end up like our brothers and sisters on the reserves in the south: continually powerless, threatened and impoverished.
>
> Only community ownership of the land, land which has belonged to our people for thousands of years, can give us the ability to determine and follow our own way.[32]

The two philosophies of development competing in the arena of the inquiry, the "colonial" philosophy and the "community" philosophy, were to weigh heavily in the outcome of the struggle between the Natives of the Northwest Territories and the federal government.

The driving force behind the Native unity and the land-not-money movements is a 30 year-old Dogrib Indian from Fort Rae, about 80 miles from the territorial capital of Yellowknife on Great Slave Lake. James Wah-Shee is articulating fluently in two languages a philosophy for his people that puts the federal government on the defensive. It states that extinguishment of land title and the consequent extinguishment of all other rights is not necessarily the best way of settling grievances. The old style of giving up everything to the federal government in return for something like beads and blankets, no matter how elaborate the beads and blankets may be, is no longer acceptable to people like Wah-Shee.

The minister of Indian Affairs insists that his mandate is only to extinguish title. He has offered the Yukon Natives a settlement similar to James Bay. He has said that Wah-Shee's approach is so unrealistic it cannot be seriously considered and that, furthermore, if the Northwest Territories Natives pursue this route, DIAND will have no other recourse than to refuse funding. The pressure from government and petroleum companies is incessant. Judd Buchanan wants to settle the "Native problem" once and for all. The oil companies want to see a settlement so they can go about their business unimpeded by cloudy land titles hanging over them. The whites want a settlement to end the conflict and tension in the North. The Native people respond by asking why the time pressure? Why should they, the owners of the land, be pressured into a hasty, ill-prepared settlement which will be of little benefit to the Natives of today or of future generations?

Wah-Shee is anxious to dispel the notion that the Indians, Metis, and Inuit are anti-development. "We are being accused of trying to hold up all of Canada from sharing in the gas and oil resources of the North. We are not really against any development, rather we are afraid of being engulfed and destroyed by development, as emerging people have elsewhere. We fear for our land, our culture, and our children. We only want to protect ourselves. Government and industry want to move ahead with development, as do the white people of the North. Only the Native people and their land settlement seem to stand in the way, and serious confrontation seems inevitable. "We need time, but neither government, industry, or the local white population seems prepared to wait," Wah-Shee told us shortly after his election as a territorial councillor from Great Slave Lake riding early in 1975.

He pointed out the complexity of the Alaska settlement, the dissatisfaction with the James Bay settlement, and the constant pressure to get it over with in the Northwest Territories. "The sole apparent emphasis for us in the Northwest Territories today is, get it done with the least possible disadvantage to groups or interests other than the Indian people." But clearly, something new is called for. Land research money has been given by DIAND for two years, totalling about $700,000, but any further money would have to come in the form of a loan against any settlement. In other words, the Indians would negotiate with their own money. The major problem here is the constant threat that, if the proposal goes against what the government has in mind or if the negotiations get tough, then the funding can be cut off.

"The irony of the whole exercise," says Wah-Shee, "is that we are being denied the time to fully work out and determine exactly what kind of settlement we want. To work out all the details with the fullest confidence that nothing has been forgotten is a formidable task." The issue is not cash; so the settlement will not be an enormous burden on the Canadian taxpayer. The figure of $3 billion to $5 billion that is bandied about the North—the rumor was started by DIAND officials, the Natives charge—is not true. "I repeat, the issue is land, not money," Wah-Shee told us.

"A land settlement that would not cost Canadian taxpayers what a settlement similar to Alaska cost the United States is not what the Natives are looking for. What we seek is the means to avoid the destruction of ourselves and our people in the economic, social, and political life of the Northwest Territories of the future."

Wah-Shee sees the land settlement, if it can be negotiated in an open, conscientious, and straight forward manner with DIAND, as benefitting all the residents of the Northwest Territories. "Full participation by the Indian people in the regional economy of the Northwest Territories will mean a dramatic increase in local control and locally generated expansion. White businessmen are extremely shortsighted if they cannot see the advantage of full economic involvement of a large segment of the population who might otherwise be a drain on the regional economy."

Wah-Shee might be called a visionary, almost prophetic, the way he looks at his people, his country and its future. Others would call him a young opportunist, out-of-touch with his people, but these are, almost to a person, whites who are confused when they see products of their system rejecting it and turning to something altogether foreign, until recently, to the colonial patterns of life in the territories. For Indians to tell whites that they can benefit from anything devised by Natives is too much to swallow.

"The general public of Canada should also look to the land settlement as an exciting challenge. The mistakes of the past must not be repeated in the North. A land settlement is a unique opportunity to bring the Indian people into the economic, social, and political mosaic of Canada in a way that would be a source of pride to all Canadians. The Minister, Mr. Buchanan, and most of his top officials have failed to grasp this point. They instead still seek to extinguish our rights and with them the basis for our own development."

Wah-Shee is a quiet-spoken, almost shy person who wears his Indian leadership easily and lightly. He sat on the end of a bed in the Yellowknife Inn one night, talking late, trying to convince, and to articulate the solution. The white man's attempt—our attempt—to pin it all down, tie it all up in a neat package, sign it, seal it, and get on with the next job is so foreign to the Natives' way that how Wah-Shee talks about the solution is as important as what he says. The one constant is that Northwest Territories Natives, unlike some others in Canada, will not be trapped into a dollar figure or an acreage figure without long and careful thought, study, and research *before* negotiations start.

"We are working on a solution now. It's a solution being worked out in the 26 settlements along the Mackenzie by the Indian and Metis, the Déne—the people—and it's a solution we feel might avoid the conflict and bitterness of other places. Our model may be the answer—a unique and novel answer which reacts to our history."

"I agree with those people who say that the Alaska settlement is the most dramatic, the most generous in North America. But it is really only similar to what has been going on for years. Indian land is secured for settlement or economic exploitation by Europeans and North Americans of European extraction. As in the case of all those 'beads and blankets' treaties, it is a 'once-and-for-all' solution."

It is this "once-and-for-all" solution that Wah-Shee insists will not work in the Northwest Territories. One reason is the time pressure, another is injustice of a final solution when no one can possess the crystal ball needed to foresee the needs of anyone, let alone the Native people, in the future. The "once-and-for-all" extinguishment of the rights model is out-of-date.

"There must be a solution that takes into account the change in philosophy which has taken place in connection with the colonization of lands of indigenous peoples in the modern era. The other policy, solve it here and now and forever, is based on a centuries-old colonial policy which the United Nations rejected when it recognized the land rights of indigenous people."

The approach, although not spelled out in detail, that Wah-Shee will talk about for hours and which is being incorporated into the research of the Native peoples into their land claim, is the opposite to "once-and-for-all." Instead of surrendering their aboriginal land rights forever, those rights must be formalized by creating an aboriginal title which clearly recognizes the ownership of the traditional lands by Native people. It sounds so simple yet so devastatingly threatening, because it opens up new vistas for Native people.

Gone are the welfare cheques that keep people in bondage, gone are the reserves, gone is paternalism, gone is second class citizenship.

Downstairs at the Yellowknife Inn, the entrance to the lobby was crowded with the sterotype of the drunken Indian—shabby, thin, broken, and hopeless. Upstairs a slim, long-haired (in Indian fashion) young man was talking about how this could end, at least for future generations. Gone would be the scorn and contempt of the white man who sees Yellowknife's main street as a slum, and gone would be the cringing, lurching drunks who have no future in a white man's world.

"Immediately," Wah-Shee tells us, "with clear recognition of land ownership, conflict is prevented, and then development [take heart, all you petroleum companies] can proceed according to the terms and conditions agreed upon between the owners of the land, the Native people, and those interested in developing or using those lands.

"The advantages flow to everyone. Subject to agreements to be negotiated from time-to-time with the owners of the land, government and industry and local whites will see an end to the conflict created by unresolved land settlement questions."

This on-going negotiation model gives the Native people time to work out among themselves, through the consensus method they are so accustomed to, the complex question of a land settlement. There will be time for them to determine how and through what agencies the settlement should be administered. Mistakes and conflict can be avoided. This new approach is the only one being considered by the Natives—Metis and Indian—in the Northwest Territories.

DIAND through Buchanan has made it clear this is not possible, at least at this moment in history, and Wah-Shee is perhaps the most moderate of Indian leaders when he says this won't work. "If the government feels our position is not worthy of their consideration, and if they try to impose Alaskan or James Bay models on our neighbors in Yukon and British Columbia, then they are sadly deluding themselves. If DIAND feels that it need only ignore our position and eventually we will be forced to accept, then they are badly mistaken. A settlement will only work—and to prove this you only have to look at the results of the traditional treaties—if developed to the satisfaction of the people who have to live with it. Any attempt to impose a settlement on us which ignores the deeply felt conviction of our people will have serious and negative ramifications for years to come."

A reporter in *The Hub*, the weekly newspaper at Hay River, Northwest Territories, Ray Lawrence, put it more bluntly and perhaps more threateningly after an interview with Wah-Shee on April 9, 1975.

> If, in time, a cash settlement is forced on them, the cost to the country and corporations will be truly staggering as nothing less than compensation for all minerals and resources already used plus generous royalties in all future extractions will be acceptable.
>
> The Brotherhood finds it most regrettable that Judd Buchanan does not consider the Indian claims to be realistic. They have come to realize that the Minister's negotiating stance has come to be paralyzed by a hardening of the mental arteries, with no room for considering just Native claims. In fact, it appears to the Brotherhood that the main government strategy is to attempt to put forth foolish offers which will turn the Canadian taxpayers against the Indian land claims.[13]

Buchanan disagrees with such a harsh position but says there is no clarification as to what "ownership" means. If it means clear "fee simple title," the same kind of title that any property owner holds in Canada, the government will not negotiate, because then the control of 450,000 square miles of land would go to Native Canadians, and sovereignty of the North is already of prime concern to Ottawa. It ignores, of course, the fact that most of the oil, gas, and pipeline companies, anxious to develop the north-south transportation corridor beginning with Arctic Gas, are American controlled.

Buchanan says that if ownership means a share in the benefits of development, that is another matter, one with which he can agree. The government, Buchanan explained, recognizes the Natives' right to unrestricted use of the land, but this cannot be converted to "fee simple title." When it was suggested to the DIAND that the threat to cut off Native funding for their land claim was a form of blackmail, officials countered by saying it was merely an attempt to have the Natives' position clarified.

"If they [the Natives] are seeking fee simple title, then there is no way the government will negotiate further; therefore, there is no reason to continue funding negotiations which will not be continued," a DIAND official told us. He was unwilling to be named and unwilling to answer the question we asked him in Ottawa in May, 1975. He did not consider it odd that the government's position to refuse Native or white Northerners a real say in planning development was irresponsible but to grant this same control to Americans and to southern Canadians was responsible. His reply was a meek "I don't feel qualified to answer that."

The feud will continue for some time and positions are hardening every day. Whites misread the firm resolve of the Natives and the support that the brotherhoods have in the villages. Government is too removed from the situation and apparently too committed to resource development to change course. The Natives see it as survival.

In April 1975, Prince Charles made a highly publicized visit to the Northwest Territories as guest of the territorial administration. He went to Colville Lake, north of the Arctic Circle, for a dog team ride. Colville Lake people are part of the Fort Good Hope Band of Hareskin Indians. Their young chief, Frank T'Selie, 29, went to greet the prince and asked him to accept, and support if he could, a petition from the Hareskin people, supporting Native land claims. It contained more than 100 signatures. But before Charles could read it, the rolled up paper was snatched away by Commissioner Stuart Hodgson who told T'Selie it was bad protocol to involve the prince in political matters.

"I couldn't explain about it," T'Selie told us quietly. "I only wanted to tell him that we have lived peacefully here for 10,000 years, and we have never fought a war, and we don't want to be driven into that; so Prince Charles we want your help in getting a peaceful and just settlement from your mother's government."[14]

Charles eventually saw the petition, but his reaction, if any, was private. T'Selie is only strengthened in his belief that land is the only hope for his people, following this example of white insensitivity where protocol overrides peoples' feelings.

"Every day we listen to the radio, and we hear about rapes and murders and violence and war in your world, and we wonder why you want us to join your society."

"About two weeks ago I was talking to an old man in our band, and he told me that the government wanted to make Indians into white men, and he said to me, 'You can't do that. It's like trying to make a rabbit into a dog. A rabbit is a rabbit and a dog is a dog and an Indian is an Indian.'"

Dene Declaration: Statement of Rights

Shortly after the manuscript for this book was finished, the Indian Brotherhood of the Northwest Territories and the Metis Association met for their Second General Assembly at Port Simpson, a community of some 1,200 people at the forks of the Mackenzie and

Liaird Rivers. More than 300 delegates from 25 communities along the Mackenzie Valley debated, and then unanimously approved, a statement declaring themselves to be a nation within Canada—a Dene or "people" nation. Because the Inuit, Metis, and Indian people are in a majority within the Northwest Territories—and this majority exists nowhere else in Canada—they feel their special status is justified.

We believe this historic document says, better than anything, what the aspirations of the Northwest Territories Natives' are, and for this reason we include the entire document, approved by the Second General Assembly on July 19, 1975.

We the Dene of the N.W.T. insist on the right to be regarded by ourselves and the world as a nation.

Our struggle is for the recognition of the Dene Nation by the Government and people of Canada and the peoples and governments of the world.

As once Europe was the exclusive homeland of the European peoples, Africa the exclusive homeland of the African peoples, the New World, North and South America, was the exclusive homeland of Aboriginal peoples of the New World, the Amerindian and the Inuit.

The New World like other parts of the world has suffered the experience of colonialism and imperialism. Other peoples have occupied the land—often with force—and foreign governments have imposed themselves on our people. Ancient civilizations and ways of life have been destroyed.

Colonialism and imperialism is now dead or dying. Recent years have witnessed the birth of new nations or rebirth of old nations out of the ashes of colonialism.

As Europe is the place where you will find European countries with European governments for European peoples, now also you will find in Africa and Asia the existence of African and Asian countries with African and Asian governments for the African and Asian peoples.

The African and Asian peoples—the peoples of the Third World—have fought for and won the right to self-determination, the right to recognition as distinct peoples and the recognition of themselves as nations.

But in the New World the native peoples have not fared so well. Even in countries in South America where the Native peoples are the vast majority of the population there is not one country which has an Amerindian government for the Amerindian peoples.

Nowhere in the New World have the Native peoples won the right to self-determination and the right to recognition by the world as a distinct people and as Nations.

While the Native people of Canada are a minority in their homeland, the Native people of the N.W.T., the Dene and the Inuit, are a majority of the population of the N.W.T.

The Dene find themselves as part of a country. That country is Canada. But the Government of Canada is not the government of the Dene. The Government of the N.W.T. is not the government of the Dene. These governments were not the choice of the Dene, they were imposed upon the Dene.

What we the Dene are struggling for is the recognition of the Dene Nation by the governments and peoples of the world.

And while there are realities we are forced to submit to, such as the existence of a country called Canada, we insist on the right to self-determination as a distinct people and the recognition of the Dene Nation.

We the Dene are part of the Fourth World. And as the peoples and Nations of the world have come to recognize the existence and rights of those peoples who make up the Third World the day must come and will come when the nations of the Fourth World will come to be recognized and respected. The challenge to the Dene and the world is to find the way for the recognition of the Dene Nation.

Our plea to the world is to help us in our struggle to find a place in the world community where we can exercise our right to self-determination as a distinct people and as a nation.

What we seek then is independence and self-determination within the country of Canada. This is what we mean when we call for a just land settlement for the Dene Nation.

Notes

1 *Time Magazine* (Montreal) April 1, 1974.

2 The Mackenzie Valley Pipeline Inquiry, Preliminary Rulings by the Honorable Mr. Justice T. R. Berger, Yellowknife, Northwest Territories, July 13, 1974.

3 *Time Magazine* March 17, 1975.

4 The Mackenzie Valley Pipeline Inquiry.

5 *Hansard Debates*, The House of Commons, Ottawa, March 4, 1975.

6 The Mackenzie Valley Pipeline Inquiry.

7 James Wah-Shee, president of the Indian Brotherhood of the Northwest Territories, to the Mackenzie Valley Pipeline Inquiry, Yellowknife, Northwest Territories, April 23, 1975.

8 The Mackenzie Valley Pipeline Inquiry.

9 *Time Magazine*, March 17, 1975.

10 James Wah-Shee, to the Mackenzie Valley Pipeline Inquiry.

11 Charles Furlong, a Native of Aklavik, Northwest Territories, appearing before the Mackenzie Valley Pipeline Inquiry at the first community hearing held in Aklavik, April 3, 1975.

12 See Chapter 1, note 1.

13 *The Hub*, (Hay River, Northwest Territories) April 9, 1975.

14 Chief Frank T'Selie expressed his frustration again when he testified before the Mackenzie Valley Pipeline Inquiry at Fort Good Hope, Northwest Territories, August 6, 1975. He told Judge Berger, "My nation will stop this pipeline. I am willing to lay down my life." The pipeline route could come within two miles of Fort Good Hope.

Here is what one chief said to a Catholic priest who was trying to convert his band, "You tell us there is but one religion can save us, yours. The Anglican minister tells us that he has got it; now which of you white men am I to believe?" After pausing and consulting with his people, the chief added, "I will tell you the resolution I and my people have come to; it is this—when you both agree and start to travel the same road, we will travel with you. Until then, however, we will stick to our own religion. We think it is best.

Treaty Days
Manitoba Indian Brotherhood
Winnipeg, 1971

9

The Churches

From the Paternalism of Yesterday
to the
Liberation of Today

Missionaries invariably followed colonization, and Northern Canada was no exception. The fur traders and explorers, the prospectors and railroaders, and later the settlers brought fire arms, alcohol, and the concept of private property to the Natives of Canada. Hand-in-hand with these people came the missionaries, usually with great devotion and zeal, who introduced the gospel, which many Natives accepted readily as an extension of their own supernatural beliefs.

The stories of peace and harmony, freedom and love were not foreign to the Natives of Canada. The idea of a supreme, omnipotent God who cared for all people, who was the Creator of nature, who saw all men as equal, was close to their own traditional concepts of Kitchie Manitou, one of many names they gave to the Creator. The father-child teachings of the church were no problem.

> Kitchie Manitou took care of them in those days. He held them in the palm of his hand, as if they were frail as an eggshell; when there were storms and tempests, and in winter time, He would cover them with his other hand and shield them from all harm.[1]

This beautifully tender description of God by an old Indian who lived before the days of the treaties could easily have come from the Bible, and no theologian today would argue with its soundness in terms of a caring, loving, liberating God. But unfortunately, many of the missionaries also had cultural backgrounds which their com-

mitment to the gospel had not altered and so they very often tried
to lure or even bribe and coerce the Natives to accept cultural,
ethical, and religious systems which often bore no resemblance to
the gospel of Jesus Christ in its purest form.

The Natives were often confused, too, by the various stripes
and shades of European Christianity. Roman Catholic and Anglican missionaries, in particular, vied strenuously for souls, each telling the Natives that his particular brand of Christianity was the
right one and the only one. As if this were not bad enough or confusing enough, the missionaries—in particular the Oblates of Mary
Immaculate (OMI) for the Catholics and the evangelical or "low"
Church Missionary Society (CMS) for the Church of England (now
Anglican)—angrily told the Natives that the other was all wrong,
even evil.

In their zeal to save souls and convert the "savages" to Christianity, in itself a laudable goal by 18th century missionary standards, the missionaries tragically believed that it was also necessary
to try and wipe out all vestiges of cultural, religious, and economic
values that Natives had practised "since time immemorial" and impose in their place incomprehensible foreign beliefs.

European values of "work" or "property" and "ambition"
became as much a part of conversion as the gospel. Generally the
notion was—and unfortunately still is in some quarters of the church
today—that Natives were lazy, obtuse, and very much deserving of
contempt. G. E. Mortimore, former newspaper reporter, anthropologist, and long-time observer of the Indian scene on the west coast,
sums up the attitude of the early white man in these sharp words:

> Indians were looked on as allies to be courted, souls to be saved, as
> fur-trapping, wealth-supplying machines and obstacles to be coaxed
> out of the way of settlement, as sickly inmates of a human zoo, to be
> protected until they died, and as substandard creatures who pro-
> vided an outlet for charitable impulses.[2]

Stories of Anglican and Roman Catholic missionaries leap-
frogging each other down the Mackenzie River, establishing mission
posts at alternate villages, or racing each other by dog team across
the Arctic Coast to get their particular brand of the faith into a
settlement, made heroic reading. But unbelievable feats of derring-
do and human endurance little enhanced their reputation for the
prime Christian virtues of unity and brotherhood. There are still
those in the churches who see the early days of missionary endeavour
as an era of great witness for the faith—and coincidentally, of great

fund-raising for the brave and isolated missionaries. But there are others who now honestly admit that much of the disruption and destruction of Native culture and social life was caused by the European clerics.

At the same time, to be honest, Native leaders also admit, albeit somewhat reluctantly, that many of the missionaries and their successors, the doctors, nurses, and teachers, did something to pick up the remnants of a social system that had been smashed by traders, police, and government administrators. But while it is true the churches were the only institutions that tried to help the Natives adapt to the European system introduced to them by fur traders and the government, it may be argued that the churches should have been working to help maintain the Native culture rather than merely teaching young people how to adapt. In the long run, the only reason for Natives to abandon their indigenous ways was to make them more productive in terms of supplying furs and buying the products of the traders—largely the multi-national Hudson Bay Company—or to make them more manageable in terms of government administration.

Many of the Natives, in particular the Inuit, accepted Christianity at first as a superior kind of magic, probably stronger than the old shamans, but generally speaking the churches rejected any infiltration of the "pure" gospel with Native religions and customs. The pressure on the British Columbia government to pass a law making all Native religious ceremonials and symbols illegal is just one example of the inflexibility of early church involvement with Natives. Marriage, work habits, nomadic life-styles, and especially education were other areas where European custom was confused with religious belief.

On the positive side, the herculean task of learning many different languages fluently and committing them to a script so that the scriptures and services could be more easily transmitted showed a resourcefulness that to this day is unique. Practically the only white people in the North who can be said to have any long-term fluency with the various Native languages are the Roman Catholic and Anglican clergy. Still, one of the most controversial areas of church involvement with the Native way-of-life is the educational system which was operated through residential schools and hostels until only a few years ago. Over the years, many thousands of Natives— Indians, Inuit, and Metis have gone through the church-operated residential schools across Canada, and while they were once the pride of the churches who used them to recruit and finance large missionary outlays, they are now often considered a blot on the church's history in the North.

Education has been a problem since the white man first arrived, and because it was always white-dominated it had—and still has— little relevance to most Natives. Statistics in 1974 reveal that across Canada, 94 percent of status Indian children dropped out before finishing high school, as opposed to 12 percent for white young people. Less than 40 percent of Natives finish grade eight. While these abysmal statistics are not solely to be blamed on church resi- dential schools, they illustrate the contempt that most white edu- cators have had since the beginning of the assimilation process for anything Native. Curricula were designed by whites and taught by whites in an environment whose primary purpose was to make "apples" of all Natives—red on the outside, white on the inside.

The resentment and bitterness that marks the reactions of most Native people who went through the residential school system is clear and can be found anywhere in Canada where this system was in vogue. A young Indian lawyer in Manitoba told us of being slapped repeatedly whenever as a boy he was caught speaking his native Cree. Now in his early thirties, his story illustrates how re- cently these repressive practices took place.

The aim of the schools was assimilation. The children usually were forced to spend at least 10 months-a-year without seeing their parents, due to the high costs of transporting them from the cen- trally located school to the villages and settlements they called home. They had to learn to speak English and to regard the life their par- ents and relatives lived as dirty, pagan, and uncivilized. Even when residential school staff came in contact with those who could man- age to visit parents, we were told, there was an attitude of coldness that made them seem like intruders.

One attractive woman at Whitehorse, in her early 40's, told us of having her hair cut off for the entire year, because in her lone- liness, she had run away from the Carcross school. A soft-spoken but quietly bitter person, she said that many of the difficulties that Indian people were living through today, especially those of early or middle-age, could be attributed to the harsh and often inhumane treatment they received at church-run schools.

The staff members of the schools varied. Many were dedicated if poorly trained and had, according to their own lights and the strict rules laid down for them by the churches, the best interests of their charges at heart. But the sisters, lay brothers, and priests of the Roman Catholic church and, to an even greater degree (because they were often more inflexible and pietistic), the lay men and women and priests of the Anglican Church, dealt with their students as "charges" or wards in a most autocratic and paternalistic fashion.

The residential schools were run efficiently and with great frugality, since until late in their existence they were supported almost entirely from church funds. Only in 1958 was considerable government money put into their operation, and by 1969 church contacts with the government had been terminated except in the Northwest Territories.

While many ex-staffers of the school system react angrily to suggestions that they performed less than adequately, former students claim that any incentive they had to independent action or thought was promptly squelched. Pupils were told what to do down to the last detail.

Former employees of the church-school system, regardless of denominational affiliation, tend to attribute complaints by their former pupils to a lack of gratitude for what was done. "Sure we made mistakes and there were failures. Perhaps we were too strict. But if the churches hadn't gone in and brought those kids out to school, the very leaders of the Native organizations today wouldn't be able to read or write. They never acknowledge that," a former administrator pointed out to us.

But most of the "graduates" we talked with said the standard of instruction was in many cases so low that few people ever reached an academic level that enabled them to enter high school. It is noteworthy that most of the few university graduates and professional people have come from the post-war years when students started to go to schools in the communities and more-and-more of the church schools became only residences. Even then the structured life at the church hostel and the irrelevance of public school curricula for Native pupils did little to raise the standard of this education.

Even today, with massive amounts of money being spent on buildings and equipment, the dropout rate is staggering, and more-and-more Native organizations want the school system brought under their control. During a tour of an Inuit-white high school in Frobisher Bay, we saw classrooms, labs, and vocational training rooms that rivalled anything in southern Canada. The only problem was that girls were being taught to cook southern foods in radiant heat ovens, when they would have to return to settlements to cook Native foods over oil stoves. Young boys were given mechanical and wood-working instruction in shops with the latest equipment available, when they would probably have to return to settlements and repair a snowmobile under much more primitive conditions. The educational system today may have higher academic standards and better qualified teachers, but its relevance to the social structures of the Native people of the North is little better than it was 30 years ago.

Heavy criticism of the divisiveness of the churches on reserves and the lack of equal opportunity within the ranks of the clergy is voiced in many quarters. There are few Native clergy in any church, and they come mostly from a period prior to World War II and have generally been relegated to isolated or smaller parishes. There are no Native bishops in either Anglican or Roman Catholic churches and none on the immediate scene. In the Anglican church a couple of clergy have been close contenders for bishoprics in predominantly Native dioceses but in both cases were edged out by white men in elections where whites predominate in the synods. A major breakthrough in the Anglican church came a few years ago when it appointed a Kwakuitl priest from British Columbia, the Reverend Ernie Willie, as an executive on its national staff.

Churches have often been justifiably accused of dividing tribes, bands, reservations, and even families, when one group would adhere to the Anglican church, another to the Roman Catholic, and perhaps a third to the United Church. In recent years, definite inroads into communities where people have belonged to one of the older churches have been made by Pentecostal, Nazarene, and B'Hai sects, causing further disruption and confusion in already fragmented villages. The disruption stems not only from denominational rivalries but from various churches buying up or acquiring large tracts of land in reserves which today are considered valuable and which the churches are not always prepared to give up, although the three larger denominations have a very recent policy of turning over church lands to the local bands, retaining only the immediate land the church building sits on. Very often, a kind of caste system was introduced, either deliberately or accidentally, in villages where the missionary sat at the top of the social heap, and the catechists, church wardens, deacons, and so on down the ladder held their status from their association with the European missionary.

While this critical look at the church can be mitigated by the many flexible, humane, and humble men and women who dedicated their lives to serving their God, it is of little consequence to a race of people who feel disrupted, alienated, and threatened with assimilation—to many this implies real or cultural genocide—in which the church assisted, albeit with the best motivation.

In 1969, the Anglican Church of Canada commissioned Dr. Charles Hendry, then director of the School of Social Work at the University of Toronto, to assess its work with Native peoples. In looking at Anglican involvement—about 25 percent of all Indians and 85 percent of the Inuit in Canada are Anglican—Hendry, in dispassionate and sociological terms was highly critical.

> The church (as well as government) in its official structure and policy took on increasingly an attitude of paternalism towards the Indians who were treated as children rather than as adults, with the focus being on conversion in another worldly context. The educational process tended to emphasize institutional membership in a white society and "in church" responsibilities such as being lay reader or catechist, etc. There was little real evidence of development towards indigenous and self-reliant leadership that would assist the Indians to assume responsibilities to deal with problems confronting them in a changing pluralistic, Canadian society.[3]

The list of the churches' past sins of omission and commission could go on indefinitely, but much of that has changed although individuals still retain many of their rigid and autocratic attitudes. The main thing is to realize that the early days of all the churches in the Canadian North and West represented much of what society at that time itself believed. There was bigotry and even racism. Natives were clearly thought to be an inferior race to be assimilated as quickly as possible into white, European society, or at least, taught to accept the cultural, religious, and moral values of that society. The churches achieved this goal only too well.

But today, more-and-more Native leaders see the church as one of the few institutions left in the Canadian scene that is prepared, at least at the policy-making level, to stand unabashedly and in penitence at their side against the encroachment of big government and big business. Only this year, all the major denominations have made Native affairs and the violation of Northern resources the major emphasis of their social action departments.

The Canadian Catholic Conference of Bishops made this subject the topic of their eloquent and prestigious Labor Day message to the Canadian people,[4] sharply criticizing the role of both government and multi-national corporations for allowing a rampant consumer society to place Northern resources of hydro, oil, and natural gas ahead of the land claims of the Natives.

The Anglican Church of Canada's General Synod, the top

level of more than one million church members, stated bluntly and unanimously that there must be no further Northern development of any kind until land claims were settled, and that present projects must be limited so that negotiations can be undertaken without fear.

The United Church of Canada works closely with the other two denominations, and in 1975, allocated national staff and some $70,000 to programs requested by Native groups. It also flatly stated that Northern development must not be a priority for Canadians at the expense of Native land claims.

Mennonites, Lutherans, Presbyterians, and other churches also have turned their backs on paternalism and assimilation in favour of self-determination for Natives.

In Northwest British Columbia, Northern Manitoba, and the Northwest Territories particularily, full-time and part-time clergy and lay people are assisting Native organizations in fighting specific projects where Native rights and lands are in jeopardy.

The change in attitudes came slowly, but by the time the Indian residential school contracts were terminated at the request of the churches in 1969, the dye was cast and new directions indicated. Perhaps the "Centennial Profile of Indians and Eskimos," presented to the General Synod of the Anglican Church of Canada at Ottawa in 1967, summed it up for all the churches when it called for "forgiveness regarding Anglican participation in the perpetuation of injustices to Indians."

Certainly the report bears out the thesis, long held by government and many white Christians, that it was only a matter of time before the Native would disappear from the face of Canada. The report stressed, and other denominations have followed suit to a greater or lesser degree, the indigenization of Native leadership. This was to become the keystone of the new social policy of the churches towards Native people, while it gropes towards defining some old problems and dealing with new ones. Its first tentative steps sound mild in the context of today's more militant demands by Native organizations, but in the light of Canada's Centennial year, given the essential conservatism of the churches, they were enlightened and forward-looking, clearing the way for today's more sincere support.

After encouraging the churches to take a new approach to Native people within their own constituency and to experiment, research, and plan ways in which the church might discover what it can learn from Natives, the report appealed for the churches to support "emerging new Indian organizations at the federal and pro-vincial levels, even though they are non-sectarian." Even then the churches were realizing that Natives had to start the course towards determining their own existence.

It was in the late 1960's and early 70's that the term "red power" was picked up as a follow-through to the black-power move-ment in the United States. The churches of that time saw something positive in this manifestation of a new sense of identity among Natives, supporting what they chose to call "Indian power" as a method of social action that should be regarded as a creative step toward self-determination, and called for encouragement rather than passive reaction.

It was the Anglican Church, not usually known for innovation, that continued the impetus for changed attitudes towards the Native people, partly because of the times, partly because of its leadership, partly, no doubt, from a genuine sense of penitence at having failed the Native people in both a political and cultural sense. The Hendry Report made—and the church subsequently adopted—some sweeping recommendations based on three major imperatives: the churches must mobilize their members into determined political action at all levels; they must co-operate with all interested agencies in running development and social service projects; and they must be prepared to try new experiments using "social and behavioral sciences." His nine recommendations stressed ecumenical partici-pation, changed attitudes, new personnel policies, new training poli-cies, adequate funding for Native involvement by the churches, and above all, an ecumenical "facility" for implementing the Hendry Report, known now by its popular title, *Beyond Traplines*.

Interestingly enough, while the Hendry Report was seen by many Christians as a radical document for any national church to buy into—and certainly, most did—there was no emphasis on land claims or resource development. But now, six years later, with many aspects of the Hendry Report fulfilled, the churches have gone "Be-yond Traplines" in their support for Native land claims and a more planned Northern development process and are in the vanguard of reform.

While the churches were engaged at many levels both indivi-dually and jointly, nationally and locally, there were three major developments in 1975, two involving denominations (although with distinct ecumenical overtones) and a third an interchurch project, that make it clear why Native organizations across Canada say the change in the churches in the last six years casts them in the new role of ally and partner rather than the more traditional paternalistic approach.

The Inter-Church Task Force on Northern Flooding

Concerned with the lack of information on Northern Manitoba's Churchill River diversion project, a group of United Church, Mennonite, and Roman Catholic people formed this inter-church project and named a Roman Catholic priest, the Rev. Bryan Teixeira, as its secretary. Its stated purpose was "to find ways and means of arriving at equal negotiation procedures between the Northern communities and the government of Manitoba." It quickly moved to expand its base from Manitoba to get support from national churches, and the Anglican, United, and Roman Catholic churches responded.

One of its major endeavours was to sponsor, in September 1975, under the leadership of C. Rhodes Smith, former Chief Justice of the Province of Manitoba, public hearings into the project. This procedure, while lacking the power of subpeona or hearing evidence under oath, was conducted publicly to draw attention to the obvious failings of the process. The process of public involvement in the Churchill diversion had been effectively halted some time ago (see Chapter 6) and as the project progressed, the Inter-Church Task Force, in their investigations, became increasingly more aware of the urgent need to provide some kind of vehicle for the people of Manitoba to voice their concerns to government and Hydro policy makers. The model for these hearings was based on United States citizen-called hearings which were quite often connected with developmental and environmental controversies and based on tribunals set up in London and Stockholm by Bertrand Russell to try International war crimes coming out of Viet Nam.

For three days in Winnipeg and another day in Nelson House (one of the Native communities that will bear the brunt of the diversion), Mr. Justice Smith and his six member independent panel,[5] with expertise in law, engineering, biology, anthropology, and ethics, listened patiently to some fifty submissions—some oral, some written —by concerned people from all over northern and southern Manitoba. Church groups, citizens groups, chiefs, and old men from Northern communities, environmentalists, and engineering consultants moved to the microphones and probed every angle of the pro-

ject from the impact of land, wildlife, people, and the exploitation
of human rights, to the rationale used by the power planners.

Officials from Manitoba Hydro were invited to submit a brief
but refused, saying the hearings were a "put up job." Two representatives from the provincial government—Stewart Martin, special
advisor to Premier Edward Schreyer, and Sidney Green, minister of
Mines, Resources and Environmental Management—appeared before the hearings to answer questions and ultimately stick to their
previous positions that the Churchill River diversion was right for
all Manitobans. Justice Smith and his panel now face the formidable
task of considering all the features of the Hydro development and
of presenting a report and recommendations to the task-force—and
Premier Schreyer has promised to review the briefs! But whatever
the outcome, the voice of the people is at last beginning to be
heard.

But the real impact of the Inter-Church Task Force was to
raise the ethical questions—a practice which the churches might do
well to emulate elsewhere, for in our opinion, one of the things the
churches could do best, and do least, is to focus, for Canadians, the
moral issues implicit in the actions and consequences of big government and its handmaidens, industry and Crown corporations. What
are the ethical questions lying behind the actions of Manitoba
Hydro and the NDP government?

Speaking to the inter-church project last year, Cass Booy, one
of the group of academics opposing the Churchill River diversion
project, proposed these issues for the committee. They are valid, as
they relate to any Northern resource project.

> I would not expect the churches to judge whether the project (the
> Churchill River diversion) makes economic sense; I would not expect
> them to declare themselves on issues of resource development or the
> quality of the environment except in rather general terms. Even the
> social development of the Native communities is a topic where the
> churches are well advised to tread carefully. But the churches cannot
> avoid the moral issue involved in the Churchill River diversion, nor
> may they avoid being very specific about it. And, regarding the ques-
> tion of extending real and practical help to the communities in-
> volved, the first step is to stand openly and officially and wholeheart-
> edly beside them. Only then can the work of restoration begin.[6]

It is this moral position that has been the churches' strongest justi-
fication for taking on the might of government, the resources of
Hydro, and the utter indifference of southern Manitobans.

The first moral issue the inter-church committee has tried to face Manitobans with, is the morality of the expropriation of Indian land. The theory behind this particular expropriation is the belief that all Manitobans will benefit from the diversion and subsequent production of power; therefore, the Natives should be compensated either by negotiation or through the courts. The basic assumption underlying any expropriation is that there is a community of concern for the whole province, and therefore, expropriation is valid. The analogy is sometimes used, with perhaps more truth in it than most of us would care to consider, that if the United States should decide that keeping all oil and gas reserves in Canada for the benefit of Canadians is against the best interests of the North American continent, we would not talk about negotiation. We would reject the North American continent idea as rubbish, and rightly so!

A similar moral situation exists in Manitoba, one which the government declines to even consider. Indians have been exploited for so long that they have never been considered, either by whites or themselves, as part of the province of Manitoba, except in some vague geographical sense. They do not see their interests as part of the total community, which it is alleged will benefit from the diversion.

The other moral issue—and again one which does not win the inter-church committee any popularity contests—is that of equal treatment for all members of that larger community that is known as Manitoba.

A few years ago when the levels of Lake Winnipeg were being altered to become part of Hydro's power source, the waters were not raised beyond a level which was considered safe for cottagers, most of whom come from southern Manitoba. It was not an economic decision, since it would have been of more benefit to Hydro if the water levels had gone higher. The decision was purely political. But when it comes to dealing with the property rights, treaty rights, reserve rights, life style rights of the Indians of the North, the only consideration we hear about is economic. Obviously the people and resources of the North are mere commodities to be dealt with as economic "things."

The inter-church committee raised, and continues to raise, the question of fair compensation. The expropriations without previous discussion amount to legalized robbery. How does one compare an estimate of the loss of fisheries, based solely on the decline in the fish population, with the development of a Hydro project? Such factors as the difficulty of marketing, securing, and finding fish

as a result of the flooding is not considered. The moral issue, therefore, the inter-church group says, is not just expropriation and compensation; it is the whole question of the loss of an essential resource
and an established way of life. The basic question, the basic moral
issue—the outcome of which is crucial to all Northern development—
is whether power (gas, oil, or transportation) can be developed without destroying the natural and human resources. It is more than
just a power hungry economy versus a quaint way-of-life. But it still
takes millions more dollars to develop resources *after* land claims
are settled, and without devastating the lives and the land of the
people who live there.

The inter-church committee, having raised these and other
moral issues, is faced with the question that all concerned groups
must grapple with. The Northern communities of Manitoba are
faced with a traumatic situation, regardless of whether the churches
pose the moral questions or not. So what can be done? Two things,
the inter-church committee has decided.

In the *long run* the church must stand, as Booy suggested to
them, beside the Native people morally, financially, and officially,
during the hard struggle through the courts and the negotiating
process. What is happening in Northern Manitoba—and in James
Bay, the Northwest Territories, and Northwest British Columbia—is
a perpetuation of what has been going on in Canada for 100 years.
It will take a long time to rectify, and the churches can do much to
re-establish their credibility with the Natives by not deserting them
in the long run, when they are beginning to feel more and more
isolated.

Using a biblical parallel, the inter-church committee says that
on the *short term* they must, like the Old Testament prophet, Na-
than, stand up alone, if necessary, and point the finger squarely at
the Manitoba government and Manitoba Hydro and say, "thou art
the man." Only then can the process of rebuilding begin. In other
words, as Cass Booy told them, you start by aligning yourselves
clearly on one side. There is no way the churches can support the
Natives in their just cause and at the same time remain straddling
the fence.

The Anglican Church of Canada

This is where it might be said to have all started—this new
wave of concern for Natives and for *their* aspirations—at least as far

as the churches are concerned. The Anglican Church is both a regional (diocesan) and a national (General Synod) church, and it was on both these fronts that it showed a new and refreshing approach to implementing the now six-year-old Hendry Report.

Out in Northwest British Columbia lies the huge, sprawling Diocese of Caledonia, starting at Prince Rupert on the coast and including the Queen Charlotte Islands, and running east half way across the province to Fort St. John, and north to the Yukon border. It includes, ironically, almost the entire area to be "developed" under the Northwest British Columbia plan (described in Chapter 7). It has had, historically, a long and sometimes repressive association with the British Columbia coastal Indians, dating back to pre-Confederation days. But its relations with the proud and independent Nishga, especially in the last decade, have been strong. In the last 10 years the priests serving in the Nass Valley, where the nation has its deep ties with the land and the rivers, have been adopted into the tribe according to its customs. The bishop, Douglas Hambidge, is an adopted Nishga and takes his membership in the tribe seriously. This is not the same as being made an "honorary chief" during an election campaign; it has deep spiritual meaning both for the recipient, as well as for the family bestowing the adoption.

Ancient religious ceremonials, including dancing, music, and the beautiful "button blanket" robe, are now part of all major feasts, both of a tribal and church nature. Much of this ancient ceremonial had been lost during the repressive days of the Potlatch Law, but now, with the encouragement of the church, it is being revived and honored. So it was natural, when the Nishga became alarmed at reports that development was about to move in on their land claims settlement, and perhaps encroach on their valley without their permission, that Bishop Hambidge should be asked to appoint the Rev. John Stokes, in 1974, as liaison officer (see Chapter 7) to help interpret the scheme.

After Stokes had been in office about a year, the synod of the diocese met in Fort St. John, bringing together clerical and lay representatives, including a number of Indian delegates and a strong group from the Nass Valley. Perhaps prodded by Stokes' work, but also under heavy pressure from both clerical and lay delegates, the synod passed a number of resolutions—aimed at the national church and two levels of government—that if implemented, would leave no doubt in anyone's mind where the Anglican Church of Canada stood in regard to Native people.

The meeting urged all Christians in all churches to be prepared to support, if requested by the Natives, all non-violent acts of protest or direct action aimed at settling land claims. This would include sit-ins, blockades, and other forms of demonstration and protest. The synod went one step further and demanded that the federal government halt any planned development on any unsurrendered land until aboriginal claims were settled. It then moved out of its own area and asked that this resolution apply anywhere in the North. And, turning to Victoria and its own provincial government whose foot-dragging has slowed the negotiation process to a standstill, it asked the British Columbia government, as a full partner, to start dealing with aboriginal claims. The intended effect of these resolutions was to discourage any excuse by any levels of government to delay dealing with the issue.

Other dioceses have taken more cautious steps, often leaving individual clergy to fight the battles without the full weight of the synod behind them. At the national level, as an extension of the Hendry report, a number of concrete steps had been taken prior to the General Synod of 1975 at Quebec City.

Back in 1971, the church had granted $10,000 from its prestigious Primate's World Relief and Development Fund (a special fund outside regular church donations, under the chairmanship of the primate, which supports relief and development projects around the world) to help the Nishga appeal their action against the British Columbia provincial government to the Supreme Court of Canada. In 1974 the same fund allocated $15,000, which was matched by an anonymous donor, to assist the Indian Brotherhood of the Northwest Territories in fighting the federal government's appeal of the caveat on 450,000 square miles of land.

The church had built into its national structure a sub-committee on Native Affairs, made up of Native people, to advise the national church, a Committee of Concern for James Bay, and a Council on the North; and its social action department was making the role of multi-national corporations in Northern development a matter of close scrutiny. It was not surprising, therefore, that by the time General Synod rolled around in 1975, Native affairs and Northern development was the key—and only—social issue the 350 clerical and lay delegates from across Canada studied in depth. James Wah-Shee came from the Northwest Territories to make his special plea for alternative models of development in the North; the Nishga came from British Columbia, and the Cree from the

Prairies and Northern Ontario to lend their voice to a growing demand for justice and self-determination.

The Native people of Canada, who have any connection with the Anglican Church, have a powerful ally in the person of the primate of the Anglican Church of Canada, its titular head, the Most Rev. Edward (Ted) Scott. Long before he reached his present position of leadership, Scott sounded a lonely voice in church councils, calling for the rights of Native people to be determined by the Natives themselves, rather than the we-know-what's-best-for-you attitude of much of the church.

The day the issue was to be debated at General Synod in June 1975, it was introduced by the newly elected Bishop of the Arctic, John Sperry, in whose diocese lies almost all the Inuit population of Canada and the powerful and vocal Native organizations of the Northwest Territories. The people of his diocese face the ravages of the James Bay Hydro project, the Strathcona Sound Mining development on North Baffin Island, the Polar Gas Pipeline from the Arctic Islands, the Mackenzie Valley gas pipeline and whatever transportation systems are to follow, plus a host of petroleum and mineral explorations that can only lead to further resource development schemes.

Sperry himself has spent 25 years in the Western Arctic and is a skilled linguist, speaking various Inuit dialects fluently. His introductory speech to the synod left no doubt where that august and often establishment-oriented body should go. Using the analogy of the parable of the Good Samaritan, he asked the synod what it should do about the robbed, beaten, and broken body lying beside the road, that was Canada's Native people of today, as the white population and its governments passed by on the other side.

"We must be like the Good Samaritan, who not only bound up the wounds inflicted by a cruel and heartless society that left a race of people to die, but who stood clearly beside this man and continued to support him when all others had abandoned him, and helped him morally and with action."

"If we today fail to place ourselves clearly on the side of Native people in Canada, and instead pass by on the other side by refusing to state clearly with words and actions where we stand, then we must return to our homes from this place and hang our heads in shame."

The synod gave the primate the authority he needed to tackle all levels of government and to take a clear stand on the side of the Natives. The decision-making process at all levels of government across Canada must, synod said, involve Native people in all aspects of planning and implementation. No further policies or actions which affect the lives of Native people should be developed by DIAND or any other branch of government unless Natives are directly consulted. Land claims must be settled fairly. Money must be provided by the federal government for research into treaties and aboriginal rights. The church must monitor this process with other churches and regularly contact government about the progress being made.

Reiterating Caledonia's resolution that all planned development be halted until claims are settled, the national church went further and told the federal government it believed that to take land claim positions such as the one in the Northwest Territories less than seriously was wrong, and that to attach prior conditions or threats to negotiations was not approaching the matter in good faith. The Anglican Church had come a long way from the days when Native people were invited in by the back door.

The Roman Catholic Church

The position of the Roman Catholic church, which has by far the largest number of Indian and Metis members of any church in Canada, is especially unique in terms of its response to Northern development. The position of the Oblate fathers in the far North has taken the same about-face as that of the Anglican clergy. The priests, most of whom have European backgrounds, are now among the staunchest supporters of Native land claims, and their insistent demands that there be greater Native participation in decision-making in the North are pushing the more conservative hierarchies to make their stands clear.

Early this year, the Canadian Catholic Conference, which is the national arm of the bishops of the Roman Catholic church in Canada, containing both French and English-speaking sections, issued a working paper on Northern development, which posed, as did the Manitoba inter-church group, a series of ethical questions which church people, especially, should consider. While it takes the Native land claims just as seriously as do the other churches in Canada, it attempts to set them in a wider context, especially in the area of natural resource development and the uncontrolled use of energy in Canada and the United States.

The ethical issues of northern development constitute the major challenge for the social mission of the Church. In particular, the Church in the north is faced with a formidable task. The proposed industrial developments threaten to transform the basic social, cultural and economic way of life in northern communities. It would be premature to readily accept these changes as being inevitable. In any case, the mission of the Church in the north will have to be re-examined and revitalized in order to meet the test of what lies ahead.

The major responsibility, however, does not rest alone with the Church in the north. For the resources of the north are being made to serve the affluent energy demands of the south, both in Canada and the United States. It is our own southern controlled institutions that are primarily responsible for the exploitation of northern resources. The proposed industrial developments of the Canadian north, therefore, are properly social justice concerns for the Church as a whole.

In effect, the ethical issues of northern development challenge the Canadian Church to strengthen its mission for social justice in this country. The social mission of the church, in general, might be aimed at pursuing northern development policies based on reponsible stewardship of energy resources and the liberation of the Native peoples. This would call for co-ordinated action of the Church at both regional and national levels.[7]

Following this approach, the Canadian Catholic Conference agreed to make the subject of its annual Labor Day message for 1975, the exploitation of the Canadian North. Written through several drafts which were submitted for revision to the more than 100 bishops across Canada, the document *Northern Development: At What Cost?* when finally released in September, was a major social and theological statement for the whole country. Its language is poetic, almost biblical, and lends an air of prophecy in keeping with the magnitude of the poetry so often associated with the expressions of the Native people of Canada.

It deals with the energy crisis and the land—the Native peoples' attachment to it and the church's involvement—and offers concrete suggestions for a different approach. It is blunt in its condemnation of government, and private corporations. It raises questions that cannot be avoided by any serious Christian. It is without doubt the most dynamic, hard-hitting statement to come out of any church in support of Native people, and its challenges are applicable to any Canadian citizen, regardless of his involvement with any religious movement.

It remains to be seen whether Canada's "last frontier" will be developed according to the principles of justice and stewardship.

The next two years will be a crucial testing period. In some cases, final and irreversible decisions have already been made. In other instances, there may still be a chance to alter the course of development. The Mackenzie Valley pipeline proposals presently being reviewed by the Berger Commission and the National Energy Board could provide the real test.

As Christians, as citizens, we have a responsibility to insist that the future development of the Canadian North be based on social justice and responsible stewardship. As responsible citizens are *we* prepared to:

a) *study* one or more of the industrial projects in the northern parts of our provinces or the Territories?

b) *actively support* Native Peoples' organizations and public interest groups currently striving to change the policies of northern development?

c) *engage policy makers*, both federal and provincial, and local Members of Parliament in a public dialogue about the ethical issues of northern development?

d) *raise ethical questions* about corporations involved in northern development, especially those corporations in which church institutions may have shares?

e) *seek a just settlement* regarding specific church landholdings that are subject to native claims?

f) *design* education programs to examine personal life styles and change the patterns of wasteful energy consumption in our homes, churches, schools, and places of work?

g) *collaborate* with the other Canadian churches, in every way possible, in a common Christian effort to achieve the above objectives?

In the final analysis what is required is nothing less than fundamental social change. Until we as a society begin to change our own life styles based on wealth and comfort, until we begin to change the profit-oriented priorities of our industrial system, we will continue placing exorbitant demands on the limited supplies of energy in the North and end up exploiting the people of the North in order to get those resources.[8]

Churches with a history which included paternalism, attempting to wipe out Native culture, and which allied themselves with the white social values of their day, could hardly have been expected to make judgements such as the Canadian Catholic Conference has done in the preceding statement or take the unequivocal stands of the Anglican Church or raise the moral issues that the Manitoba inter-church group has done. Giant strides have been made, at least in rhetoric, to rectify the wrongs of the past.

What remains to be seen, and what the Native organizations are watching carefully, is whether the churches are prepared to put money, personnel, and corporate and individual action behind these brave words so that justice may actually be done.

Notes

1 *Treaty Days*, (Winnipeg: The Manitoba Indian Brotherhood, 1971), Preface.

2 *Beyond Traplines*, Charles Hendry, (Toronto: The Anglican Church of Canada, 1969), Page 6.

3 Ibid, Page 42.

4 *Northern Development: At What Cost?* the 1975 Labor Day Message, (Ottawa: Canadian Catholic Conference, Sept. 1, 1975.)

5 Serving along with Mr. Justice Smith was a panel of six: Mel Watkins, economist and consultant to the Indian Brotherhood of the Northwest Territories; Sandy Beardy, a trapper from Cross Lake, Manitoba; Dr. W. W. Koolage, assistant professor, department of anthropology, University of Manitoba; the Rev. Ernest Willie, consultant in Native Affairs, the Anglican Church of Canada, Toronto; Bishop H. J. Allan, Anglican bishop of the Diocese of Keewatin, Kenora, Ontario; and Dr. K. M. Adams, associate professor, faculty of engineering, University of Manitoba.

6Professor Cass Booy, addressing the Interchurch Task-Force on Northern Flooding, Winnipeg, Manitoba, November 25, 1974.

7 Tony Clarke, "The Development of the Canadian North: New Challenges for the Social Mission of the Canadian Church," (Social Affairs Desk, Ottawa: Canadian Catholic Conference, 1975.)

8 *Northern Development: At What Cost?*

The only way out of [our] dilemma is to change our manner of thinking. We do not have any energy crisis or a growth crisis. We are at a watershed and we must decide whether belief in man or belief in numbers will be the dominant philosophy of our public actions. The technocrats, down in the bowels of every government, believe in numbers and they send out their philosophy in economic analyses and demands. They get away with this because economics has become the religion of modern man.

Douglas J. Roche
Member of Parliament for
Edmonton-Strathcona in
To Care . . . To Share
Toronto, 1975
page 19

10

Alternatives

A Search for New Policies of Northern Development

From the beginnings of the fur trade, through the gold rushes, and up to the latest exploration programs, the North has always been looked on as a breadbasket for the south. An area of inhospitable climate fit only for Natives and a handful of hardy whites, the natural resources of the North have provided an opportune investment for the populated areas of Canada to exploit and deplete as rapidly and as economically as possible. This is a colonial style of development. It never occurs to government or private enterprise to return anything to the North. Secondary industry, long-term investment, and conservation are simply too expensive in that harsh country for profit-motivated development.

First, it was the fur-traders who, by the systematic slaughter of a once vast animal population, had decimated the fur-bearing species by the 1940's to a point where only a few people can now eke out any kind of existence from trapping. Today, even those who would live off the land find it so disrupted that only a handful of Inuit and Indians can still survive in the traditional ways. The fluctuations of the white population, following such booms as the Yukon gold rush, construction of the Alaska highway, and now oil exploration with the attendant "busts" that send hordes of "transients" south again, adds to the instability of the permanent residents of the North—the Natives and a small number of whites.

There is nothing to attract most whites except high wages and a sense of adventure. Once these largely temporary motivations are fulfilled or found wanting, the majority of people flee south to the more "civilized" parts of Canada. Outside the restrictive confines of government, there is too small an economic base to hold most southerners.

For the Native people, the loss of their land-based economy is further compounded by the deliberate herding together of small groups of people into larger, more easily administered settlements and the introduction of the wage economy. But, since even the wage economy in many Northern hamlets is small and fluctuates with the development market, many of the Natives quickly find themselves in the permanent state of being welfare recipients.

With the destruction of much of the opportunity to live off the land, they turn to alcohol, and their children, through the school system, pick up a taste for southern "amenities" without the means to buy them. Their Native languages are denigrated, and their parents' traditional ways are seen as inferior to the white man's ways; and the disrespect children have for their parents is even more apparent than it is in the south. For Natives, the family and the extended family unit has always been one of the strongest social ties in the culture.

When the school system has completed its work of destroying their ways, the children are then pushed out into the home settlements where there is no work or move to the few larger Northern towns or go south, where they quickly join the ranks of the urban poor and dispossessed. Contrary to the protestations of major resource developers, who in order to receive their licences from government will promise almost anything, the extraction of resources in the North does little for the people there except on a most fleeting basis.

The pattern goes something like this: first, a resource, say oil or natural gas, is explored and "discovered," next, if there is sufficient quantity to cover the higher costs of extraction and transportation, a "crisis" conveniently comes along, and then, the rush is on. The current energy crisis in Canada may end when Northern oil and gas are exhausted or when the energy giants decide to switch to another source of supply. But then the permanent residents of the area will be abandoned or driven to welfare following resource depletion, their survival skills destroyed or blunted; and there will be no possibility of their developing a viable economy of their own.

They become dependent on government, whose services must consequently be expanded, thereby increasing the bureaucracy and its attendant support systems, furnishing more jobs for southern social workers. Yellowknife and Whitehorse get bigger and better government housing and concrete buildings. The artificial towns of Frobisher Bay, Cambridge Bay, and Inuvik also grow, with increased alcoholism, prostitution, and degradation. As one "rush" for a Northern resource succeeds another, the depletion continues until there is nothing left but the mighty rivers, and in Northern Manitoba and Northern Quebec, we have seen what happens when there is only water left. It too is diverted south.

The future could not look bleaker for the Native people of the North. If the colonial concept of development continues, they will be reduced to a life of marginal semi-existence in sub-standard social conditions, the entire fabric of their culture destroyed. As matters continue there is no hope for any form of independence or self-directed activity. If this brief description does not equal cultural genocide and welfare slavery, then what does?

It is precisely the same pattern that was to be found 25 years ago in much of what is now called the Third World. Colonial powers extracted resources—both renewable and non-renewable—and returned only a colonial bureacracy to look after the "white man's burden"—the Native people of Africa, Asia, or Latin America. Even with independence, economic colonialism continued to the point where today we see 80 percent of the world's resources owned or controlled by 20 percent of the world's western white nations. And even when the OPEC countries raised their prices for oil to a level at least fair to them, the industrial West rose up in holy horror, turning its covetous eyes to the North, which they believe has no hope of achieving political independence.

It is our contention that Northern Canada, be it territorial or the area at the tops of the provinces, is a colonial outpost of the south, exploited and depleted in exactly the same way and with exactly the same policy—with a few modern refinements—as the African nations of the last century.

The future of the Native people though, lacks even the unifying goal of independence, since they are in a minority everywhere in Canada, except the Northwest Territories. It can only be through their land claim settlements, if they are allowed, that some measure of economic, and hence, cultural independence will come their way. At least they will have an opportunity to choose whether they will go the western-industrial-technological route or take a new and more truly indigenous direction such as has been postulated by Julius Nyerere, president of Tanzania in East Africa. It might be called the development of a Fourth World model, a name that George Manuel of the National Indian Brotherhood has given to the amalgam of Native peoples of Canada.

Before examining this alternative to colonial development though, there is a need to reassure white Canadians, especially Northern white Canadians, that to allow Native people the right to self-determination will be to their advantage as well.

Self-determination requires an economic base. Self-determination for Northern Natives, indeed for all Natives, requires, they say, that their economic independence be based on a new model of development which will incorporate many of the ideas of their ancestors while retaining the reality of the 20th and 21st centuries. One does not need to be a romantic to see that the present course of Western industrial development is a dead end. The crying need to alter course, to search for what the poor nations of the world are already calling "a new international economic order," corresponds to the Native peoples' demands for new policies of Northern development for this country. If it means a simple reversal of the present slavish devotion to technology, consumerism, and bigger-is-better, then Canada could do worse. Our present directions are towards larger cities and greater concentration of people and power in fewer centres. The Native suggestions that people live simpler, less complex lives in smaller centres, for example, would improve the quality of life for most people.

The opportunity exists to break the treadmill we are presently frantically running on, where possession mistakenly becomes the sum total of life. The treadmill keeps running because we refuse to challenge the assumption that we must keep churning out an endless supply of consumer products, all of which exhaust our natural resources at a suicidal rate. The Native people of Canada, perhaps unwittingly, are offering us the opportunity to take the risk of challenging the basic economic order and the basic assumptions of the Ottawa bureaucracy, which indicate the present course is the only one and it can continue indefinitely.

The second major reversal that alternative models of development might force us to look at would be of course to return ownership and control of Northern resources—particularly oil and gas—to Canada, and this way we would once again own the fossil fuels in the ground. All Canadian people would then reap the benefits of these commodities and see that they were used in a planned and responsible manner, rather than existing, as they do now, for the profits of giant corporations in the United States and elsewhere.

The North is no longer a forgotten giant populated by a few Natives. It is the "last frontier," the last great untapped repository of natural resources almost anywhere in the world.

If we follow present policies, which are developed on an ad hoc "crisis" basis, then outside control and ultimate depletion with no real benefit to Canada will result. But if we listen to the cries of the poor and oppressed people of the world and the demands of the Natives of our own country—that there is a better way of distributing the wealth and resources of this nation for the benefit of all Canadians—then we must take action immediately. Or it will be too late.

Shortly after the Anglican Church of Canada passed resolutions at its General Synod, asking that all planned development projects on the North be halted until Native land claims were settled, Jack McArthur, financial columnist for the *Toronto Star*, wrote in his June 20, 1975 column, that the church was advocating nonsense. He said to halt planned development in the North at this time would break faith with the oil companies, change the ground rules for exploration, and waste millions of exploration dollars already spent. In this incredibly myopic analysis, Mr. McArthur has missed the point. This is precisely the problem. Canadian energy needs are based on projections by energy companies on the invalid principles of a consumer-oriented society which assumes there are unlimited supplies of non-renewable resources.

The church is not saying these resources should never be developed, nor are the Native organizations. They are simply saying that land claims must be settled first, without the pressure of imminent construction, and secondly, that until proper planning and rational needs are developed, a pipeline, for example, will adversely interfere with the ecology, wreck what little is left of the traditional way of life, and block any hope of a new form of non-colonial development. What the churches and Native organizations are saying is that, if the present patterns continue, serious under-development of the Canadian North and its people will result, and Canada will have a "Third World" within its own boundaries.

Before any further massive industrial and resource development schemes are allowed to progress, the land claims must be settled, of course, but that will take time, and in that time an opportunity could be made available for the Canadian government to ask, and then try to answer, the serious questions raised from the Native claims. It is much more than a simple proposal to build a hydro dam or construct a pipeline. Technology has the ability to do these things. The questions to be raised involve the quality of a Canadian life-style, the right of minorities, the fragility of Northern eco-systems, consumption of energy, and accurate assessments of what our energy requirements and reserves really are.

To the colonial mind, these are "bleeding heart" generalizations which say that values based on human needs, as opposed to economic growth, are unrealistic. We insist that to continue in a mind-cast such as this is more unrealistic. All over the world, the poor and dispossessed are taking the law into their own hands and violently forcing decisions. We have an opportunity to prevent such desperate measures, by declaring a moratorium on massive projects such as James Bay, Nelson-Churchill, Northwest British Columbia, or Mackenzie Valley, until all the people of Canada have had an opportunity to decide whether such projects are in the public interest.

Informed discussion, under the present colonially-oriented bureaucracy in Ottawa with its cozy relationship to industry, is next to impossible, because they both ignore questions or respond to them with dishonest, partial, conditional, confusing, contradictory, or misleading answers. But however, we could take the time— all the time needed by the Native people to properly prepare their land claims with adequate funding—to have a full scale public and independent inquiry into Canada's energy needs and reserves.

In 1971, Joe Greene, then minister of energy, mines, and resources, told the Canadian people that Canada had 923 years' supply of oil and 392 years' supply of natural gas, and that we had better expand our exports before alternative energy sources made these fuels obsolete.

In 1974, just three years later, the National Energy Board was telling us we would have to start importing oil by 1982. The discrepancy is so unbelievable as to demand the most rigorous explanations, and underlines again the utter lack of any rational resource policy in Canada.

It is increasingly clear that it is not just the Natives who need time—based on their long-time occupancy of the land—to research and plan for their just share of the North's resources, but also, that all Canada needs the time to get some straight answers and new policies. Clearly the Native land claims will benefit all people. The consumption policies of the Canadian government should be changed to conservation policies. Alternative sources of energy must be developed. Just royalty and tax provisions, giving Native people a fair share of the revenue and reducing the exorbitant profits of the oil companies, must be set. Natural resource revenues must be used to improve the quality of life, instead of merely being pumped into economic growth. Exports of oil and gas to the United States should be halted and surpluses exported (at below international prices) to struggling Third World countries.

The model for Northern development that we would like to present for consideration, therefore, is the radical departure suggested by some of the Native land claims, particularly in the Northwest Territories. This radical departure is away from a tradition of land settlement that means extinguishment rather than preservation of rights. It is based on the growing awareness of the political consciousness of Native people, and the subsequent recognition of their needs and aspirations. Like the colonies of the new Third World, Native Northerners are demanding the right to initiate and control their own programs that affect their own lives. The latest "energy crisis" and the renewed focus on the North provides them with a unique opportunity to suggest—yes, and promote—an appropriate Northern development philosophy for Canada. The settlement of their land claims constitutes, in reality, a development plan for all the Canadian North.

The word development is bandied about in much of the emerging world, both in Canada and overseas. Its meaning varies with individuals but essentially there are two kinds: the colonial model, which we have described throughout this book, and the new model (sometimes called the Third World Model), which is essentially self-determination of economic development by the people of the country or area involved, with a sense of interdependence with other parts of the world or nation.

In September of 1967, the Tanzania African National Union (TANU) meeting in Arusha, prepared a declaration signed by Julius Nyerere, which set this former colony of Great Britain on a course of self-determination and self-control, which in the short run may make its material wealth less than those of its neighbors

(who opted for western-style capitalism) but in the long run promises economic, social, and human growth for all. The Arusha Declaration said in part:

> Any action which does not increase the people's say in determining
> their own affairs or running their own lives is not development and
> retards them, even if the action brings them a little better health
> and a little more bread.

It is this philosophy that underlies the alternative form of
Northern development for the Native people. Native people, and
anyone else on the economic fringe, have been the objects of a
development policy which may have raised their material standards
in a marginal and questionable way, but in return has taken away
any independence they had. There is no form of mental acrobatics
or high-flown rhetoric that can call that development.

Today there are vast and expensive socio-economic studies
underway just about everywhere that energy projects are planned.
Consultants, all with masters degrees in sociology, are getting rich
by confusing people and governments with the jargon of their
trade. It is as if a deliberate attempt were being made to con the
North with rhetoric. The argument advanced by the consultants
to government and industry, knowing full well who pays their
fees, is that the impact of Northern development can be "ameli-
orated" and "counter-balanced" by enormous outlays in the public
sphere. That means, in plain English, welfare and dependency. It
means, in plain English, independence can be bought. It means, in
plain English, assimilation will be forced once more on Natives
where the reserves and Indian Act failed.

What people who accept this type of jargon fail to recognize
is the historical fact that what has passed in the hinterland of
Northern Canada for development exists solely for the benefit of
multi-national petroleum corporations. There is not one Northern
development project that we know of that can be said to exist for
the benefit of the people in the region, and it is highly questionable if any exists solely for national benefit. When all the fog of
jargon and rhetoric has lifted, the essential question of land claims
and Northern development policy is the same. The answer lies in
what development philosophy each side subscribes to.

A development philosophy which seeks to make the hinterland dependent on and exist for the urban south will result in
the kind of economic and resource policies we have today in Canada
and the kind of Native land settlements that have made the south-

ern reservations one of the worst blots on Canada's unearned reputation for justice and equality. On the other hand, a policy of development which puts real value on regional needs, increased self-determination, and economic independnce puts the emphasis on control rather than compensation when dealing with land claims. This means ownership within the region of the resources and the resulting economic independence from their development. The provinces of Canada already have this right.

The minister of Indian Affairs has a philosophy, if it may be graced with that name, of compensating the Natives for the loss of the traditional and continued use of their land over which they have aboriginal title. The Native people have a philosophy based on the Third World model which seeks formal recognition of their rights over the land which they have been using and continue to use.

As James Wah-Shee puts it, "We are not interested in being paid off for loss of a way of life but for the right and the freedom to construct our own alternatives for development from the bedrock of our past. We even reserve the right to be wrong about some of our directions. Certainly we are not going to be bulldozed into putting a price tag on our freedoms."

Natives are rejecting the attitude that money will purchase anything in return for laborers' jobs on pipelines initiated outside their land and outside their sphere and largely irrelevant to their needs. It would be 100 percent accurate to say that if the Indian people of the Northwest Territories had been asked to accept the responsibility for designing the shape of Northern development over the next 50 years, the last project they would have suggested would be the pipeline they are being forced to consider.

The shape of Northern development, if the government is willing to negotiate in good faith, cannot be decided any longer without the essential input of Native people. Such a role is their right on two counts—ownership of the land and Canadian citizenship. The development of their land claim is a process that the Canadian government would do well to emulate. Contrary to charges that Native leaders have become "professional Indians," out of touch with their communities, the Northwest Territories is taking the stance that the eventual land settlement will be rooted in the communities. It is a long process involving band councils and Metis locals in each village, then a regional process, and finally the 14-member negotiating team elected by the status and non-status Indians. Each community is being asked to prepare and record its land-use patterns, economic base, and eventually to look at the economic future they wish to develop. It is a slow process, but one which Native people have always uniquely employed— CONSENSUS.

This is true community development and bears a striking resemblance to the Nyerere model in Tanzania, Africa, a country many of the Native people have never heard of.

The alternate model of development is emerging from the locality for development, the community, and this is where the initiative should lie, not imposed from above by government or industry. It is a process that citizens' groups in many urban centres of Canada are beginning to study, as they see themselves swallowed up by forces they can no longer control. It is a way of preserving the heritage we so cherish—the heritage of individual freedom and democracy.

As this process slowly unfolds—and it has now been going on for two years—the reason for the Northwest Territories slogan, "land not money," becomes more clearly apparent. The land-use surveys, laboriously worked over with people in the villages, many who cannot read or write, none of whom is a sociologist or anthropologist, are being transferred to regional maps, and a pattern of usage is beginning to emerge.

What appears on a white man's map, no matter how detailed, as a roadless, uninhabited wilderness, when inscribed with the activities of Native peoples, begins to show a tangle of lines that at first seem aimless and insignificant but slowly develop into a pattern of thorough use and occupancy. This design of development differs radically from that usually employed anywhere in Canada today. People are presented with proposals for high-rises, airports, and throughways and told they must only "react" to these specific proposals initiated in the ivory tower planning offices of industry and government. If the reactions of people opposing the Pickering airport or the Nelson-Churchill River diversion indicate that the project is totally bad, then government moves to deny them any further initiative and simply imposes its wishes. Occasionally modifications can be pushed through if opposition is too vociferous and an election is in the offing, but generally speaking, citizen-participation is discouraged and apathy encouraged.

Through this process, thousands of projects both large and small but equally undesirable from a human viewpoint are approved each year in Canada, a nation which proudly boasts of its "participatory democracy," a phrase which will haunt Liberal administrations for years to come. What's more, by abdicating their right to participation, Canadians are watching their country drift dangerously close to a total lack of cohesive—and coherent—national, regional, or community policy on anything, especially in terms of resource development.

It is nothing short of dishonest for the Canadian government or the multi-national and Crown corporations to argue that pipelines, hydro projects, and other colonial-style development projects will have a beneficial impact on Native people, or even that they fulfil regional needs. Of the thousands of workers on the James Bay hydro construction site, there are only 70 Natives employed, and they fill the most menial positions. There is no known benefit except colored TV for the people of Northern Manitoba, and of course, the Mackenzie Pipeline case is uncertain as yet. And while the federal government is committed to the Mackenzie Valley pipeline in principle, there are many indications that it too is not a national priority or that there are urgent Canadian needs that must be filled. The priority exists in the investment needs of multi-national corporations and their accomplices in Ottawa.

Alternative models of development, based on the philosophy that colonialism is not an acceptable practice in Canada, anymore than it is in Africa or Asia or Latin America, mean that Canada must be prepared to take the hard decisions necessary to control its own resources for the use of human rather than economic advancement; it must be prepared to deal justly with Native land claims, and it must be prepared to involve the people of this rich nation in decision-making.

To implement these new models of development, we suggest the following resumé as a pattern that could start the process of dismantling colonial development and support the Native people in their attempt to reach fair agreement which will, ultimately, be in the best interest of all Canadians.

——Social, cultural, and economic well-being cannot be separated, and such well-being for Canada's Natives will result in a better quality of life for all Canadians if they will press all governments to allow Natives to achieve their goals.

——The land is the key to this social, cultural, and economic well-being for Native people, and without economic control of the

resources of the land they have historically and traditionally occupied, they face genocide.

——The legal rights to this land, either through treaty or
aboriginal title, should give undisturbed possession of the land to
the Natives, and formal recognition of this must be enshrined in
law.

——Whether the Natives wish to pursue their traditional
land-based livelihood of hunting, fishing, and trapping in an inti-
mate relationship with nature, or whether they wish to use the
land as a base for economic development, it must be their decision.
In either case it is only when they have direct control of these
lands that they can ensure themselves of a life style in keeping with
their own aspirations.

——The federal government has a constitutional obligation
to protect and promote the best interests and rights of the Native
people. Therefore, it is their responsibility to provide adequate
financial and other resources, without strings attached or threats
implied, to allow the Native people to undertake the necessary
research to document and present their claims.

——Time pressures must be removed so that sufficient time to
clearly prepare their claims is provided.

——All development projects currently planned or underway
must be halted or postponed wherever it appears that Native
people have a valid claim on the land, either by treaty or by aboriginal rights. These projects must be delayed until the full extent
of title has been established, and Natives must not ever again be
forced to negotiate under the pressure of these projects, no matter
how loudly multi-national petroleum corporations might scream
or governments threaten.

——Each negotiation process must be treated on its own
merits, whether it be the reassessment of a treaty or the aboriginal
claim, and one settlement should not necessarily be used as a precedent or guideline for another.

——Treaties signed in the period prior to 1923 should all be
reassessed on the basis of fairness, understanding, interpretation,
and fulfilment of promise, and wherever any of these criteria fail,
the treaty should be renegotiated and reparations paid where violations are clear.

——There must never again be any decisions made involving
the policy or programs for any Native people without prior consultation and involvement of the Natives.

——The Indian Act must be rewritten by Natives and the present DIAND dismantled, giving Native Affairs its own portfolio.

For too long the attitude of government, industry, and individual white people is that a Native person fits a stereotype— poor . . . lazy . . . dirty . . . drunk . . . undernourished . . . irresponsible . . . parasite . . . liar. A shocking list! For this reason, combined with what seems to be an innate racism among many Canadians, the argument has always been that Natives cannot be trusted to run their own affairs and that the only people who know best are white civil servants.

After reading the annual reports of the auditor-general, one wonders if this argument holds water for any level of government. But the truth is, we are afraid to entrust the lives and land of Canada's Natives to themselves. They might make mistakes; they might spend their money foolishly; they might not pander to the oil companies; they might educate their children their own way. So for these, and a host of other reasons, we must keep them under our control. Maybe yet, they'll go away and assimilate, and then the Indian problem, which is really a white man's problem, will go away.

Instead, why not let the Natives do things their way for a change. Instead of always patting Native people on the head, why not try to learn something from them? Our way hasn't worked. We might be surprised at what they have to offer!

Acknowledgements

This book has been the product of many thousands of miles of travel by the authors. We talked with hundreds of people in both territories and four provinces. We spent many hours in Ottawa and covered innumerable meetings and conferences. To acknowledge the help we received from every individual would take many pages, but a few people were especially important to us, as much for the support we received as for the information they supplied us.

Without the financial and staff support of the Anglican, United, and Roman Catholic churches, the book never would have been researched or written. Elizabeth Loweth (United Church), Tony Clarke (Roman Catholic), and Russ Hatton and Ernie Willie (Anglican) kept us in touch with the churches. Kitson Vincent at Canadian Arctic Resources Committee in Ottawa was invaluable in helping to sort through the maze at DIAND.

Travelling across Canada we gradually got to know the Native people: James Wah-Shee, Gina Blondin, and George Erasmus at the Indian Brotherhood of the Northwest Territories, Willie Joe in the Yukon, Bill McKay of the Nishga Tribal Council, Ken Young and Joe Keeper in Northern Manitoba, and many others. Without the exceptional co-ordinating ability of Mary Parisian, executive secretary of the Canadian Churchman, the manuscript might not have reached the publisher in any usable state.

But there is one acknowledgement which, above all else, must come from our hearts. It was Ted Scott (Archbishop Edward W. Scott, Primate of the Anglican Church of Canada) who first felt that what we knew needed to be said. It was his deep grasp of, and wholehearted empathy for, the Native people of Canada that inspired us to write this book. But mostly, it was his patience and faith in us over the five or six months of long hours, when this book occupied almost our every moment, that made it so deeply and so personally the right thing to do.

AREA OF JAMES BAY DEVELOPMENT

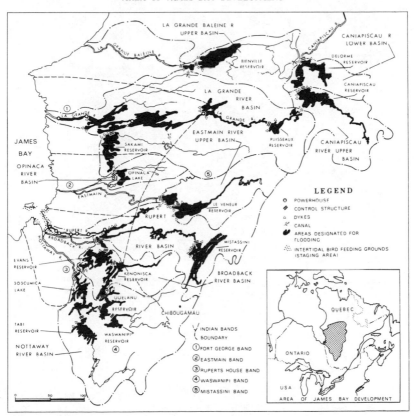

The above illustration is from "The James Bay Power Proposal", an article written by Valanne Gooschenko for the Canadian Nature Federation. This illustration shows two additional drainage areas which could be developed, thus bringing the total area affected to over 170,000 square miles.

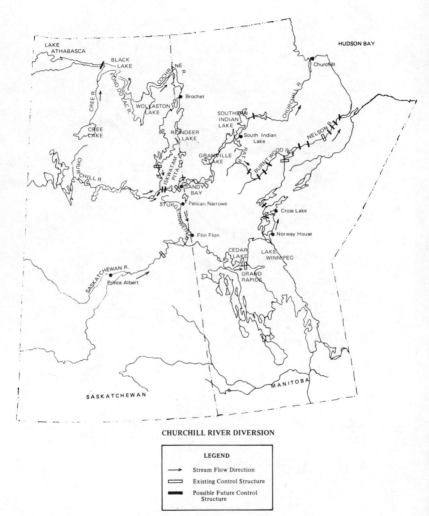

CHURCHILL RIVER DIVERSION

LEGEND	
→	Stream Flow Direction
▭	Existing Control Structure
▬	Possible Future Control Structure

The above illustration was not drawn to scale, therefore shows only the general location of existing and proposed control structures.

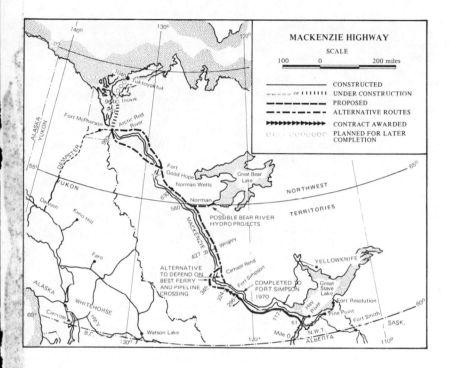

The above illustration is from The Financial-Post, Toronto, Ontario.